# Identity&
# Identification

wellcome
collection

black dog
publishing
london uk

# INTRODUCTION

Ken Arnold
James Peto

Recent advances in scientific, and particularly biomedical, techniques have made the task of uniquely identifying each of us easier and easier. Finger prints, voice recognition, iris scans and DNA profiles all enable the establishment of databases that record what distinguishes you from me from everybody else. But at the same time, we find the simple question "who are you?" agonisingly difficult to answer. "It depends", we insist. Each of us, of course, is an amalgam of multiple selves, some of which do not care for, or even know each other. And while we are adamant that there is much more to us than the simple accumulation of distinguishing features, we seem at times to be hovering on the edge of a collective identity crisis.

We are insecure about the nature and significance of our biological, socio-political, national, professional, religious and sexual identities; but we are also more generally unsure about which category of distinction is most important. Are we mostly what our genes have made us, what our parents wished us to be, what we work at, where we were born, or some combination of our class, gender, race, and age; or more flippantly just what we eat? So while bioinformatic instruments can pick each of us out from an unimaginably large crowd, we are nevertheless undecided about what exactly makes us ourselves. Maybe it is this tension between precise external data and vague internal feelings that has created an age obsessed with questions of identity, ceaselessly probed through art, science, politics and the rest of culture, but also through everyday consumer and lifestyle choices.

A book about identity and identification is therefore highly relevant, but also somewhat daunting, foolhardy even. What topics or ideas could legitimately be left out? Far from attempting either a comprehensive survey of the themes or a robust analysis of the relationship between identity and identification, the material collected in this volume is instead presented in order to suggest new perspectives and juxtapositions. To that end, two sets of resources are gathered here. One is a series of interviews with prominent scientific, cultural, political and philosophical thinkers. The second is a selection of visual essays focused on historical and contemporary figures whose lives and careers shed particular light on key aspects of our subject.

The interviews were conducted by Mick Gordon and Chris Wilkinson. Gordon is the artistic director of On Theatre and each year he makes a piece of theatre on a given subject. The interviews in this book form the research for his latest endeavour, an exploration of English identity, which he has co-written with the singer-songwriter, Billy Bragg. It premieres at Wellcome Collection in April and May 2010. Gordon calls his work Theatre Essays—in a sense, theatrical presentations of the essay form. As with a written essay, the starting point for a

Theatre Essay is a question or series of questions. And each one draws its source material from scientists, artists, philosophers, interest groups and members of the public directly affected by the question.

The interviews presented here were conducted with experts on various aspects of identity. They include the scientist Alec Jeffreys who developed the techniques for DNA fingerprinting; the neurologist Paul Broks, who works with injured brains, that is with patients whose identity has changed as their brains have altered; the philosophers AC Grayling and John Searle, who speculate on the fundamental components of identity; the political exile Ayaan Hirsi Ali, whose struggle for the rights of Muslim women means that she lives under constant threat; and the transsexual Roz Kaveney, who was born male and transitioned to being female.

Each interview probes the same two questions: "who are you?" and "who do we think you are?" It is a deceptively simple framework, which invites each interviewee to consider a self-definition from the inside out, and then from the outside in. And it is this constantly shifting double-helix of our subjective sense of individual identity and our inherited, imposed cultural identity, that we all live with, and that some of us battle against.

In giving thoughtful answers to these basic questions, the interviewees inevitably go on to suggest numerous others. Why, for example, do we feel safer assuming that the identities of hose around us remain consistent, while we ourselves are sometimes tempted to slip between roles? How do individuals maintain their identity within the collective pressure of nations, faiths, or technologically determined environments? How differently do people throughout the world think of their identities: does it make sense to apply a universal notion of individuality to people in China or Egypt, Greenland or Ghana? What about those who lived in earlier centuries and civilisations? And finally which, if any, animals exhibit a sense of identity?

The exhibition presented at Wellcome Collection during the same season as Mick Gordon's and Billy Bragg's theatrical piece similarly uses case studies to explore the broad topic of identity and identification. Co-curated by James Peto and Hugh Aldersey-Williams (whose introductory essay provides another ingredient in this volume), the exhibition tackles the same core concerns as this book: how we know who we are, how we are identified and how the two are related. It does so by showcasing relevant scientific, cultural, philosophical and social ideas about identity captured in the lives and work of historical and contemporary individuals—figurehead personalities, guides as it were, to specific aspects of the theme. Six of them have been converted into visual essays that are interleaved with the interviews in this book.

April Ashley was one of the first people in Britain to undergo a full sex change operation. She then fought for 35 years to get the change officially recognised. Her story reflects an awkwardly drawn-out struggle to align two definitions (one defined by biology and surgery, the other by state bureaucracy) of Ashley's sex.

Claude Cahun (an artist who lived in Jersey under Nazi occupation) photographed herself hundreds of times in the 1920s and 1930s. Her images, as well as the basic details of her life, reveal how she flexed and adapted the nature of her identity and sexuality.

Franz Joseph Gall was a nineteenth century pioneer of phrenology, an investigation now dismissed as quack science and worse. Its subject was the measurement and correlation of skull-shape with human characteristics as diverse as criminality and creativity, analysed according to the criteria of normality, abnormality and deformity.

Francis Galton (Darwin's prolific and polymath cousin) was primarily a scientist obsessed with measuring and statistically analysing vast ranges of human traits (anthropometrics), who thereby, arguably, invented a 'science of identity'.

There have been twins in at least three generations of the Hinch family. The youngest 'twins' (now one and three years old) were separated through the freezing and delayed development of one embryo. Their father on the other hand is a conventional identical twin. He grew up sharing both genes and environment with his brother. But his daughters will challenge our preconceptions of what it means to be a twin.

Fiona Shaw is an actress who has played a great variety of roles, from Richard II for the RSC to Aunt Petunia in the Harry Potter films. Her work illuminates the unusual license granted to actors to transgress the social expectation that we stick to being ourselves.

This book therefore presents almost two dozen partial insights into the dizzyingly broad topics of identity and identification. They are all about people grappling in different ways with the question of what it actually means to be themselves. Cumulatively, they suggest that part of our wellbeing rests in our ability regularly to reassess our sense of who we are.

# WHO NOW
## *Selfhood & Society*

Hugh Aldersey-Williams

On 18 October 1997, a boy who had gone missing three years earlier was apparently reunited with his family in Texas after having been found in a Spanish youth shelter. At San Antonio airport, 'Nicholas' was met with hugs and tears from his sister and other relatives. His mother was there too but held back from the general jubilation. At home over the coming weeks, the boy settled back into normal life, went to school, and was able to recall family incidents. If one or two people suspected something was not quite right, the police and immigration officials were on hand to reassure them everything was in order. After a couple of months, however, 'Nicholas' began to unravel. Finally, in March 1998, five months after taking the boy in, the mother communicated her suspicion that he was an impostor and a cruel deception was exposed. The 16 year-old American 'Nicholas' was shown to be Frédéric Bourdin, a 23 year-old Frenchman with bleached hair and a talent for memorising the details of other people's lives. He was sentenced to six years of imprisonment for perjury and obtaining false documents. On his release, he resumed his career as a serial child impostor, and in 2005 was discovered once more, this time back in France, claiming to be Francisco, a 16 year-old Spanish orphan.[1]

In Rwanda, 'Claudette', like her father and his father, carried a card that identified her as one of the majority ethnic group Hutu. In April 1994, the Rwandan president was killed in a mysterious plane crash, which unleashed a slaughter of the long persecuted Tutsi by Hutu. Rumours began to circulate that Claudette was not the Hutu she apparently claimed to be. In fact, her paternal grandfather had been known as a Tutsi but had managed to obtain an identity card declaring him to be a Hutu when he settled in a new district. He and Claudette's father were killed in the genocide, while Claudette found refuge with a group of Catholic nuns. Since the genocide, she has moved to the capital, Kigali, where it is convenient to present herself as a Tutsi, although she says she now doesn't really know whether she is the Hutu she was brought up as or the Tutsi of her ancestry.[2]

In 2002, Rikki Arundel proposed to visit his young teenage daughter, Celeste, at boarding school. Rikki is Celeste's father and was at the time in transition towards a full-time existence as a woman. Celeste had already noticed certain changes—the softening of the skin due to hormone treatment, the more frequently worn women's clothes—and these caused some unease in a girl in the midst of adolescence. With the parental visit looming, Celeste felt the need to lay down some rules: "If you come as my dad, that's fine" she announced. "Or if you come as a woman, I can say you're my aunt. But please don't come as something in between." That, Celeste knew, would require too much explaining to her peers. Having grown his grey hair long and recently had it coloured, Rikki went for the former option to spare the daughter's blushes. She now runs GenderShift, an organisation that campaigns for greater acceptance of people undergoing gender transition. Because of her unusual personal history she also enjoys the rare status of being a female freemason.

Society has a desperate requirement that we be in fact exactly what we seem to be. If appearances do not correspond with what we think we know, then the rest of us—in the family, in the community, in authority—are liable to be profoundly unsettled. We may be affronted, ashamed and threatened when we suddenly learn that somebody in whom we have placed some investment is not what they appear to be. So strong is our need for people to conform to our expectation of them that many conventional statements of identity may be overlooked if to do so produces a neater fit. This is what happened to Frédéric/Nicholas. The found boy was too good not to be believed; he fulfilled that family's need and tidied up the case books of the authorities. Such was the social pressure that even the doubting mother was persuaded to accept the impostor. The appearance of a neat fit was also what 'Claudette' needed to get on with her life in the aftermath of the Rwandan genocide, and it was what Celeste needed to be able to handle her father's visit.

　　Personal identity is an act. Most of us settle into one 'character' and maintain it without too much difficulty, in part at least because that is what society requires us to do. The cognitive machinery that enables you to play your role is then always running, and may even surface into consciousness at crucial moments, such as when you catch yourself remembering how to greet people appropriately or sense the awful irrevocability of leaving a voice message. There is constant pressure to keep up the act. But, as the saying goes, even kings need holidays (Shakespeare's Richard II needs his servants to remind him of his royal role: "I had forgot myself; am I not King?/Awake, thou coward majesty! thou sleepest.") And so we set aside special times (hen nights, say) and special places (such as the stage) when you no longer have to be who you are; indeed, it becomes imperative that you 'are' someone else. It is no coincidence that people testing their identity, or determined to experiment with alternative identities, often find a safe haven in the theatre. It's a way for men to explain the mascara, as Rikki Arundel puts it.

　　In more extreme cases, it becomes impossible to maintain the act, at least at the level of consistency that the world expects. Bourdin was not able to 'be' himself, so he sought to get along by 'being' other people. Yet the underlying wish is not to pretend, but to belong—for the act to become the life. Unable to sustain the act of his true self, he tried out other selves one after another, but was eventually unable to sustain them as well.

　　Often what is most disturbing about these stories is not the impersonation, the act performed more or less successfully by the central figures, but the reaction of those around them. We onlookers, aware that a story is being related, are stunned at the apparent credulousness of these people: how can they be fooled, we wonder. But from within the story, it is clear that this apparent credulousness arises from the need of people to believe the person is really who they claim to be for the sake of social cohesion. The real psychological centre of the famous story of the return of Martin Guerre is his wife, Bertrande de Rols. Was she a simple woman deceived by the impostor, as other people were, and as (men's) accounts of the episode have suggested? Or was there—as Natalie Zemon Davis, the cultural historian who brought the episode to light, has suggested—reason enough for Bertrande to go along with the pretence offered by this alternative husband?[3] For, as long as everybody accepts their role (without too many questions asked) the life of the world can go on its way. Thus the mother may be 'reunited' with her 'son', or, in order to satisfy the public thirst for 'justice' following an especially horrible crime, an unexamined fantasist confessor may be sent to prison while the real perpetrator makes his escape.

James Hogg's 1824 novel, *The Private Memoirs and Confessions of a Justified Sinner*, demonstrates how the concept of the self in law, morality and medicine may be brought into conflict. The central character, Robert Wringhim, imagines himself to be constantly accompanied by his 'second self' who eggs him on to a series of misdeeds including the murder of his half-brother. The narrative, itself told in multiple versions, provides an acute description of bipolar disorder as well as an astonishingly modern experiment in the form of the novel. As Wringhim tells it: "over the singular delusion that I was two persons my reasoning faculties had no power. The most perverse part of it was that I rarely conceived myself to be any of the two persons." He

imagines instead that these persons are the half-brother who torments him and a companion. But he nevertheless finds that "to be obliged to speak and answer in the character of another man, was a most awkward business at the long run."[4]

In happier circumstances, we are more free to explore additional and alternative identities than ever before. For a start, quite simply we have more clothes, and so more options for dressing up. In Shakespeare's time, most people owned little more than the set of clothes they stood up in; indeed, description of their clothes was felt to be a reliable method to identify the wearer before the existence of standard documents, and sumptuary laws forbade extravagant or immoral dress.

We also have the option to work up alternative personas in virtuality, and to a great extent live that life in place of 'real life'. This can have confusing consequences. Real couples have split up because of virtual infidelities committed by their electronic alter egos, for example. What does it say about contemporary society that people do this? Is it escapism? If so, escape from what? Or is it merely a modern manifestation of something we have always sought—the masquerade, the temporary disguise which excuses the expression of another side of the self?

For the reality is that the daily business of maintaining even a single act of one's personal identity can be consuming and exhausting. It necessitates multiple viewpoints of the self. We participate in the drama of life but we also observe ourselves participating. We are actor, audience and

10/11
**12/13**
14/15
16/17
18/19

critic in one. In·the mythic first moment of self-recognition, Narcissus sees his reflection in a pool, and exclaims: "I know you now and I know myself. Yes, I am the cause of the fire inside me, the fuel that burns and the flame that lights it."[5]

Vladimir Nabokov describes this dual condition in his aurally punning novella *The Eye*: "I walked along remembered streets; everything greatly resembled reality, and yet there was nothing to prove I was not dead and that Passauer Strasse was not a postexistent chimera. I saw myself from the outside treading water as it were, and was both touched and frightened like an inexperienced ghost watching the existence of a person whose inner lining, inner night, mouth, taste-in-the-mouth, he knew as well as that person's shape."[6]

This is something that diarists understand implicitly. We may think of diaries as honest attempts to record the self, but they are necessarily more artful than that, as Virginia Woolf indicates by the title of her own published diaries, *Composing One's Self*. Samuel Pepys' diary is paradigmatic in this respect, but even he omitted much—not only the dreary, but also for example his involvement in secret affairs of state occasioned by his position on the Navy Board. Of course, which information is conveyed and which withheld, and how it is done, shines a second light on the self who is writing.

But in general we seldom stop to regard ourselves in this dual existence (to do so requires a third observing self!). We go about instead with a working idea of our self: we know 'who we are', or think we do. This hazy, unexamined conception of our self is enough to see us through much of our lives. Science and philosophy have various, more contentious definitions of the self. Their more particular conceptions seldom have an impact on us unless something goes seriously wrong, and a life-changing event—a facial injury, memory loss, a long absence and return, the discovery of a deception or some other revelation—forces us to reappraise our own self in a conscious way. It is no coincidence that drama—and especially the more stylized forms such as opera—frequently turns on these moments, tragic or comic, when identity is challenged.

Such dramas animate some of the most fundamental and puzzling questions about identity. How do we know we are the same person we were ten minutes or ten years ago? How do our loved ones and others know? Is it important to know? A Bourdin or a Guerre may give rise to doubts, but when our partner returns from work we are sure it is the same person who left that morning. How we establish this to our satisfaction is no trivial matter.

Philosophers have always puzzled over what makes somebody a recognisable individual. Significant strides were made by John Locke and David Hume, who asserted that consciousness, and continuity of consciousness in memory, were the sine qua non of personal identity. To Hume "the principle of individuation is nothing but the invariableness and uninterruptedness of any object, thro' a suppos'd variation of time, by which the mind can trace it in the different periods of its existence, without any break of the view."[7]

Sleep does not constitute such a break because we remember the previous day. But it is clear that amnesia or physical injury to the brain can derail this train. Clive Wearing is a distinguished musicologist who, as a result of a viral infection in 1985, has lost the ability to remember anything that happens more than a few seconds before. He has kept a diary in which each entry asserts his existence in the present at that time and denies the previous existence claimed in earlier entries which, so far as Wearing is concerned, have no truth to them.

Recent philosophical thought has tended to focus on hypothetical scenarios in which continuity of self-identity is suddenly disrupted, as for example when mind and body are separated and shuffled around in various ways in space and time. But these various thought experiments in teleportation and body-swapping seem to have added little understanding. We conclude, rather unsatisfactorily, that our identity resides in the person most like 'us' a moment ago or a step away—the so-called "closest continuer theory" of identity.

Interestingly, this theory was mocked long before it was articulated. In Hogg's *Confessions* a witness in court is pressed to say that certain items are those taken in a robbery. The witness refuses to confirm the identicalism that the court wishes to hear and the case has to be dropped. "*Like* is an ill mark" she says. The context of the story implies that 'like' or 'most like' is not enough to affirm the identity of either object or person.

Still today, many of these questions about the nature of identity seem to be more fruitfully—and more entertainingly—explored in novels, film and television.

A major purpose of Identity: Eight Rooms, Nine Lives is to counter the constraining influence of all those agencies that find it expedient to fit us into pigeonholes of their own devising, and to remind us that we have more power over our identity than often seems to be the case.

Assertions of identity that confound the evidence of our eyes or otherwise contradict the norms may be seen as so socially subversive that we are capable of relating to them only as a kind of performance art. People have proposed to sell their past life, their virginity and their skin colour on eBay, for example: "This heirloom has been in the possession of the seller for 28 years" wrote 28 year-old artist Keith Obadike in his pitch. (Admittedly, it is not always clear how the transaction would be completed.)

What does it mean when an individual does this? What do they lose? What does the buyer really gain? Some of these offers are clearly artistic gestures, others perhaps marks of desperation. But all suggest that aspects of a self may be gained or lost, even bought and sold, and may have value, if of a quite different kind, to people other than their original 'owners'. These exercises remind us that our identity is far more than the cipher to which we often feel reduced. We are *not* only our skin colour, our sex, our professional reputation, the sum of our possessions. We are simultaneously, and quite possibly contradictorily, many other things as well.

The deeper social purpose of identity, to which contentious things like ID cards are just a formal efflorescence, is to link each individual to humanity. According to the anthropologist Meyer Fortes, "the concept of the person relates mortal, transient human beings to a continuing social whole". It's the "mortal" that is key here. It is our unique consciousness of the inevitability of death that demands we forge these links. As John Donne put it more poetically: "any man's death diminishes me, because I am involved in mankind".[8] If the 'I' chooses not to be "involved in mankind", then personal identity not only fails to be recognised by others, but actually ceases to exist for that person. For, as the first century BCE Babylonian Jewish scholar Hillel demanded: "If I am only for me, who am I?"

Identity cannot then be formed by the individual in isolation, but must be composed in response to social surroundings. However, this does not mean that it is others alone who determine our identity. From birth essentially we are told who to be—by parents, schoolteachers, peers and role models, by advertisers, by the media, by the government. It can easily seem as if we have no choice in the matter. But we do.

Consider the surge of interest in genealogy prompted in part by the publication of public records on the internet. At first, this seems to be a search to locate fixed roots in the most immutable aspect of ourselves, our ancestral history. It is anything but. Observing people setting out on this journey into their past, it is notable how they often start with a destination in mind. For example, the BBC's popular and invariably compelling ancestry-tracing series, Who Do You Think You Are? has featured the actors John Hurt and Jeremy Irons in separate programmes. Both had a fancy their roots were Irish. Irons was delighted to find his hunch confirmed, but Hurt was crestfallen to learn there was no substance in his fantasy.

The genealogical quest is often not about finding the truth, but about finding a story. The search for roots implies a narrowing of focus to a single origin, but the roots of a tree themselves branch, of course. Every generation back leads to a doubling of stories to follow. Soon, it is clear that no one story is your true past, nor are you in any meaningful sense the sum of the stories of your ancestors. Instead, it becomes clear that what matters is almost arbitrarily finding a story, and people have considerable freedom to pick out one that suits them.

Identity: Eight Rooms, Nine Lives addresses a number of topics in personal identity and identification by selecting certain individuals to stand as figureheads for the topic. In this way, we are reminded that while a person may be chiefly regarded by the world for one trait or achievement, that person invariably has many other facets to their own identity.

Fiona Shaw, who gender-crossingly played the role of Richard II playing the role of the king, provides the prism allowing us to look at the business of acting in which we are all, in our way, employed. April Ashley, one of the first people in Britain to undergo gender reassignment, also joined the merchant navy, was a Paris showgirl, raised funds for Greenpeace, and sailed across the Pacific Ocean. The Hinch twins, Charlotte and Emily, were born two years apart (by IVF treatment); immediately, these two young girls force us to reassess our fascinated tendency to see twins as somehow less than full individuals. Claude Cahun made a lifelong series of photographic self-portraits essaying different personae but also distributed anti-Nazi propaganda in occupied Jersey.

Two more such figureheads are the scientists Francis Galton and Alec Jeffreys. Both are pioneers of biological techniques of identification, Galton of fingerprinting, and Jeffreys of DNA profiling. Both promoted their techniques for use in solving crimes and earned prizes and knighthoods. Separated by a hundred years, they illustrate differences as well as similarities in the life of a scientist as well as progress in the science. If Galton had been able to appear on Who Do You Think You Are?, he would have found the story he wanted to find in his relation to Charles Darwin, a fact of his life that fuelled an obsession with hereditary genius. Jeffreys, on the other hand, has been able to use the DNA technology he developed to tell another story, disproving a family myth that he is related to the infamous Judge Jeffreys.

Yet the entirety of these persons' identities is not their ancestry, their gender, their pairedness, or their creative output. Nor are the scientists simply the fleshly husks of their science. They are all fuller personalities than that.

The question "who are you?" invites the riposte "who wants to know?" long before it leads on to the more reflective question, "well, yes, who actually am I?" Both questions have never been more asked. It is not only the apparently inexorable expansion of the national DNA database and the prospect of compulsory national identity cards that explains this topicality.

It is also the fact that we live in egotistical times. We are constantly reminded that *our* self and *our* identity has supreme importance and constantly encouraged to think about ourselves, usually in shallow ways. From brain gym to boob job, we seek to transform our minds, personalities, faces and bodies. Implicit in this contemporary self-sense is the idea that the individual has not always been so central, that identity once stemmed from something other than conscious individuality or that it simply mattered less. It is easy to believe that in Communist China or medieval Europe the sense of individualism was less profound, but it seems impossible to test this proposition, and this too may just be the conceit of our solipsistic present. After all, recent research has established that 'I' and 'we' are among the very oldest words in many languages.

That personal identity may be altered—and perhaps improved—by consciously undertaken extension of the self is increasingly widely acknowledged. Such extension may be psychological (self-help books), physical (cosmetic surgery) and chemical (mind-altering drugs) as well as technological (virtual environments). At the moment, these possibilities are perhaps only crudely being tested. However, it seems certain that in the future it will be increasingly easy, and probably increasingly acceptable, to manipulate both the external appearance of the body and our genetic make-up, disrupting what Nikolas Rose, director of the Centre for the Study of Bioscience, Biomedicine, Biotechnology and Society at the London School of Economics, calls the "naturalness of the self".[9]

Yet at present, it can often seem as if our identity as seen by others, and especially by those in authority, is merely the sum of those aspects of our self that we don't choose for ourselves: our sex, surname, forenames, height, skin colour etc. This is the information we are asked for first when we fill in a form. The motive for asking is always the same, and so is the effect, which is to reduce the complex human individual totality to one small photograph, an iris scan, a PIN number. Identification is always a reductive shorthand. Are we no more than a snapshot or the sum of the things we say we are when we fill in a form?

So we appear to be poised at a moment in which personal identity is being subjected to unprecedented external forces. On the one hand, we find ourselves surrounded by agencies that wish to reduce us to a string of digits. On the other, we are constantly told the patent untruth that we can be whatever we want to be.

Even our gender is subject to this tension. To the world of officialdom, we must declare ourselves unequivocally of one sex or the other, M or F. We declare a baby to be a boy or a girl, and have tended to force people born with chromosomal or genital anomalies into one of these categories. As we grow aware of our sexuality, most of us accentuate our nominal sex, encouraged in this direction by the role models we find around us. In other words, we perform to our gender—another act. But this conformism—never as important in many Eastern cultures—is weakening in the West too. The trend for surgical 'correction' of intersex births had risen because it was possible to perform the operations safely, but it too is now falling again with the realisation that it was done more in response to societal discomfiture than patient needs. The concept of sexual fluidity—the notion that one's sexual identity and preferences may not be constant for all time, but may change over years or for that matter days and minutes—is gaining ground. The concept is apparently more widely acknowledged and accepted among women, according to the psychologist Lisa Diamond, to the extent even that many women find conventional sexual identity labels entirely inadequate.[10] Is it truly less in men, one wonders, or are men simply not ready to have the discussion?

Stating an identity is, as we have seen, a social statement. So too is agreeing to accept one. As the psychoanalyst Jacques Lacan has pointed out, the apparently autonomous decision to assent to a chosen personal identity is in itself a sign that we have been manipulated by another. We accede to this manipulation because it is made socially advantageous for us to do so. The identities conferred by authority—physical description, facial photograph, DNA profile, and the rest—are necessarily severe reductions of the complex, ever-changing totality that is our self. To that extent, though they may be a convenience, they are also in the manner of insults. "I am not a PIN, I am a free man" as the Prisoner of the famous television series might find himself saying today.

This insulting reductionism is part of what makes being asked for one's identity always controversial. It was so in the past when 'distinguishing marks' were the means and will be so when iris scanning or some other high-tech biometric method becomes widespread. There is no question that a DNA profile is a more complete shorthand than a fingerprint, but it is shorthand nevertheless; it is not *us*.

However, the photograph has long been widely regarded as an acceptable means of official identification. Even though facial appearances blatantly change and it offers no guarantee of unique identification, the photograph is accepted because it most closely corresponds to the way we recognise and identify people ourselves. So accustomed have we become to the idea that identity is adequately summarised in a photograph that we grossly underestimate (and do correspondingly less to investigate) the extent to which we identify people by other means: voice and language, as well as characteristic habits of movement and gesture. Photography is a demotic technology: photos are easily reproduced and easily passed from hand

to hand. And, until recently at least, they could generally be assumed to be relatively immune to doctoring. DNA profiling, by contrast, has the paraphernalia of an opaque technology and a state apparatus behind it. Perhaps when it becomes more widely used—as it surely will by consumers for domestic genealogical research—attitudes towards it may soften too.

Science is a reductionist project and naturally colludes in the process of reducing our innate complexity in its own troubled effort to understand human identity. It used to be thought that the soul, or what we now might call the self, resides in the heart (or, in some cultural traditions, the liver). Today, we are more likely to place the emphasis on the brain. This is why we are generally more comfortable with the idea of a heart transplant than a brain transplant. The idea of a transplant of the face, which is the means by which we are able to sense so much of the activity of the brain, falls somewhere in between these two.

At the beginning of the nineteenth century, the German physiologist Franz Gall—another figurehead in the exhibition—made scientific measurements of the skull in an attempt to associate regions of the brain with the mental functions. His studies blossomed into the field that became known as phrenology. Its subsequent champions, men such as Johann Spurzheim of Vienna and George Combe of Edinburgh, brought a moral agenda to the investigation, seeking the key to such loosely defined qualities as genius and criminality in the shape of the head. Though doubted by many professional sceptics and satirised by others, phrenology had enthusiastic adherents and remained the focus of science's attempt to describe the self for over a hundred years, until Sigmund Freud finally had the simple thought to ask people what was going on in their heads.

Francis Galton, meanwhile, sought his answers in facial appearance, tediously layering photographs of individuals said to represent various 'types' in order to build up composite faces that might be definitive. The list of types Galton chose for his studies is worth repeating here as it says more about Galton and his era than it does about any category of individuals: "American scientific men, Baptist ministers, Bethlem Royal Hospital and Hanwell Asylum patients, Chatham privates, children, criminals, families, Greeks and Romans [taken together!], Leeds Refuge children, Jews, Napoleon I and Queen Victoria and her family, phthisis patients, robust men, Ph. Ds, Westminster schoolboys."

How much deeper should we go mining for the source of the self? "The mind is what the brain does" is the currently fashionable, but perhaps not entirely illuminating mantra connecting thought with biological tissue. Functional MRI scanning is now able to display brain activity 'as it happens'. There is already an iconic familiarity to sections of the brain seen on a computer screen with parts of it lit up like rain storms on a weather map. But where does the high-level mental activity characteristic of the self takes place?

This powerful new technique is facilitating a great deal of research. Most of it is naturally focused on understanding neurological disease, but some work seeks to probe the mental activity that we associate with selfhood—creative behaviour, for example, or the exercise of self-control, or the acute self-consciousness experienced during adolescence. Other studies seem to exhibit a contemporary version of the moral agenda of the phrenologists, examining such behaviours as racism and truth-telling. All this work is united by the urge to distil the human character into a picture so that we can say at last: here is the self.

Will these luminous images really show us Narcissus' 'fire inside'? I have my doubts. But maybe that's just me.

1   Grann, David, "The Chameleon", *New Yorker*, 11 August 2008.
2   Longman, Timothy, "Identity Cards, Ethnic Self-Perception, and Genocide in Rwanda" in Caplan, Jane, and Torpey, John, eds, *Documenting Individual Identity*, Princeton NJ, 2001.
3   Davis, Natalie Zemon, *The Return of Martin Guerre*, Cambridge MA, 1983.
4   Hogg, James, *The Private Memoirs and Confessions of a Justified Sinner*, Edinburgh, 1824.
5   Ovid, *Metamorphoses*.
6   Nabokov, Vladimir, *The Eye*, London, 1966.
7   Hume, David, *A Treatise of Human Nature*.
8   Donne, John, *Meditations XVII*.
9   Rose, Nikolas, *Inventing Our Selves: psychology, power and personhood*, Cambridge MA, 1996.
10  Diamond, Lisa, *Sexual Fluidity: Understanding Women's Love and Desire*, Cambridge MA, 2008.

# April Ashley

Hugh Aldersey-Williams

April Ashley is one of the first people in Britain to have undergone a full sex-change operation. She was born a boy—George Jamieson—in Liverpool and grew up there in a large family during the Second World War. Treated brutally by his mother, shunned by his siblings of both sexes, and sexually abused by a family friend, George was from earliest memory unhappy in his biological sex. "Although I was brought up a strict Roman Catholic boy, I knew from the age dot that I was a girl", Ashley wrote later.

George joined the merchant navy at 15. This was a way to escape family life, but it was also an attempt to live up to a male role like his older brothers. The experience broadened his horizons, but George's increasingly feminine appearance gave rise to teasing and worse. From Liverpool, he made his way via a succession of jobs to London and then to Paris and the stage of the Carrousel night club, famous for its female and male impersonators. Now calling herself Toni April, she discovered that her sexual ambiguousness held its own appeal and brought her greater social mobility as she tried out different looks and personae. "I was not so much building my character as collecting characters."

Unlike some of the characters she met, who were content merely to seem to be of the opposite sex, April knew she really wanted to be a woman. She began hormone treatment, and in May 1960, at the age of 25, travelled to Morocco and underwent genital surgery to remove the testes and invert the nerve tissue of the penis to create a vagina. Returning to Britain, she immediately experienced the conflict between appearances and official 'fact' that fuels identity tensions between the individual and the state when the passport inspector initially refused to accept that she was the person pictured in the document.

She changed her name by deed poll to April Ashley and began a long struggle for recognition in her chosen sex. The law at the time did not permit a birth certificate to be amended in the light of later events; the position was that it should be a record of fact at the time of birth. But with the passing of the Gender Recognition Act in 2004, the position changed so that birth certificates could be amended. This enables people who have undergone gender reassignment to keep their former gender confidential from employers and partners. Ashley finally obtained her amended birth certificate in September 2005, thanks not least to the personal intercession of then Deputy Prime Minister John Prescott, with whom she had once worked in the kitchens of the same hotel.

April Ashley became famous largely because of her gender reassignment—she was long ago 'outed' by a Sunday newspaper. She has been George Jamieson, Toni April and April Ashley, and, by two marriages, also the Honourable Mrs Arthur Corbett and then Mrs Jeff West. She has modelled for *Vogue*, has met film stars, Salvador Dalí, Elvis Presley and the Beatles, and persuaded Einstein to give her his autograph. She has sailed the Atlantic and Pacific oceans, and worked at various times as an agony aunt, a restaurateur, and a Greenpeace fundraiser. Though her chosen gender is an important aspect of her identity, it is clear that it is far from all.

April Ashley backstage at Le Carrousel, Paris, circa 1959.
All images courtesy of April Ashley.

George Jamieson at the age of 10 at St Theresa's Primary School, Liverpool.
This photograph was taken on VE Day, 8 May 1945.

20/21
**22/23**
24/25
26/27
28/29
30/31
32/33
34/35
36/37
38/39
40/41

George Jamieson aged 15. George was teased by his siblings and schoolmates for his girlish
looks, and sought to make his voice break by imitating the film actor Robert Mitchum.

The 'girls' at Le Carrousel in Paris. Some were female impersonators, who dressed the part and in extreme cases had breast implants, but nevertheless wished to remain male. Others, like April (here numbered 8), were would-be transsexuals.

At Le Carrousel, 1959.

April Ashley passport, circa 1960.

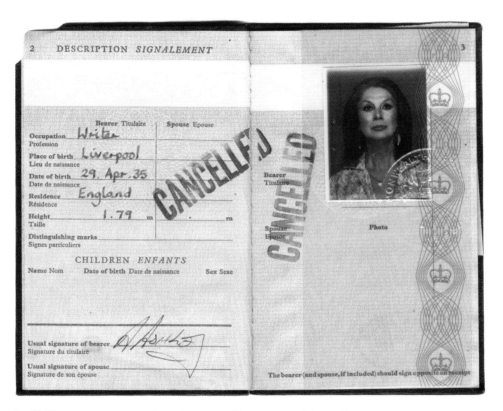

April Ashley passport, circa 1970. Notice how some of the categories of identity change or are described differently at the two times: thus, "Special peculiarities" becomes "Distinguishing marks", while Ashley changes career and her signature.

April Ashley was 'outed' as a transsexual by the *Sunday People* in November 1961 ("The Extraordinary Case of Top Model April Ashley. Her Secret is Out"). She has often been the subject of media attention since then. During this time, the coverage has gradually shifted from scandalised and sensational to more respectful as Ashley has become a figurehead for the transgender movement.

The April Ashley Jag...

# FROM NAVY CABIN BOY TO SULTRY STARLET IN ONE OPERATION!

They used to call sex-changing April a freak — but pretty soon they may be calling her a star!

NEW SPOUSE—Geoffres Ross of Germany will soon become Hubby No. 2 of sex-changeling April Ashley Corbett. April, born George Jameson, was a Navy cabin boy before operation in Casablanca.

MOTHER - DAUGHTER — Mrs. Ada Jameson poses with her daughter— who was once her son.

## BY JACK HENDERSON

Mrs. APRIL ASHLEY CORBETT—the one-time cabin boy in the British Navy who "did a Christine Jorgenson" and turned from male to female—has hit the headlines again on the Continent.

In fact, during the past few weeks, the charming—and, frankly, pretty—sex changeling has received more publicity than Liz Taylor.

It all started when she had a spat with her husband, the Hon. Thomas Godfrey Corbett, and decided to cool off with a trip to Rome.

As it developed, she did anything *but* cool off.

A few minutes after she deplaned at Leonardo DaVinci Airport, she was arrested for insulting a cop.

Then, she was jailed—in a men's prison, because the *carabinieri* thought she was merely a fag in drag.

After examination by the prison physician, she was transferred to a female jail.

But the cops were still pretty uncomfortable about the whole matter, so they voiced an official complaint to the Italian Department of Immigration and Naturalization and April was ordered out the country.

Pretty wild?

Well, hold on—the story has a happy ending. Before she left, Federico Fellini—the internationally acclaimed movie director of *La Dolce Vita* fame—announced that he was signing her up to star in his next film.

Thus, April became the first person in history ever to be born a male and wind up a leading lady of the silver screen . . . while in prison, yet.

The details in just a minute—but first, a brief dissertation on the life and hard times of our heroine.

April was born George Jamieson at Liverpool, England—a city which, it would appear, owned the patent on the production of wierdos even way back in those early pre-Beatle days.

She (he) was, in her (his) own words, "an ugly, thin, but quite hearty little boy" who liked "playing with dolls and preferred

FIRST HUBBY—Gibraltar tycoon Sir Arthur Corbett with April in happy days before divorce

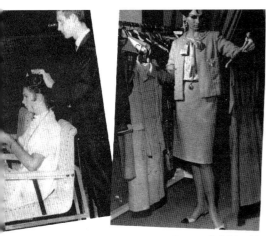

—Shortly after her sex change operation in May, 1960, April became topline British model. ...he poses in Madrid, Spain, where she got new coiffure; right, she checks wardrobe.

the company of little girls."

When she (he) was 15, however, her (his) preferences switched to boys—which resulted in her (his) being derided by peers as, in their term, "a queer."

Hating herself (himself) for this, April (George) enrolled in Merchant Navy School with hopes of becoming "an able-bodied seaman." A year later, she (he) got a job aboard a cargo vessel, the *Pacific Fortune*.

April's (George's) life aboard the *Fortune* might best be characterized as *un*fortunate. For one thing, the rest of the crew thought that she (he) was, in her (his) own term, "soft"—or, in their term, "a bloody faggot." For another, April (George) experienced great emotional conflict at the thought that the virile-looking young men to whom she (he) was attracted weren't equally attracted to her (him).

When the ship docked in Los Angeles, the despondent misfit sailor tried to commit suicide. Apparently, though, she (he) didn't try hard enough—because, a few days later, she (he) was discharged from the hospital fit as a fiddle.

A few days after that, she (he) got another discharge—from the Merchant Navy, as "unfit on medical grounds."

Back in Liverpool, she (he) went to Walton Hospital and requested treatments to make her (him) more manly. It didn't work and there was another suicide (Continued on page 36)

**LITTLE BIRD TOLD HER**—Coccinelle, whose name means "Little Bird," hipped April to sex change scene when both of them were boys working in the same Paris "gay" bar.

14

(Continued from page 14)

attempt, which didn't work either.

This rapid-fire series of failures, surprisingly, resulted in a change for the better. April (George) decided that "I'd try making the most of my life—just as I was." And it worked.

The teen age boy who wanted to be a teen age girl took a job as a waiter in a hotel. Not long after, she (he) met what she (he) calls "my first love."

This is her (his) accounting of the experience:

'I was wearing jeans and a sweater and had no trace of a beard. He was a tall and very handsome Jewish boy who believed I was a girl.

"We spent some happy, innocent hours together. But then, one day, he telephoned me and said: 'You fascinate me.' And I thought it was time to enlighten him."

The enlightenment brought his fascination to a screeching halt. The just-jilted April (George) then went to London. It was here that the ex-cabinboy, whose sea cruising had met with such dismal results, took up a different kind of cruising—as a homo-sexual transvestite.

The London period is described by April (George) as "an interlude of horror." She (he) went to "grotesque, wierd parties night after night," numbered drug addicts "among my friends" and lived generally in "the twilight world of the half-men and half-women"—in other words, among the swish set.

When the pleasures of this kick palled, she (he) moved on to France. She learned of a Paris night club, the Carrousel, which featured female impersonators and decided to give it a try.

The manager took one look at her (him) and said: "But we don't employ girls. Only men."

Says April (George):

I proved to him that I was a man and the job was mine."

While working at the Carrousel, April (George) learned of the phenomenon of sex-change operations. Immediately, she (he) set her heart on having one. While saving enough money to pay the doctor, she (he) lived the "good life"—travelling around France and Italy in the company of show business celebs and jet-set swingers.

**"MY FIRST LOVE"**

"I mingled happily and freely," she (he) recalls, 'with people like the late Belinda Lee, Van Johnson, Bob Hope, Shirley Bassey, Juliette Greco ad scores of other international personalities."

Josephine Baker even gave her (him) a picture of herself autographed: "To the most beautiful girl in the world."

But her (his) pleasure still wasn't complete—because, no matter how readily she (he) was accepted while in drag, she (he) still woke up every morning with irrefutable proof that she (he) was a male.

A conference with Coccinelle, the famous Parisienne sex changling, changed all that. The blonde bombshell of the Paris switch set put April (George) on to a Casablanca surgeon who had performed her own operation. An appointment was made and April (George) finally became Apri—

out into legit society. She adopted the last name, Ashley, and got herself legally declared a woman.

Unlike many of the changlings, who really look more like grotesque parodies of femininity, she *was* beautiful

—so much so that London photographers began offering her modelling jobs.

Soon, the Hon. Thomas Godfrey Corbett, a British lawyer with headquarters in Gibraltar, married her—and it looked like she would live happily ever after.

Them came their lovers' quarrel and she left their luxury villa at Marbella, Spain, for a jaunt to Rome—which brings us to the present.

As she left the airport, a car pulled alongside her and the driver asked if she would like a ride. Thinking the auto was a taxi, she got in.

"But," she recalls, "instead of taking me to my hotel, the driver drove me into the country. Then he stopped and I had a devil of a time persuading him that I was not his type.

"He told me that he wasn't a taxi driver, but that he just haunted the Via Veneto—the starlets' stomping ground—hunting for beautiful foreign girls in his car."

After she escaped his clutches, she ran into a policeman—whom, for reasons unexplained, she insulted, resulting in her arrest.

**IN A MEN'S JAIL**

"The police wanted to put me in a men's jail," she says, "because I told them I had been a sailor. They made me submit to a physical examination before sending me to a women's prison. I was so humiliated."

All, however, was not pain and agony.

'During the five days I was in jail, I received wonderful messages of sympathy, flowers and even offers to become a movie actress."

The offer which she accepted came from Federico Fellini, who will feature her in his forthcoming "Juliette and the Spirits." The Oscar-winning director has nothing but the highest praise for her.

"Before seeing her for the first time, I thought she would be one of those freaks, but I found she was a beautiful, charming woman. A *real* woman."

The feelings of admiration are mutual.

"Fellini has the strangest look in his eyes," says April. "He seems to look through you. I could never lie to a man like that."

Of course, the Fellini picture will not be the pretty changling's first experience before the movie cameras. She played a bit part opposite Bing Crosby and her old friend, Bob Hope, in *Road to Hong Kong*.

'I was a Chinese girl, but I was a little too tall for the part," she recalls.

As to the reasons for her spat with her hubby:

'Arthur loves his little zoo—(a menagerie that includes dogs, cats, a porcupine and "all sorts of other bugs"). But a zoo isn't enough for me. I prefer to be with people. And in the film world you meet all kinds."

Her plans for the future?

Well, she says, she'd just sort of like to drift toward international stardom—which is quite a task, even for those who were born women. But a lot of people think her chances are good.

Says Italy's leading fashion designer, Emilio Schuberth:

"Not only is she lovely, but if she were not quite so tall I wouldn't hesitate to give her a job."

So, as was noted earlier, despite the hard times of youth and the recent, publicity-getting period in Rome, Mrs. April Ashley Corbett appears to be on the road to success, happiness and all those other nice *desiderata* people (sex changlings included) dream about; the worst is behind, the best is yet to come.

And, as her Italian captors of late might have said, *bona fortuna*—here's lookin' at ya, kid.

THIS SULTRY STARLET WAS ONCE A NAVY CABIN BOY!

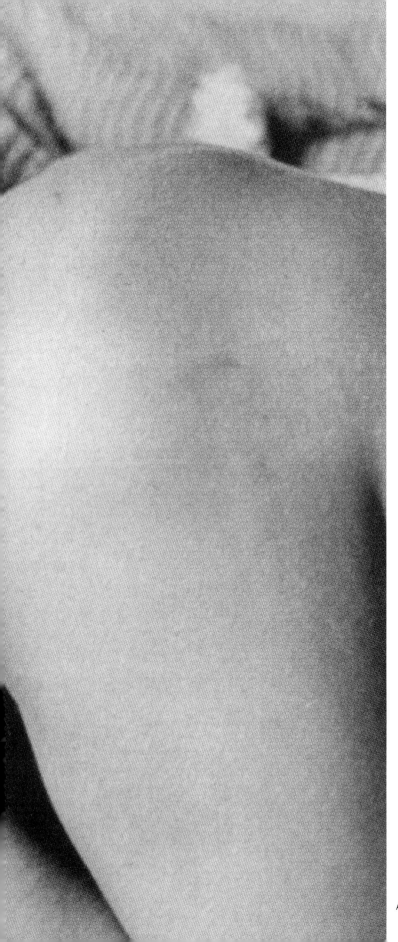

April Ashley modelling in the 1960s.

April Ashley travelled to Casablanca in May 1960 to undergo surgery to change her sex.
These photographs date from the late 1950s and were taken on the Côte d'Azur where
the Carrousel troupe toured in the summers.

As Toni April, posing with a friend before her gender reassignment.

This photograph, probably taken in 1961, is one of April Ashley's favourites.

*Below* April Ashley with her first husband-to-be, the Honourable Arthur Corbett, in 1961.

*Opposite* April Ashley photographed by David Bailey in the 1960s.

April Ashley photographed in 2006 for a feature in the *Observer Magazine*.

20/21
22/23
24/25
26/27
28/29
30/31
32/33
34/35
36/37
38/39
**40/41**

April Ashley has fought a long battle to be officially recognised as a woman. In 2004, the Gender Recognition Act provided for transsexual people to be recognised in the gender to which they had transitioned. This enables them to keep their former gender confidential from employers and partners. In August 2005, the General Register Office, having received April's Ashley's Gender Recognition Certificate, indicated that it would be possible to issue the new birth record shown here.

# Draft A

R06670/05J

| REGISTRATION DISTRICT | | | | | Liverpool South | | | |
|---|---|---|---|---|---|---|---|---|
| BIRTH in the Sub-district of ........ | | | | Sefton Park | in the ........ | County Borough of Liverpool | | |
| Columns:- | 1 | 2 | 3 | 4 | 5 | 6 | 7 | 8 | 9 |
| No. | When and where born | Name, if any | Sex | Name and surname of father | Name, surname and maiden surname of mother | Occupation of father | When registered | Signature of registering officer | Name entered after registration |
| | Twenty ninth April 1935 126 Smithdown Road U.D. | April | Girl | Frederick JAMIESON | Ada JAMIESON formerly BROWN | Corporation Tramways Conductor of 94 Pitt Street U.D. | | | ———— |

# AYAAN HIRSI ALI

is a Dutch feminist, writer and politician. She is currently a fellow at the American Enterprise Institute. In 2005, she was named by *Time* magazine as one of the 100 most influential people in the world. She has also received several awards for her work, including Norway's Human Rights Service's Bellwether of the Year Award, the Danish Freedom Prize, the Swedish Democracy Prize, and the Moral Courage Award for commitment to conflict resolution, ethics, and world citizenship. Her books include *Infidel* and *The Caged Virgin*.

---

*Who are you?*

I am many things all at once. I'm a woman. I was born in Somalia. My skin colour is black and I'm one metre, 72 centimetres tall. That's what my passport will tell you! These are aspects of my identity that are a given, that are static. And then of course there's the dynamic aspect of being a Somali, a Kenyan, an Ethiopian, a Dutch person and now an American *all* at once.

*Are their expectations associated with what you call your static identity—being a woman, having black skin and so on? Could you talk a little bit about that, and then about how you have experienced the dynamic aspect of your identity?*

Well, when I was born I was a girl, and I lived in the context of an extended family. And the expectation was that you were going to grow up to be a young woman and while growing up, you would learn to be a good wife and a good mother and a good cook and a good cleaner, all because of your gender. So, being born a woman, where I was born, had a lot of expectations tied to it. And in the West those expectations are not a given anymore, they've become more of a personal choice that you make.

*So, you feel that your gender identity has become less of a pressing issue for your day-to-day life since you came to the West.*

Yes—since I switched contexts.

*The question of switching contexts, arises in your book* Infidel. *You wrote about moving from Somalia to Saudi Arabia—where you were suddenly seen as a black person and that that was seen as being a lesser form of human from the Arab point of view.*

Well, in Saudi Arabia, blacks descended from, and are still seen largely as, slaves. Slaves and slavery is allowed in the Islamic religion and in the Arab tribal context, and the slaves that they know of, and knew of, were black-skinned. So, when people with a darker skin colour emigrated to Saudi Arabia in search of jobs, the Saudi's first reaction was: "slaves".

And yet my mother would also view certain people as slaves. She saw people with black skin who had a flat nose and kinky hair as slaves, because from the Somali tribal context, those communities represented at first sight slaves or people of a lower order, and people you don't intermarry with. And this too was difficult for me, or contradictory, because I was also brought up to believe that God created all of us and that God was just. In Islam, God is constantly referred to as being just. So it was a difficult contradiction for me: to be unfortunate enough to be born a girl and then black and still think of God as being just!

*And this is something you struggled with?*

Well I don't think I would call my early response resistance, because I wasn't resisting—I was just disgruntled. The first questions came at the age of eight or nine years to my father and my mother. And the answer from the adults was to say that you should show forbearance and patience and perseverance in the role that God has put you in—a role which they all expected to be static. And the belief was that forbearance would lead to rewards in the hereafter. So everything that I envied—being male and free—that was something that I was going to get in the hereafter.

*After Saudi Arabia you went to Ethiopia. Who were you, and who did other people think you were there?*

Well, in Ethiopia I was a child, still, a girl, and a stranger. And I think that that first sense of not belonging, which I felt in Saudi Arabia, became much stronger in Ethiopia. Ethiopia and Somalia were at war, so we viewed the Ethiopians as enemies, and they viewed us as enemies. The contradiction in Ethiopia was that the Ethiopians treated us much better than we treated them.

My mother spoke of the Ethiopians as uncircumcised, un-Islamic and selfish. And yet they gave us, members of the Somali opposition, a huge compound. And there were Ethiopian servants who had to taste the food before they served us to make sure that we didn't get poisoned. They gave us a car, a Land Rover, that took us to school, and I remember that the driver, the Ethiopian driver, had to bear us children repeating all the prejudices that we had from my mother and all the other female Somali refugees, and how he just laughed off those remarks. In hindsight, we weren't as kind to them as they were to us.

*Then you went to Kenya. Who were you then? And how did other people see you and treat you in that context?*

On arrival in Kenya, I remember the first time I went to school. At school I was referred to by the Kenyan children with a name that means something between a pirate and a thief. And that's how the Somalis were all seen. It means raider. So, I was labelled a "slave" in Saudi Arabia by the little Saudi girls at school. And I then called the Ethiopians by the same name. Then, in primary school, the Kenyans, sometimes in a friendly way, referred to us Somalis as raiders.

So I felt excluded and yet the crazy thing is, because of my accumulated prejudices, I and the other Somali children felt superior to the Kenyans, because they had kinky hair and flat noses and we referred to them as "slaves"! So in a crazy way being a "raider" was a much more comfortable position than being referred to as a "slave"!

So, who was I? I was, by the time we arrived in Kenya when I was 11 or 12 years old, already a person of many identities. I'm still a girl, and there are still those related expectations from my mother and my grandmother. So compared to my brother, who's free and roams round the streets of Nairobi, I'm kept inside, and my mother made sure that, after school hours, I go straight home when she picks me up. And I also have a whole new consciousness now, because I've become aware of my sexuality. And the older I become, the closer I get to becoming a teenager, the more nervous my mother and grandmother and everyone else becomes, so they feel a need for more control over me. And the kind of control gets harsher—so they say to me: "you cannot go outside" and "you've got to cover yourself" and "you cannot mingle with the opposite sex", and all of that, but they don't explain why. And that's the interesting thing, that part of the development of my identity is not explained to me. That part I got from Western books.

*And so how does that make you feel?*

Confused! And it left me in a constant state of guilt, because I didn't understand. I seemed to have crossed an invisible boundary. And then Sister came into our lives. That was in secondary school. At the height of my teenage years, with all my teenage hormones, Sister came in and she took on a position which was very different from the other individuals of authority in my life—my mother and the other teachers and my grandmother and my absent father and all of that. Instead of just barking down orders, she sat down at our level and explained things to us.

*This is a Saudi-trained religious teacher who taught you in Kenya?*

Yes, we called her Sister. Well, she explained things differently. And this is another contradiction because I think this is where my psychological autonomy comes from, if I can say it that way. It was with her that I learnt to think for myself.

For example I and some of the other Muslim girls, if we were made to cover our hair, we would only do so until we reached the corner of the house and then, when the person of authority disappeared, we would just remove the headscarf! But Sister explained to us why, if we did that, even though our parents could not see us, God could see us. So we might have thought we were not doing anything wrong, but actually we were seen and would be punished for it. And God's punishment was going to be far harsher than our parents would ever be, and it was going to be permanent. I know it's appalling to the Western ear, but this is how she persuaded us to develop some form of a conscience. So now, instead of removing the headscarf on the corner of the street, I started to cover even more, and the other girls did the same, because now we were no longer covering for our parents, we were covering for God.

So I was asserting a sense of identity but also finding a new group or a new community to belong to. And those of us who actually understood her message considered ourselves superior to those who did not get it. And it did require a bit of mental exercise, because you had to read the Koran and then answer the question: "what do you think now—should you do something or you should not do something?—such as pray five times a day or observe Ramadan and all of that." So, once we got practised at that, those of us who got into it felt strong and superior and wanted to assert that sense of superiority and that sense of power. You can cover

your hair in many different ways that doesn't attract that much attention, but we went about covering ourselves with this black, shapeless thing like a big tent. And this clothing attracts a lot of attention and that's a political and a religious and a moral assertion of identity.

*You eventually became an asylum seeker and a refugee in the Netherlands to avoid entering into an arranged marriage to a cousin in Canada. What was your experience of how that was affecting your sense of self and how other people were seeing you?*

I have to confess that before I came to the Netherlands, before I took that train and decided that I didn't want to marry the man I was supposed to, the only thing I was worried about was how other people would see me. I was only worried about how Somalis and my family would see me.

Again, what was coming into conflict was my personal identity versus my group identity—or my various group identities. My personal identity was becoming stronger, because I could suddenly imagine very clearly how my personal life would look if I had to go to Canada and spent the rest of my life with this man who I didn't like and wasn't attracted to. So, in Nairobi, even though I was developing a very strong group identity, somehow underneath there was also a personal identity developing too. And it sounds contradictory to say it, but in a way I really think that Sister somehow strengthened my sense of personal identity. And it also had to do with the Western books that I was reading. So my Somali identity, and my belief in "the will of God" had somehow weakened. And for me, to succeed in escaping that marriage, I needed to be in a context where I wouldn't be judged constantly. So, I couldn't escape my father's destiny for me, in a place where there were other Somalis. Because then I would be shunned, I'd have to face the consequences of saying "no" to tradition and to custom. Whereas, in Holland, surrounded by white people whose opinion I really didn't care that much about, and who probably didn't agree with arranged marriage anyway, I was more comfortable. And that's where I could reassert myself as an "I" instead of part of a "we".

*And how did you do that?*

I took the train from Germany, and asked for asylum in Holland, and I was put in an asylum-seeker centre for 11 months. And there was a large community of Somalis in all asylum-seeker centres, because of the civil war in Somalia. And so when I left the asylum-seeker centre I cut off all ties with the Somalis there and just rented a flat. I changed my telephone number and refused to answer the door when Somalis knocked on my door. I physically removed myself from that social control.

*Did severing yourself from your religion feel like it was a conclusion of a process that you'd started when you were severing ties with Somalia?*

You could look at it that way, but I would say one is an intellectual process and the other is an emotional process.

*The intellectual process as being the break away from religion?*

Yes. Because before the 11th of September, I really managed to avoid ever asking myself questions about the possibility of not being a Muslim, even though I was surrounded by non-Muslims. My boyfriend, with whom I lived together for five years, was an atheist. And still, I avoided the question altogether.

*So you felt an emotional connection to your Somali background, but your relationship to your faith didn't feel emotional in the same way?*

No. It was very intellectual. It was only emotional in as far as the emotion *fear* is concerned—a fear of hell, and of the hereafter, a fear of being burned and boiled and a fear of a God who would become very, very angry just because I had a glass of wine. But for me to have reached the intellectual conclusion that this is absurd was, obviously, an intellectual process. The five years I spent at university helped with that. All the little things I had gone through—Ethiopia and secondary school in Kenya and all the questions that come up, all those experiences, were, somehow, reordered at university.

So, education mixed with life experience helped. I only ended up going to university at age 25, I don't know how I would have reacted to that same amount of education if I had gone when I was 18. And by then I had been to all these countries, and I had been translating and interpreting for Somalis who had come as asylum-seekers to the Netherlands. So, as a very, very mature 25-year-old, I went to university in search of answers for myself. I had all these questions like: "How come *they*, the uncircumcised, filthy, impure, white infidels are wealthy and peaceful and we are coming to their countries?" It was all just very confusing and it didn't add up. And I came from the highest clan, from the highest religion, and from the best and most superior background. So my self-impression did not fit in to this reality, because I could see that all the other Somalis were on welfare. So I think that things would have gone in a different way if I had gone to college when I was 18, because I would have been too immature, and would not have reached that level of questioning.

*So when you shut the door on Somalia in the Netherlands, what were you thinking of? How were you constructing your identity behind the closed door?*

Firstly, I had to get away from the pain. It was very painful to constantly meet with these disapproving eyes and disapproving tongues.

*From Somalis?*

From the Somalis, yes. I remember I wanted to learn Dutch, and that required going to bed by at least 10 or 11pm, so that I'd be fresh and able to attend class at eight am the next morning. And, of course, I could stay awake for two or three nights until three am, but not every day of the week. So, I would have a conversation with some Somalis and say, "I can't come out tonight," and they would say, "Oh, you've become just like them. You've become like the white infidels." And there's a very strong moral judgment there. And I had to go through that to understand when people talk about dilemmas between modernity and the tribal life. Modernity takes away this kind of tribal way of life.

*You made a decision in May 2002, while drinking a glass of wine, that you would become an atheist. You say that was an intellectual decision. How did that decision and the repercussions of that affect your sense of self?*

There's more consistency now between what I believe and how I behave. And that is very peaceful and very calming. I've lost the fear of hell since 2002, but also, of course, I don't have the comfort of going to heaven. I've become stronger emotionally, so that I feel I can stand up to members of my family and say, "this is what I believe, this is what you believe. I am prepared to respect what you believe, but are you prepared to respect my choices?" And that is a source of strength.

*How do you think that Western societies should relate to different identity groups within societies, particularly within a multicultural context?*

I believe that if we take as a starting point the group, we will get into a lot of philosophical but also practical trouble.

If we look at Western legal systems, whether in Holland, the US, the UK or Australia, the assumption is always the individual: individual responsibility, individual rights and freedoms, and individual obligations. If you introduce a group element into that, and you say, "this religious group will be exempted from a number of obligations", or "we're going to ignore the rights of this group within the group", then you'll get into philosophical trouble, and you'll also get into practical trouble. And you can see this in the UK now, with the introduction of, or at least attempts to introduce, Sharia. So, the best way to go about it is to maintain the assumption of individual freedoms and individual obligations. So, multiculturalism is bad for the individual, and multiculturalism is especially bad for women and girls from tribal societies, who, like their male brothers, are seeking a better life when they come to the West. Where in this case, the men at least get the opportunity, and the women have one more hurdle—they have to go past their men-folk. And the proponent of multiculturalism will say, "leave them to their culture". But what they're actually saying is, "these people, women and girls and sometimes children do not have the same rights as everyone else."

*In 2006 you made a comment to a Dutch newspaper, proposing the screening of any Muslim applying for a job for a possible link to terrorist groups. Is that an accurate representation of what you said in that interview?*

It's not accurate! It's completely taken out of context.

*What was the context, then?*

Well, the context in fact, is the Dutch Parliament. And I was saying that as a Member of that Parliament. I said, "in the US there is screening, they are having a debate over ethnic and identity screening. But we in Holland are not having a debate, yet we have implemented ethnic screening." And so the question was, "what should we do?" And I said, "we should have the debate, just like they're having in the US. We should be open about it." And also, I mentioned, Islam is not an ethnicity. So if they thought you were from an Arab country, or were North African, or Turkish, or Somali, then you'd be screened more, and that, by the way, feels much worse. So people should open about it. But as Members of Parliament we knew that that was going on, yet we were not having the debate. I mean one of the 9/11 terrorists who learnt to fly in the US, and who lived in Hamburg as an architect, did not look like a typical stereotype of a radical Islamic fundamentalist. "So," I said, "if we're going to screen, then we need a debate on what we're going to screen for."

*Johann Hari, who interviewed you for* The Independent, *talked about there being two Ayaan Hirsi Alis: the revolutionary Ayaan, who feels that there is no distinction between Islam and radical Islam, and that Islam needs to be defeated, and the reformist Ayaan, who feels that it is still possible for the faith to be reformed from the inside. And he felt, speaking to you, that there was a kind of battle going on within yourself between those two positions. Do you think that's fair?*

I don't make a distinction between radical Islam and Islam in general or moderate Islam. I prefer the distinction of philosophy. And if you take Islam as a philosophy for life, politics, economy, as a political theory, then it's not compatible with human rights and it's not compatible with modernity. The idea of Islam as a way of life, and those agents who would impose it on others, need to be defeated. But defeating them doesn't just mean military defeat, it means defeating Islam in terms of ideas. And I am convinced that the Muslim mind can be persuaded to see alternative ways of life and society than just Islam.

*Where do you consider home?*

My home is the US. It is the place where I've decided to live and hopefully spend the rest of my life.

# JULIAN BAGGINI

is a writer and co-founder and editor of *The Philosopher's Magazine*. His books include *The Pig That Wants to be Eaten and 99 Other Thought Experiments* and *Welcome to Everytown*. He has written for many newspapers and magazines, including *The Guardian*, *The Independent* and *Prospect*, as well as being a frequent guest on BBC Radio. He is currently writing a book on the self and identity, picking up on the theme of his PhD, awarded by University College London in 1996.

---

*Who are you?*

I would say that I am a history and collection of thoughts, feelings, memories, sensations and so forth. But to say that is slightly misleading, because all these things are embodied. All the thoughts, feelings, ideas that I have are, or seem, part of me because I am in a body. A typical example of what I mean by this might be if someone was feeling horny. After all, they wouldn't be feeling horny if they weren't a mind in a body!

*Who do we think you are?*

It depends on your point of view. We tend to think that there is something at the core of every person which is fixed, definite, determinate, and that this comprises the essence of who someone is. The general idea is that this 'core' doesn't change from birth to death, despite anything else that might happen. So I think people have an idea that there is some core of self which is fixed and makes you who you are. I think most people make that assumption.

*What specific events or experiences have made Julian Baggini who he is?*

Well, I mean, it's everything. I think, again, that one of the things we believe about ourselves, which is probably false, is that it's only a few major facts about us that fix who we are. Whereas in fact, identity is being formed all the time, particularly in younger life.

I mean, I suppose the answer I've given so far is a very philosophical answer—on the basis of me approaching the question through John Locke, David Hume etc. But it's also true that if you ask, "who do people think we are?", people reach for categories. You know, you're the sum of your categories. So people might say to me: you're a man, you're white, you're, I suppose, middle-aged now, you're European, British-Italian, whatever it might be. And I think that there is a sense in which people see identity as being the sum of these things, and that if you list enough of those things then you've got a person.

*Do you identify yourself as English?*

Well, I think I'm a typical Englishman, though I slip between English and British as though they're interchangeable—which, of course, I know intellectually they're not. But actually when I'm talking I can say the two things meaning virtually the same thing for me. I think 'Englishness' is an identity which is unclear. I don't think a lot of people have grown up with a clear sense of it, so I think this is why it gets a bit vague. And, of course, I wrote a book on Englishness, called *Welcome to Everytown*.

*What compelled you to do that?*

I guess it was because I did not really feel that I had that identity very strongly—British or English. Yet I knew that that was what I was. I have lived in other countries, and I have got Italian family. But I know I'm not Italian, and I know I'm not Spanish. And I know it would be very difficult to go and live in those countries, because I'm the type of person who quotes from Alan Partridge and Fawlty Towers and all that kind of stuff.

So, in a way, I did feel a sense of unease with that. And I guess the book was partly an attempt to come to terms with my Britishness and my Englishness. I wanted to try and have a more sympathetic view of a part of me which I really didn't like. I didn't want to just think of Englishness as being all about drinking beer, falling over and being a bit ignorant!

*Is that something that you felt a connection to, even if you didn't approve of it?*

There are certain stereotypical aspects of English and British behaviour which I do feel a disconnection from—the whole drinking thing, and stuff like that. But I do feel on other occasions, in subtler ways, that I nevertheless am more like the average typical Brit than I am like the average typical Italian or Spaniard.

So there are these continuities. I think the book was mainly a desire to look again and more sympathetically at a part of my identity which I think I had kind of tended to disown over my life.

*Why were you trying to disown it?*

Because I didn't feel it very strongly. And when I did think about what it meant, it tended to throw up things that I didn't like. For instance British identity is all still very class-ridden. So, the question for me was which class do I identify with? And I'm a typically class-confused person, because I have a working-class background on one side, very, very solidly. But

on the other hand, my dad's Italian and entrepreneurial, and also a man who is interested in books, and all that kind of stuff. So I'm confused. I look at working-class British culture: at tabloids, and ITV, and beer, and that's not me. And I look at upper-class English culture and think "well, that's definitely not me". And I look at that aspirational *Daily Mail* middle class thing and I can't stand that either. So, again, it's this curious thing of knowing that I am more British and English than I am any other kind of nationality, but not finding any connection with it.

*When researching your book* Welcome to Everytown, *you spent six months living in Rotherham, in a district that you took to be a statistical microcosm of England. You said you wanted "to understand the English mind, what we think, what we believe, what we want and what we value". And one of the intriguing things about your book is that you seem to have a great deal of empathy for people, even when they're saying and doing things that you don't approve of, while at the same time maintaining a real sense of distance between yourself and the people you're observing.*

Well, from the outset I decided I would be a sympathetic observer, and not just see the downsides, but also see the upsides. I think this is something which always happens with identity. When people are repelled by an identity—which I suppose is what you're talking about when people say, "ooh, I really don't like Englishness"—the repulsion is always stronger if you're able to depersonalise it in some way. As soon as you get a more personal interaction with anybody, then any antipathy you may have to those things which gives a person an identity tends to dissolve. And it's a cliché in relation to the art of mediation, when people say, "the thing that works best is actually to bring people face to face". They're trying to do it in the Middle East, they used to do it in Ireland. The idea is always that, once things are made personal, then you stop seeing people primarily through their identity. But of course, the funny thing is that it's not true that those identities have nothing to do with who they are. They do. So, it's not like these identities are just stereotypes which, once stripped away, allow us to see the real person. It's rather, once you see the real person, their individuality and humanity come through in addition to their identity.

People often ask, "what are the critical things about identity?" And they'll talk about things like religion, as if what matters when there's a religious conflict is that one side believes that we contact the Lord directly, and another believes that we contact Him indirectly. But I think, when it comes down to it, it is much smaller things that bind people culturally. For example, look at humour—people always talk about their culture's sense of humour. I think everyone who is British has had the experience of being abroad and cracking a joke and nobody getting it. So you know that you've got a cultural connection with somebody when you sense it. And you know it when you don't have it. But it's very hard to put your finger on what it is. And despite having written a book, I'm not sure I can tell you exactly what it is.

Anyway, I went to Rotherham because it is somewhere that has the same racial mix, and the same representative spread of age, income, and all these other factors as the country as a whole. I asked companies who do demographic profiling to tell me which postcode areas have the mix of household types that most matched the mix in the country as a whole.

Now, of course, this is not scientific, and everywhere has its particularities, so nowhere is exactly the country in miniature. But it's funny how many people said, "you can't take Rotherham as typical, because it's in Yorkshire." And I said, "well, how would it be more typical if it were London? London's very different to the rest of the country." But many people have this default belief that the South is a benchmark of normalness, and the North is a diversion from it. But nonetheless I started by looking at hard data, from opinion polls, surveys, and statistics. And the point of going to live in Rotherham, was as it were, to try and get a sense of how, in the experience of living there, things were borne out.

So, I guess it was like a case study, where I was trying to test objective facts against the experience of life. My thought was that without any sense of how people actually live and do things, the data itself wouldn't be self-explanatory. So, if you get

a statistic which says that 80 per cent of a given population think there are too many immigrants, for example, that in itself wouldn't tell you whether or not people are actually bigoted, or whether they just really wanted a sense of continuity in their demographic— it wouldn't tell you *why* they don't want immigrants to live in what they think of as their home.

So on things like attitudes to immigration, ethnic minorities, and so forth, the statistics might tell you that there's suspicion and hostility towards immigrants, but they couldn't give you a sufficient explanation for that. If you want to get a sense of what really lurks behind these attitudes you have to meet those people. And again, my overall view was that, most of the time, this suspicion didn't come from anything like a violent hatred of immigrants, but actually it had much more to do with ignorance and a little bit of fear.

But then sometimes it worked the other way around. Sometimes what happened was, I'd get an impression from living there, then try and check it out statistically. So, for example, you'd clearly get the impression that, despite all this Jamie Oliver school dinner stuff, most people's eating habits there are still actually very poor, and quite like what they used to be. So, then I'd contact Tesco, and say, "well, what are your best-selling items?" And they say, "value orange juice, sliced white bread, bananas", and a few things like that.

*What did you look for and what did you notice?*

Well, remember I wasn't trying to look for an identity as such. If that emerged, then so be it, but I was really looking for people's dominant beliefs and values. So, what I was really trying to do, in terms of just living there, was be a sponge.

*In your writing you basically exclude London from England.*

Yeah, London's very different. It's a world city. Anywhere you go in the world, it's always the same—the people in the capital are different from the rest of the country. The capital tends to be the international representative of the country, but it is always different to the normal life of most people in the country.

One of the things that stimulated Billy Bragg to write his book was the rise of the BNP in Barking and Dagenham.

The BNP are doing quite well at the moment because they are distancing themselves from the far right. I went back to see two BNP councillors recently. And, I think, the BNP are being quite clever because their current message is "the mainstream parties have abandoned you". And in a sense, they have, because the electoral logic means that they're chasing people in the middle. They're not chasing the poorer, white, working-class demographic. And so these people feel that they've been abandoned. And they are worried because they have certain beliefs, which are generally untrue, about immigrants taking resources. So, people might say, "I've got nothing against people of colour, blah blah blah, but they're getting preferential treatment and we're not." Now, they're wrong about that, but there are so many stories knocking about that you can hardly blame people for believing what they're told and what they hear, and not believing politicians and the newspapers which, quite rightly, they don't trust. So essentially, the main reason that people vote for the BNP, is that they feel that the BNP is going to speak up for them. I spoke to the councillor who was elected there, and he really seemed pretty ignorant of the explicitly racial nature of the BNP manifesto. But they do believe that too much ethnic diversity's bad—they do believe in maintaining a certain gene pool. And its funny how, when they are making this case, they appeal to arguments that people use about biodiversity in the world. A lot of environmentalists talk about the need to preserve certain species and things like that. So they say, "if they're not bigoted and prejudiced, why are we?"

Can you choose your identity?

Well, I think so up to a point. But the problem is that people can get into terrible difficulties by denying what is part of their identity. It's interesting—one of the phrases people often use as a great commendation of someone is that they don't forget their roots: "he's a good lad, he hasn't forgotten his roots." I heard people say that up in Rotherham. And in a way, you

can ask: "well, why do they think that's a good thing?" I think partly because it's about an honesty, isn't it? The persons who do forget their roots, or pretend they don't have roots, even if their life now is so different, and even if they're never even going to go back, are in a sense denying something about themselves. And that goes back to my first answer, because who we are is, in so many ways, the culmination of all the experiences that we've had. That's why you can never entirely escape your background, I don't think.

You seem to have come to the conclusion that if English identity is changing, then it is changing extremely slowly.

Well I don't want to predict the future, but it seems to me that people always exaggerate the extent to which things change. Over a long period of time, things do change. So I suppose when I say that things haven't changed I mean that things haven't changed as much as people say they have. Take England's relationship to alcohol for example. I mean, I quote the book, *Beer and Britannia*, on the Battle of Hastings. So it's 1066, the night before battle, and while the French are praying for victory, what are the British doing? Getting pissed. Hence the result of the Battle the next day.

I just think that people tend to exaggerate the extent to which things change. And that occurs on the individual level as well. When someone says, "I've really changed" a lot of the time they haven't changed as much as they're saying or pretending they have. I had an experience recently, when I met up with people I shared a house with at university, and I've seen some of them on and off over the years, but not a lot. And in a sense it was quite depressing, and interesting, for various reasons. There was something paradoxical about it all—on the one hand, we had all changed in lots of ways. I would say I've changed. But then when you actually get together in a group like that, you see there are fundamentals about your personality and the way you interact which actually don't change. And it was a bit of a downer for my preferred theory of identity, in which I talk up the extent to which identities are not fixed. Because even though it's neurologically true to say that we have no fixed, immutable essence, or core self, and that it's actually all to do with connections and patterns in the brain—experience shows that those connections are remarkably stable. Families are brilliant examples of this. As soon as people go back to their families, they tend to revert to the role they had as children.

People like the way of life they're comfortable with. Now, I think that's pretty much universal. People find a way of life they like, and they don't want it to be changed. They also tend to gather around people they find like themselves. Now this should be uncontroversial. But people often talk about how it's appalling that certain minorities are living in ghettos. Yet they don't talk about literary ghettos up in Hampstead or media ghettos in Brighton or British ghettos in the Costa del Sol.

It's the same in any English town. Whatever town you live in—name an area of that town, and, if you know the town, then you will know roughly what sort of schools people go to, where they go to on holiday, what supermarkets they shop at and so on. Generally, you will be right. People often think it's terrible that kids go to school where the majority of the people there are Muslims or Jewish or whatever. Yet they don't think it's terrible that some people go to schools where there are kids there who have never played with a child who doesn't have a nanny. That's also segregation, but of a social kind. So, I think the uncomfortable fact is that people like to live amongst those with whom they identify as being like themselves. Once they have a way of life they're comfortable with, they like to keep it. I think people are now afraid that their way of life is under threat. And the point is, in a way, that they are right. They are right, because things do change. Different ways of life are always under threat. Now middle-class Londoners can get around that problem, by moving, and things like that, but other people can't. It's really difficult to talk about these things, because you get accused of being an apologist for racism if you even dare to do this sort of stuff. My Wikipedia entry was hacked by someone who claimed that I had written an article defending the BNP in *The Independent*. This was an *absurd* statement, but that's the kind of criticism you open yourself up to when you even dare to try and discuss these things.

*You argue in your book, that the Chinese community in this country doesn't usually come up against any racism, whereas, say, the Muslim community or the black community does.*

Yeah. I mean, there are Chinatowns all over the country. But imagine if there was an Islamatown in the middle of London. That said, things may change as China grows as a global power. One could imagine a situation where people become fearful of China taking over the world, and then people start looking fearfully towards the Chinese in this country. I hope that doesn't happen, but it could do.

*What is your attitude to multiculturalism? Is it right to allow for different communities to be protected, tolerated and to exist autonomously?*

I think there's a balance to be struck when it comes to these things. There's a mistaken view that essentially what one must do is never challenge the other, never challenge difference—that one must always respect difference. And that's not true. There needs to be enough communality in a society for it to rub along. At the same time, at the other extreme, there is the assimilationist view which says that if someone's going to live in this country, then they've got to adopt our way of life. And that needs to be challenged too. I mean, what exactly is our way of life? If I go down to the Cotswolds this weekend, our way of life might involve picnic hamper by the river. If I go to inner London, it might involve a night down the Cock and Bull and a knees-up. "Our way of life" is a myth. There's huge diversity.

The point is that everyone has to agree on the minimal, essential, shared values that are needed for society to survive. And some of those can be tough. Because they might include things to do with sexual equality and things like that, which not everyone might be keen on. But everyone has to agree on them nonetheless.

People generally tend to assert identities most strongly when they're under threat. And the fear that comes out can be legitimate or it can be illegitimate. So, for example, when people are asserting their identity as gay, on pride marches and all that sort of stuff, well the reason why people have to have a festival of it is that it has not historically been very easy to be gay. So, that community felt a great need to assert that identity.

*Do you find that you now define yourself differently because of your experience in Rotherham?*

Well, as I've said, I think people tend to exaggerate the extent to which something or someone is changeable. I remember going to East Africa, and my then girlfriend's mother said, "it'll change you" and I said, "I don't think it will." What happens is, you go somewhere, you come back, and within three weeks you're back in your own routine. People have an amazing ability to have their sense of identity stretched and pushed and everything, but then we tend to revert back. It's like a memory cushion, isn't it? Like a memory mattress! It remembers your shape, and you only have to lie on it for a bit, and then you just revert back into that old shape. So I really don't know. I think it changed certain ways of thinking I had about right approaches to multiculturalism, and it certainly clarified thinking I had about the role of identity in social cohesion. So, it's changed certain views I had, I think. But has it changed how I *feel* about myself? Not really. But I suppose I feel slightly more *at ease* in the country I live in. I would say that.

# BILLY BRAGG

is a singer/songwriter who has been performing his own unique brand of politically inspired alternative rock which blends punk, folk and protest music since the late 1970s. In 2006 he published his first book *The Progressive Patriot—A Search for Belonging.*

*Who are you?*

Well, first and foremost, I'm a name—I'm Billy Bragg. That marks me out as an individual. Then, I'm from Barking, which is a place in East London, which is also in Essex. So, I'm both a Londoner and an Essex man. And Barking's in the East End, so I'm also an East Ender. And West Ham are the local football team, so I'm a West Ham fan. I'm also a Southerner because I now live in Dorset in the South of England, or rather, the South-West of England. So I'm English. Which means I'm British. Which means I'm European. So, these are some of the simple levels of identity that I have.

Now, there are other things that inform my identity that aren't so readily discernible from my postcode or my accent or my CV. My mother's grandfather and grandmother were born in Italy and came to this country at the turn of the nineteenth century. And even though all my mum has left of her Italian heritage is her Catholicism, it still informed my upbringing and is part of my background. And my great-grandfather on my father's side was involved in the first industrial militancy in the Beckton Gas Works in the 1880s. So, that also informs a little of who I am. But most people wouldn't know me from any of those things. If you said the name, "Billy Bragg", they would say, "lefty". They know me from my politics. So depending on who I'm talking to, depending on where I am, depending on what the context is, all those things change and interact with each other and inform the position that I'm coming from and other people's perceptions of me. Because I'm all those things at the same time, and others.

*You're also male, white and you're also famous. Why didn't you say any of those things?*

Well, because I don't feel my racial identity very strongly. As a white person, I live in a white society; it's not an issue. If I were a black person, living in a white society, it would be an issue. If I were gay, I'm sure it would be a strong part of my identity. If I felt I was in a minority, if I was disabled for example, I might feel that strongly. And yeah, I'm famous, but no one's coming up and talking to me, no one's spotted me in here, have they?! So, I never really think about that.

There are other things, as well, that are part of my identity—that I don't have to dwell on. I didn't identify myself as working-class, either, but I do feel working-class. Even though I live in a nice big house by the ocean in Dorset, I still think of myself as working-class as that was my upbringing. Perhaps in the old days, distinctions of class would have been much more significant. But now, in the time of rampant individualism, identity moves on to other things. Class becomes less significant and the focus moves to local and national identities. These are the contested identities, now, whether we like it or not. And I happen to not like it. I wish I didn't have to write about this shit, but unfortunately I do.

*Why?*

Well, because everyone knows, without me having to point it out, that English nationalism is a sleeping dragon that people are scared of. And as a result people say to me, "you shouldn't really talk about these things, because it gives a platform to nationalists, it brings racists out the woodwork." But if we don't discuss the issue of the politics of identity, then it will be the nationalists and the racists, it will be the BNP, that define who does and who doesn't belong in England. And unfortunately, in the past we've been guilty of ignoring the problem in the hope that it will go away. We haven't discussed it. We've left a vacuum. And the far right has filled it. And unfortunately, we have to contest that ground now. And I say "unfortunately", because the far right knows that ground like the back of its hand but we don't. It's unfamiliar to us. We're internationalist, but we need to engage in the debate about national identity, yet we're not used to arguing for it. Just bringing the subject up can alienate people who come from a traditional leftist background. Immediately—just the mere mention of it. So, it's complicated. But the fact is that immigration has now risen up the political agenda, so we have no choice but to engage. It's not enough just to keep saying to people, "well, we're internationalist, we're all in this together, we're all one great, big family." That doesn't wash any more. We have to take on the BNP on their terms, to fight them for our heritage, our English dissident heritage. We have to fight for the culture of dissent that's been the key vehicle for fundamental change in this society, all the way back to Magna Carta.

*You have described the idea of the British Empire as being about capitalism.*

Empire is always about exploitation. The British didn't conquer India. It was conquered by a private, limited company. Exploitation is the driving force. Therefore, I think, rather than look at the English as a people who went out to conquer the world, to 'civilise' other peoples, I think of them as capitalists who went out to exploit people in order to put stuff in shops.

One of the terms that it's really difficult to talk about these days is 'socialist'. Because if you say you want to live in a socialist society, you've got to explain to people that it's not going to be like totalitarianism, that it's not going to be like Stalinist Russia. Whereas, if you say you want to live in a compassionate society, people understand where you're coming from.

I'm a socialist, and what I mean by that is that I believe that the individual is the most important person in society, but that the rights and the potential of each individual can only be guaranteed and realised by the collective provision of education, healthcare, decent, affordable housing and proper pensions. That is why I define myself as a socialist, because I believe in that passionately. I'm not against the individual; I just don't believe that you should have a society based purely on individualism. One of the many mistakes of the Soviet Union was that they denied that people have spiritual needs and that people have material needs. Whether we like it or not, they do. But what you don't want is a society based purely on theology or a society based purely on consumerism, which is what the US is aiming towards. So, in that sense, creating that fair and equal society is not about suppressing the individual. It's about supporting the individual. But recognising that each individual has a collective responsibility to the other—that we are in this together, whether we be ever so rich or ever so poor, whether we be black or white or Muslim or Christian or whatever. Ultimately, it's our responsibility to one another that is the thing that defines us. And it's that sense of responsibility that's been completely undermined by the marketisation of society, by the cult of the individual, which says, "you're the most important person in the world, this is all for you, get these great things, never mind anybody else, forget all those other people, they're a pain in the arse." That was the message of Thatcherism and shamefully, it has not been dismantled by New Labour.

*What place does religion have in your definition of socialism?*

To be frank, I don't think that religion is fundamentally, in and of itself, a bad idea. You look at the great revolutionaries in British history—many of them were driven by the Bible, particularly by the New Testament. The Diggers, the Levellers, the Abolitionists—it was a crucial component of what inspired them. But fundamentalists, whether they be religious or political, are always a danger. People who have all the answers, people who have no doubts, are a danger. So, I have faith. But my faith is in humanity. I'm not sure I'd feel comfortable living in a world where faith becomes abolished and where everything is a matter of reason. I would find that a rather troubling world. After all, the Holocaust wasn't perpetrated by religious fanatics. It was perpetrated by people who thought they have reinvented reason in the form of Nazism. Extremists of any kind, whether they're the Spanish Inquisition or the Crusaders or the Nazis, are the real danger. So rather than denying people their religious beliefs, I'm trying to make room for those aspects of Englishness that are both secular and sacred. If you live in a multicultural society, you have to respect some things you don't necessarily adhere to. That includes the

Royal Family, that includes Morris dancing and that includes the Church of England.

*So interpretation of Englishness or socialism, relies on cherry picking certain aspects in favour of others.*

Well, isn't identity all about cherry picking? Isn't your identity those things that have happened to you, and the social and familial and local environment that you choose to identify with? Why do you dress like that? Why does that guy over there wear a suit and a tie? Because he chooses to, in order to make a statement. I put this shirt on this morning because I cherry picked this identity to present today. I took into consideration where I was speaking, and I cherry picked the clothes to go with who I would be in that context. In a few nights from now, I'm going on stage with Richard Hawley at the Royal Albert Hall, as a surprise guest. I've got a great black shirt, a country-and-western shirt, with music notes on it. And in that context, I'll be going in with a kind of Johnny Cash vibe. So, I think identity is all about cherry picking. And when you're trying to make a case about patriotism, there are as many different types of patriotism as there are socialism. And so, when I say "I'm a socialist", I need to explain what I mean by that, what I have cherry picked. It's the same with Englishness. Someone said to me, "how can you write a book about Englishness and not mention cricket?" Obviously for that person, their personal notion of English identity is very strongly connected with cricket while mine is not. And that's why, to some people's frustration, the book doesn't define Englishness. Instead, I put forward the idea of a modern Bill of Rights that unites us in our diverse identities. Rather than subscribing to a national identity based on stereotypes, some of which will be unfamiliar to many, a Bill of Rights would provide a universal definition of what it means to be British, based on values that we as a society subscribe to.

*Isn't there a risk with a Bill of Rights, however carefully one is put together, that it will force an identity on England? If you think of some aspects of the American Constitution, like the Second Amendment for example, the right to bear arms?*

Well, that's absolutely true, but you have to remember that the US Bill of Rights was written at a time when notions of individual rights were just being formulated. The Americans were writing a Constitution for a fledgling State, so the right to bear arms probably made sense to them. They also lived in a very wild country where you could get eaten by a bear, so the idea of carrying a gun was something that most people in that society subscribed to. Now, the Universal Declaration of Human Rights is less prescriptive, more universal in its content.

*In your book,* The Progressive Patriot*, some of the most moving passages explore your own family tree.*

Yeah, I sat down to write the book, and I thought, "well, I can either write an academic overview of English history, which I've not really got the wherewithal to do or I can explore the reasons why I am who I am, and hopefully people will relate to that. I wanted to respond to this terrible thing that happened in my home town: the British National Party won 12 seats on the local borough council. That was a terrible shock to me, in 2005, a real shock. It really made me question who I am. I mean, I finish my gigs—every night, wherever I am in the world—by saying, "my name's Billy Bragg, I'm from Barking, Essex. Thank you very much, good night", so it really undermined my sense of who I was. So, the book became an exploration of how I ended up being born there. I really needed to get to the bottom of that. "Yeah, I am from Barking, but *why* am I from Barking? What forces—historically, socially, politically, economically—resulted in me being born there?" And were these forces the forces of fascism, or were they the forces of progress? And that's why a lot of it was history, our national history, but also trying to piece together little fragments of my own family history.

*How did you start?*

Well, I looked at my grandfather's diary. I never met him: he died before I was born. His father, I discovered, worked in the Beckton Gasworks in East London at the time of great industrial action in the 1880s. And then I also found an ancestor who was a Baptist, refusing to sit in church on Sunday behind the squire, instead attending meetings in barns and open fields. I lighted on those people who, in some way, I felt a sense of strong connection with, or who, in some way, gave me what you might say was a sense of continuity. These ancestors of mine chimed in with my own sense of identity. There may have been others in between who didn't share my politics, but I chose to identify with these two.

But then families construct their own narratives don't they? My missus, her father was Spanish and although she had never lived in Spain—she had been born in Trinidad—she has a strong sense of Spanish identity. Her father had left Spain as a child with his cousins—they were refugees from the Spanish Civil War. When my missus was growing up, the presence of her Spanish grandmother—her *abuela*—was a very important part of forming who she was. Recently the last of the cousins died, and left a manuscript of the family history. He'd had the prescience not only to write their story down but also to put it on disc.

My missus made copies for her brothers and sisters and when they came to stay with us at New Year, she got the laptop out on the table and her elder brother read the manuscript to us. It was mentioned in passing that their great-grandfather was working in London as a Spanish lawyer, at the turn of the century. This caught my attention. If their ancestors were in London in 1900, there was every chance that they would appear on the 1901 UK census. So without saying anything, I went and got my laptop and as my brother-in-law continued to read from the manuscript, I was searching the 1901 census online for references to their great-grandparents. With an uncommon Spanish name—*de Valero*—it didn't take me long to find them. There they all were, living in East Ham, on the same page of the *London A to Z* as my great grandparents. The best thing though, was that the census revealed that their Spanish grandmother had been born in Buckhurst Hill. Their dear *abuela* was from Essex, just like me.

And my missus and my in-laws could not believe it. So, they rang up their mum, and she said, "oh, yeah—actually, I did know about that"! So, does my missus feel any less Spanish now? Not at all, although she does have to put up with a bit of 'Essex girl' leg pulling from me. The fact is that if you are prepared to do the research, your identity may be a little more ambiguous than you think.

*Are there contexts in which it is acceptable to say to somebody, "you're not who you say you are"?*

I don't think there are. Identity is a personal construct. It doesn't really become an issue until somebody tries to tell you who you are *not*, based on your skin colour or accent or religion or allegiances.

Our son has a dual heritage. His mother was born in Trinidad and his father was born in England. During the last World Cup he supported Trinidad and Tobago. He was 12 at the time and noticed that they had a white English guy playing for them. He asked me why and I said "Oh, his mum is from Trinidad." He got excited at this news "My mum is from Trinidad—I could play for Trinidad and Tobago." The missus just smiled at me, and I was like, "Oh my God, what have I just done?!" But there's no point in me saying to my son, "no, no, no, you can't do that." Because it is his right to draw upon any facet of his identity in order to be himself. And if he plays football for Trinidad and Tobago, I'll be just as proud as if he played for England.

*Who is excluded from the group that you belong to?*

As a socialist, I wouldn't want to see anyone excluded. Yet as someone who wants to redefine what it means to be British around a new Bill of Rights, I am aware that there are some who would exclude non-British passport holders from access to those rights. Rights have to be universal, available to everyone no matter what their colour, creed, or politics, otherwise they are nothing more than privileges. The trick is to strike a balance between liberty to speak your mind and the responsibility not to cause deliberate offence. Because, paradoxically, it is those who wish to exclude others on the basis of race that are the most vociferous in defence of their own rights.

*Does this fuel your idea about reclaiming the flag, and other ideas of Englishness?*

Well the flag either belongs to all of us, or none of us—just like the rights we inherited from Magna Carta.

Each generation has sought to push back the barrier that divides those who do belong from those who do not, to make our society more inclusive. That's what the Chartists were trying to do, to get the right to vote for all men, regardless of their social standing. The Suffragettes sought to do the same thing for women and over the past 50 years as more and more people have come to our country, the definition of society has expanded to accommodate them.

There are those who wish to turn back the clock of course, to exclude these people, but we have more in common with recent immigrants that many give credit for. Basically, what all these people who come here want is to work hard, get paid for it, and have a better lifestyle for their children. And that's the reason why my ancestors came to Barking: one from Essex, the other one from Italy, but both for exactly the same reason.

*How has your exploration as an artist, as a singer-songwriter, informed your sense of identity?*

It's been very, very important. My first ever feelings of Englishness were engendered by Simon and Garfunkel singing "Scarborough Fair" when I was 12 years old. That song awoke something in me that I hadn't experienced before: it was a very deep sense of timelessness and a connection to place, and that was something that was overwhelming when I first felt it. Now, how two Jewish geezers from Queens playing with Bob Dylan's backing band in New York can make me feel more English, as a 12-year-old... well I don't know—go figure! At the time, Martin Carthy, who taught "Scarborough Fair" to Paul Simon, was doing gigs in London, in the city of my birth, my countryman, performing songs from my culture. Yet I never heard the songs of my ancestors from him, I heard them courtesy of CBS Records in New York.

So what is this process, whereby foreigners take your culture away, reanimate it and then send it back for you to connect with? This is the key thing The Beatles did. Think about it: what would The Beatles have sounded like if they had grown up listening only to English music? Just think about it—it would have been awful. Everyone knows they were inspired to write songs by listening to the music of black America, which, conversely, led them to write perhaps the most

English music of the twentieth century. So, there's an historical process at work here, a constant exchange between cultures, which *we* generate.

This seemingly modern idea of multiculturalism is in fact the driving force in popular music. And when you've lived through such a fundamental coming together as punk rock and reggae, in 1977, then you can't fail to be aware of these things. Of course the knock-on effect of that coming together was Rock Against Racism, which provided me with my first experience of political activism and attuned my radar to the politics of identity.

On the other hand, as a writer—because I try to write songs that are quite personal—I have often used the architecture of the English tradition in some of my songs. Although, sometimes it has all been a little bit inside-out. For instance, it's ironic that the Billy Bragg who made a career talking about politics, and writing at great length on identity, should be most famously known for a song that says, "I don't want to change the world, I'm not looking for a New England, I'm just looking for another girl."

*Where did that lyric come from?*

Well, really you've got to see that lyric in the context of when I wrote it. It was right at the end of punk, when everything had fallen apart, and I was like, "well, we tried our hardest to change the world, it didn't happen. England is as it was before punk. So I just need a shag. I can't do this any more. I just need someone to hold. I can't do this any more."

*And has it been the resurgence of the BNP that made you think, "actually, it's worth trying again"?*

To be honest, as early as 2000, you could smell 'em—they were out there again spreading their cynicism and hatred. I guess if your entire political life has been built around fighting against racism and fascism, if that's what first brought you into political discourse, your antenna will be highly tuned into that sort of thing, so you will quickly pick it up when the language of racism and exclusion starts creeping back.

As a political artist you have to make a choice to either make art that panders to your audience's convictions, or to use your platform to challenge

them. And I've always wanted to try and offer a different perspective to the mainstream one, so I decided to challenge them.

How do I do that? By writing songs about subjects that are taboo on the left, like national identity. When that was well received, I sought to take things a step further by introducing the symbols of Englishness into my performance. On St George's Day in Wolverhampton I brought the flag of St George onstage and held it up. And there was an audible gasp from the audience, and a silence. But I said, "look, if we're serious about reclaiming Englishness from the neo-Nazis, we've got to get used to seeing this. We've got to be able to hold it. It's not kryptonite." And I kept that flag on the entire tour and I did it every night. It's a tough one, because some argue that 'Englishness' cannot be 'reclaimed' (its a debate with a lot of inverted commas). But I'm not trying to make everyone salute the flag of St George on April 23rd. I'm trying to encourage a broad debate about identity and belonging; about other ideas of what it means to be English, so that those who feel excluded might actually realise that it is their right to be English if they so choose and that no one can take that away from them.

*Can you envisage any circumstances in which you would actually renounce your Englishness?*

Oh, yeah—I mean, there are aspects of it that I renounce anyway. There are plenty of things that I'm ashamed of that England did. And there are plenty of things that we do now that I'm ashamed of. But to renounce that part of my identity which I define as English would be to surrender to the bigots on the right and to the cynics of the left. Instead I'm determined to engage with both sides and to challenge their perceptions of what it means to be English. I guess that's what makes me a patriot.

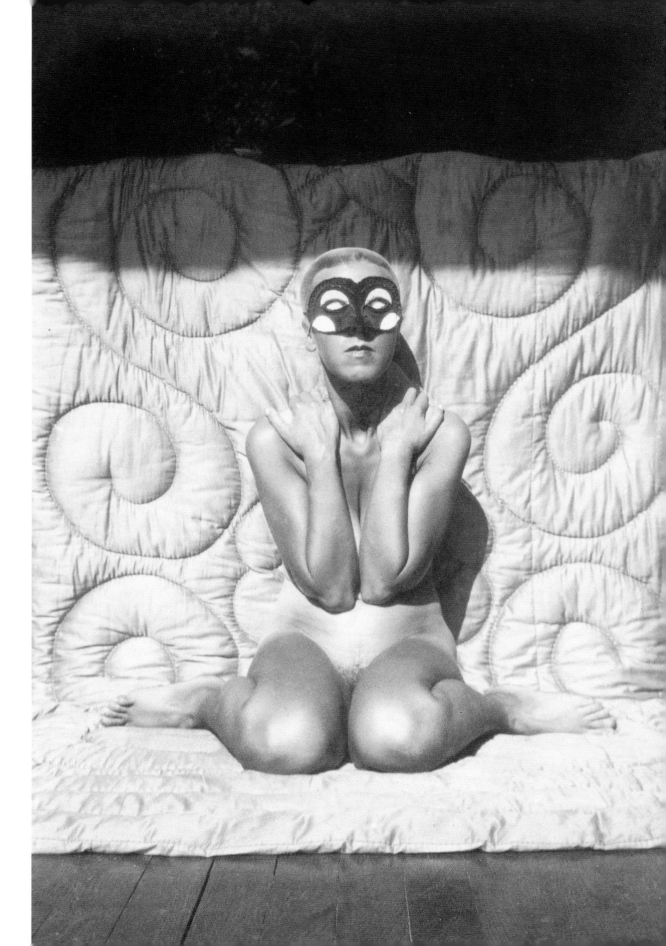

# CLAUDE CAHUN

Emily Jo Sargent

The photographer and writer Claude Cahun was born Lucie Schwob in France in 1894. Her paternal grandfather was the director of a large regional newspaper in Nantes and her father and brothers were among the founders of an all-male intellectual group. Influenced by, although seemingly excluded from, her family's interests she went on to study literature at the Sorbonne. By 1914 she had begun to publish articles exploring symbolist imagery and themes associated with identity under the name Claude Cahun. Her choice of pseudonym was a deliberately ambiguous one and her apparent interest in moving towards an androgynous identity was reflected in her appearance. She cut her hair very short and wore trousers—a radical departure from early twentieth century society's expectation of women.

It was around this time that Cahun began to make the photographic self-portraits for which she is now best known. Portraying herself in a variety of different poses and costumes, this lifelong project can be understood in terms of her femininity, sexuality and religion. Her apparent and continued rejection of fixed identity markers ('female', 'lesbian', 'Jewish') coincided with the rise of National Socialism and the increasing tendency to judge the individual using those precise terms. Rather than treating the self-portrait as an opportunity to present a 'true' identity, Claude Cahun's work looks towards a position outside traditionally fixed notions of identity. Responding to Rimbaud's "Je est un autre" (I is another) Cahun writes "Je est un autre—un multiple toujours"—"I is another—and always multiple".

Although universally acknowledged to be Cahun's own work—composed and framed by her—the photographic portraits, by their very nature, imply a collaborator or accomplice. This is widely understood to be Cahun's long term partner (and step sister) Suzanne Malherbe, an illustrator and designer who worked under the similarly ambiguous alias of Marcel Moore. Some photographs survive with Moore in place of Cahun—a rehearsal for her self portrait perhaps—while in others Moore's presence is betrayed only by a shadow.

Cahun and Moore moved to Jersey in 1937 and remained there despite the Nazis' occupation of the island in 1940. They launched their own anti-Nazi propaganda operation, distributing pamphlets designed to appear as though written by a reluctant German soldier. These were signed "a soldier without a name".

Cahun's work is often discussed in the context of the exploration of fractured or multiple identities by more recent artists like Cindy Sherman. Not widely known in her lifetime, Cahun's photographs remain a fascinating and early example of a particular kind of self portrait—one that resists the idea of a single selfhood.

Cahun often made use of masks in her work, both literal and metaphorical. Each identity she created for her photographs was a kind of mask, continually changing but never revealing a 'true' or single identity. In this photo, taken in 1928, her face is concealed but her naked body is revealed.
Courtesy of the Jersey Heritage Trust.

Untitled, 1928.
Courtesy of the Jersey Heritage Trust.

**FEMALE.**　　　　　**REGISTRATION CARD.**

(1) NAME (Surname first in Roman capitals).

S C H W O B　　Lucie Renee.

ALIAS

(3) NATIONALITY　　French.　Born on　25/10/1894.　in Nantes France.

(4) PREVIOUS NATIONALITY (if any)

(5) PROFESSION or OCCUPATION　Independent. (single)

(7) Address of last residence outside U.K.　Nantes France.

(2) IDENTITY BOOK OR REGISTRATION CERTIFICATE.

No. J. 6010

Date 15/7/1922

Issued at Jersey.

(6) Arrived in U.K. on　1 / 7 / 1922

(8) GOVERNMENT SERVICE.

(9) PASSPORT or other papers as to nationality and identity.

Passport issued at Nantes France 27/6/1922 No.389.

(10) PHOTOGRAPH.

(11) SIGNATURE OR LEFT THUMB PRINT.

Lucie Schwob

Claude Cahun's Jersey alien registration card, bearing her birth name: Lucie Schwob.
Courtesy of the Jersey Heritage Trust.

(12) REMARKS.

(*6303) Wt. P. 361—S.P.D. 22. 4,000. 5/20. J. T. & S., Ltd. **162.**

| (13) Date. | Registration District Serial Number. | ADDRESS OF RESIDENCE OR REMARKS. |
|---|---|---|
| 15 July 1922. | Jersey. | St.Brelades Hotel Jersey. |
| 22 Sept. 1922. | Jersey. | Left for France. |
| 6 Aug. 1930. | Jersey. | St.Brelades Hotel, St.Brelades. |
| 23 Sept.1930. | Jersey. | Left for France. |
| 29 July 1931. | Jersey. | St.Brelades Hotel, St.Brelades. |
| Sept.1931. | Jersey. | Left for France. |
| 30 July 1932. | Jersey. | St.Brelades Hotel, St.Brelades. |
| 23 Sept 1932 | Jersey. | Left for France |
| 2 Aug.1933. | Jersey. | St.Brelades Hotel, St.Brelades. |
| 29 Sept.1933. | Jersey. | Left for France. |
| 18 July 1934. | Jersey. | St.Brelades Hotel, St.Brelades. |
| 18 Sept 1934 | Jersey | Left for France |

N.B.—A Continuation Card was added by the Police on

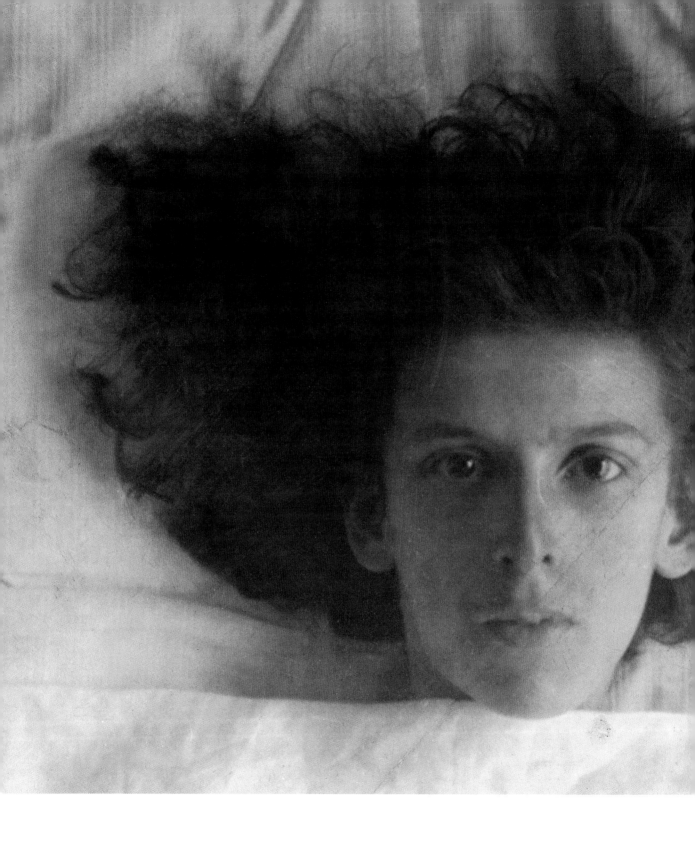

A photograph dating from 1914 in which Cahun confronts the viewer, staring directly out of the frame with her hair fanned out, medusa-like, around her head.
Courtesy of the Jersey Heritage Trust.

Untitled, 1938.
Courtesy of the Jersey Heritage Trust.

In this photo from 1947, Cahun appears triumphant in front of the graves of German soldiers. An infant's skull, a traditional memento mori or symbol of death, sits in the foreground of the image.

Courtesy of the Jersey Heritage Trust.

Between 1925 and 1927 Cahun and Moore became involved in the symbolist theatre in Paris. This image was taken in 1927 at a cultural centre founded by the Theosophist Society, an organisation dedicated to 'universal brotherhood of humanity without distinction of race, creed, sex, caste, or colour', where the Théâtre Esotérique productions were staged.
Courtesy of the Jersey Heritage Trust.

Image from *Aveux non Avenus* (photomontage prefacing Chapter III).
Courtesy of the Jersey Heritage Trust.

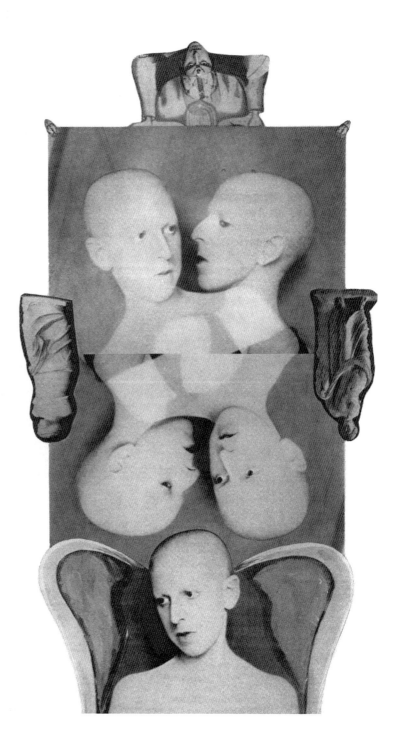

Cahun and Moore created these collages from Cahun's photographs to illustrate *Aveux non Avenus*, a non-narrative collection of essays published in 1930. The text in the image reads "Under this mask, another mask. I will never be finished removing all these faces".
Courtesy of the Jersey Heritage Trust.

*Keepsake* Discovered stored in an envelope marked "Jersey 1932", these images show an increasing interest in Surrealism. Cahun was introduced to members of the Surrealist movement around this time and remained an active member throughout the 1930s.
Courtesy of the Jersey Heritage Trust.

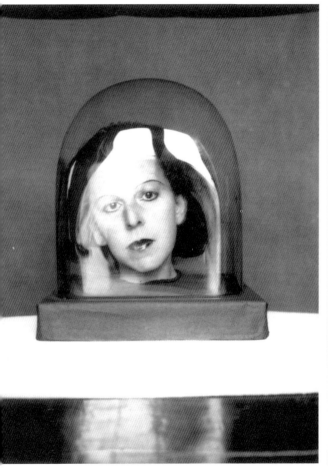 

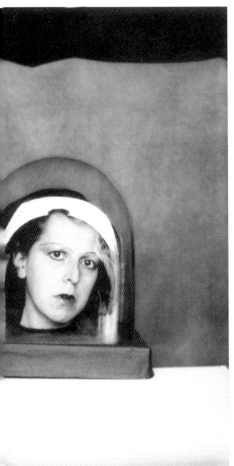

A selection of the anti-Nazi propaganda leaflets produced by Cahun and Moore during
the occupation of Jersey for distribution amongst the German forces.
Courtesy of the Jersey Heritage Trust.

UNSERE REVOLUTION SOLL VON ALLEN, NICHT VON

EINEM,

UNTERNOMMEN WERDEN. organisiert die Waffen OO

Brod und Gewissensruhe, Vater und Mutter

der Kultur.

Vater und Mutter müssen wir versöhnen.

Ein Universalvolk aus welchem alle geistige
Durst geboren wird.

S těmihle slovy nejsou žádné žerty.

Jsme schopni konat plně

svou revoluční povinnost.

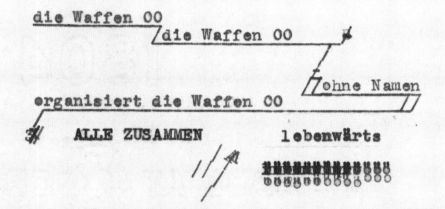

die Waffen OO

die Waffen OO

ohne Namen

organisiert die Waffen OO

3/    ALLE ZUSAMMEN          lebenwärts

Whilst in prison, Cahun and Moore formed a trusted relationship with their guard
Otto, who gave Cahun the badge she holds between her teeth, as shown in this
photo dating 1945.
Courtesy of the Jersey Heritage Trust.

60/61
62/63
64/65
66/67
68/69
70/71
72/73
74/75
76/77
**78/79**

# PAUL BROKS

is a neuropsychologist and science writer. He is currently Senior Clinical Lecturer at the University of Plymouth and Honorary Consultant in Neuropsychology. He is a regular contributor to *Prospect* and has written for *The Times*, *Sunday Times*, *Daily Telegraph*, *The Guardian*, and *Granta*. His book *Into the Silent Land—Travels in Neuropsychology* was shortlisted for the Guardian First Book Award 2003. He has co-written two plays with Mick Gordon: On Ego and On Emotion.

*Who are you?*

Well, that's a very interesting question. I'm the stuff in the draw marked "Paul Broks". So first of all I am a name. And when you open that draw, you find all sorts of different kinds of files in there. You find that I'm a middle-aged white man who's a psychologist, who is a father, who is a husband, who is a homeowner, who is an atheist, who is a son, who is introverted but occasionally extroverted, who is industrious, etc, etc. So I'm lots of different things. There isn't a single answer to that question, "who am I?"—it will depend on who's asking the question. It will depend on the circumstances, and on who wants to know what about me. So, I don't think there's any kind of definitive answer to the question, let alone a very concise one.

*In relation to this, then, who do we think you are?*

Well, you think, or rather you probably know that I am most or all of those things. But there are some things that you might not know that I am, which I may lay claim to. So, again, it depends on the circumstances—it depends on the kind of interaction you have and the kind of relationship you have. So, we might know each other as friends but I know other people as students, or as parents, and so on. And their perception of me is influenced in different ways, according to the person and their circumstances.

*What is a person?*

That is a question that's certainly interested me in recent years. And I don't think there's a very clear answer. I've approached it from the perspective of neuropsychology. We have, in neuropsychology, lots of pretty good operational definitions of things like memory, language, action, agency, and things like that. But what we don't really have is a really good theory of how it all comes together to produce the person, or the sense of self. And I'm using "the sense of self" and "the person" as different sides of the same coin, although they might be used quite differently by other people. It's only recently, actually, that there's been any real concentration of effort on the question. It's still a very new question for neuropsychology and for neuroscience generally. So, it's a bit like the question of consciousness: we all know what it is and we all think we understand it at one level, but actually, when you come to define it, it can be very, very difficult. It eludes precise definition.

Let's think about intuitively what it means to be a person. If we just reflect on that, it is clear that we're all embodied—we have bodies. We feel we have a sense of control over the body, so we have a sense of agency. We tend to think that we're unified and singular—that there's only one of us. And we tend to think that we're continuous, so that we're the same thing, essentially, from one day to the next or one week to the next, across a lifetime. So, if you start with those ideas—that leaves open a little crack into the neurology of the problem. And we can look at how the idea of embodiment, or our sense of embodiment, is challenged by neurological damage, and likewise for the sense of unity and continuity.

Neuropsychologists have also started talking about this distinction between the minimal self and the extended self, otherwise known as "the core self" and "the autobiographical self". And they, to some extent, map onto those three categories of embodiment, unity and continuity. So, in a sense, the minimal self, or the core self, is the self at the present moment—it requires that embodiment, and it requires that sense of unity. From this perspective we are a unified point of experience, which happens to be embodied. And then we think about the extended self, the autobiographical self or the narrative self, and we get into the notion of continuity. The idea of the autobiographical self doesn't make any sense at all unless we think about its natural extension across time. So, we are a continuous being with a history, an autobiography, a sense of the future and a capacity to anticipate what's likely to happen to us, or what we hope will happen to us, or what we dread will happen to us. Partitioning the self in these ways opens up the possibility of developing scientific theories of selfhood or, at least, of making inroads into the question. We can start by looking for neurological "dissociations"—finding cases where one dimension of experience is affected by one kind of brain injury, and another is affected by a different kind of brain injury. There's not a vast literature on this when it comes to selfhood, but there are tantalising clinical observations to suggest that the

minimal and extended selves have quite different neurological underpinnings.

*So it's possible to have one without the other?*

Yes. You can have cases where people lose all sense of biography and all sense of continuous memory. And they feel like they are just a floating point of awareness. This condition has got a name—it's called "transient epileptic amnesia", and you find it particularly in cases of temporal lobe epilepsy. So, the people who suffer those kinds of experiences will tell you that they'll just walk down the street, or they might be sitting in the living room, and their sense of a continuous self, fades away. And they're left with, in some cases, quite a heightened sense of experience of the world, a heightened sense of consciousness of the world—but with no personal story attached to it.

*So, they would find it quite hard to answer the question "who are you?"*

Oh, they'd find it impossible to answer the question, "who are you?" Now those cases are quite rare. But on the other hand, you have cases, which are even more rare, where people retain their sense of personal story, but lose their sense of immediate being-in-the-moment. And that's linked with a condition called Cotards Syndrome. You find this sometimes in cases of profound depression—neuropsychiatric cases. But it can also, in rare cases, be a result of quite discreet neurological damage. These are people who'll tell you their life story and then in the next breath tell you that they don't actually exist. It's very strange, and it shows how we take for granted all of these cognitive functions that sustain our unified and continuous sense of self.

*So, these people are not lacking any short-term memory and they have a sense of their life story so their position is paradoxical, then.*

It's paradoxical, yes, to the extent that they don't believe that they exist. In fact, they will often interpret that as being dead. Not in every case—and there are some cases where the sense of degradation of self is less dramatic than that. But in full-blown cases, of which I've seen three over the course of 20 years—they will tell you that they don't exist any more. You might as well bury them. And actually, they can usually put up a strong defence of that position, if you want to get into a debate with them.

*So what if you say, "well, how can you be here to tell me you don't exist?"*

Well, they would probably tell you that this world isn't real any more, or that they'd gone to heaven, or whatever. They'll find a story, and they'll confabulate around it, but the idea is core. It's a delusional thing, effectively, so that you cannot shift them on that point. But, as with all delusions, people hold bizarre beliefs in the teeth of contrary evidence, so it shouldn't be that surprising. The interesting thing from my point of view is that different kinds of damage to the brain can produce these discrete and actually extraordinarily different kinds of effect, which actually map onto what the philosophers have been talking about in recent years, in terms of minimal self and extended self.

*So, when you say "different kinds of damage", do you mean damage to different specific areas of the brain?*

Yes. Those particular areas aren't specifically mapped, but in broad terms, there seems to be a disconnection between so-called somatosensory systems—body-sense systems—and autobiographical memory systems. People with Cotards Syndrome have a sense of story and of continuity, but there's no bodily sense of being that goes along with that or any kind of emotional response to the world that might confirm that they're actually in it.

*You started this by explaining to us the difference between the minimal and the extended self, and then you went on to say that—in your clinical experience—you have seen that those two ideas can disassociate clearly. What implications does that have for your conception of what it means to be a person?*

Well at one level I think it doesn't have any effect at all. It doesn't affect the way I think about people, or

the way I think about me. But as for the way I think about how brain functions go together, it suggests that they're dissociable, that they operate through different and to some extent separable systems of the brain. And that's just how classical neuropsychology proceeds—by this method of double dissociation, and so on, so that your aim is to isolate particular functions in the brain. And what it can do, as I said, is to bolster these ideas that psychologists and philosophers have, and give them a neurological grounding. But it doesn't actually make any difference at all to the way that I interact with people—this knowledge that operates in one domain doesn't transpose in any obvious or direct way to the level of personal interaction, or to my sense of self. And that may be because there's a very severe disjunction between the way that we think about ourselves and the way that we actually are.

*In terms of that question of the extended self, what's the answer to the question, "am I the same person now that I was 20 years ago?" Is there a case to be made that so much changes over 20 years in any individual life that effectively we are different people?*

Well, we are and we aren't. The problem is, I think, that we expect really definitive answers to these questions, yet we may never get them. And science and philosophy don't like questions like that. Science, certainly, takes a very convergent approach and wants to find answers to things. But it's a very good question nonetheless. And I think that, in a sense, clearly, physically I am not the person I was when I was five years old. Physically, at the molecular level and at the atomic level, I'm not the same lump of matter. But nor am I the same entity intellectually and emotionally. Clearly, I have a much broader and deeper knowledge of the world, I have more skills, different dispositions—although it may be that some of my behavioural dispositions have persisted. So if you want to get down to the bottom of that question, you will find things that there are continuities with. You would probably recognise me from a photograph of me at the age of eight or nine, and probably even five or six. So, there's a pattern to the facial configuration that's persisted—there is a kind of physical continuity of the pattern. And at the psychological level, there are also patterns. But I would find it very interesting to have a conversation with my childhood self—it might be a shock. I mean, even to chat with one's teenage self, might cause a bit of a shock. I think I'm very different to how I was at the age of 16 or 17. And there are things I would do then that I wouldn't do now, and vice versa. But I guess with some of those things that I am now, you could have seen in embryo then, or you would have seen projections towards the point I'm at now. And you can trace lines of continuity there. So, it's a question of looking for patterns. And, obviously, I'm not the only person who has come round to this conclusion, but it seems to me that's probably as far as we're going to get—unless you're looking for some absolute essentialist view that there is something absolutely central and essential to what it means to be a person.

*So, when you say, "that's as far as we're going to get" you mean that the nearest we are going to get to an understanding of where our identity lies is by seeing it as a series of recurring patterns?*

Well, recurring patterns and experiences. From my point of view, the important thing is that those patterns are attached to experiences. It is the inter-subjective experience that continues on and makes us who we are as well as those box files of information about me as a father, or as a psychologist or whatever. And this goes back to that thing about the minimal and the extended self. The complete self really requires both aspects. But you can't translate the terms of one directly to the terms of the other. Although, as I suggested, the two may be dissociable, it's actually important to our perception of ourselves that they are yoked.

*So what's the problem, then, with having an absolutely essentialist view of the self? Is that something that's quite common, do you think, in our society, or as individuals, that we have that view? And why is that view flawed?*

Well, I'm not sure that I would say it's flawed. In the scientific sense, if you're asking me: "why don't you believe in an essential, incorporeal component of the self?" My answer would be: "well, I don't see it; there isn't any evidence for it. That doesn't make sense to me scientifically." But, of course, that doesn't mean to say that I don't share the intuition. It doesn't mean to say that that intuition isn't extraordinarily deep and important to us, as persons, at the level of, not just social interaction, but self-reflection. I'm quite happy to accept the idea that my self-reflections are, at one level, deeply flawed. Because it seems to me that, at a certain level, when self-reflection comes into play, there are only certain ways that we can think about ourselves. And so, we work by those intuitions. And there's nothing wrong with that. I don't see a massive contradiction there. It's a question of how we choose to think about different kinds of phenomena, or different levels of analysis of the human brain or psychology.

*Could you relate this to wider theories in neurology, such as ego theory and bundle theory? It has been said that bundle theory is an extremely depressing concept.*

Well bundle theory doesn't depress me, I just can't get my head round it. And I think it was the philosopher Thomas Nagel, who said, "it's probably true, but we're never going to get our heads round it." So bundle theory is the idea that we are a confederation of different systems and subsystems and emotions and behaviours and cognition, but there is no point at which it all comes together in a central control room. Our sense that we have a core self (which is what ego theory says) is merely part of a magical-thinking process that goes on in the brain. And ordinary waking life is just a constant flipping back and forth between reality and imagination, and the self is part of that imaginative realm. And I think the case for bundle theory is pretty overwhelming in terms of what we know about human neuropsychology. But I'm not sure that takes us very far. It's just a neuropsychological brand, I suppose, it's a logo for what most neuroscientists think these days. I don't think it is a very interesting area of scientific enquiry. I suppose it's important, because it challenges ego theory. But I do suspect that, if there's going to be any really interesting work in this area, it will actually be in the direction of ego theory. Bundle theory will be seen as true but not that interesting in the long run, I think.

*So, would it be fair to describe our deeply felt sense of an essential self, as a story that the brain tells itself in order to function?*

Yes, I think it would be. I think of it as an act of imagination. There's a lovely phrase, which comes from William James. He talks about "standing in the thicket of reality". So, we're all "standing in the thicket of reality" with lots of stuff around us, we have a body that's embedded in the stuff around us. But at the same time, we also sense that there is this other, kind of invisible world—a more spiritual place—and it is that which gives our lives significance. Now, what I'm saying is: that's fine—and that intuition is probably built into the circuitry of the brain. But to say that is not to devalue it. It may be that, as you say, it can be revealed as a composition, as a story, or as a collection of stories. But that doesn't devalue its worth at other levels of personal reflection.

*Could you say something about how notions of race and ethnicity relate to neurology? Is there a neurological basis for how we understand something like race?*

Well, actually, a lot of work has been done on this, but it is not my area of expertise! But this work looks at perception of 'in groups' and 'out groups', and suggests that there are processes that go on at pre-conscious levels, that influence the way we relate to people of different ethnicities, and so on. So, no matter how much, with the best liberal conscience, you try to avoid it, this does operate at an automatic level. And probably, politics should partly be about overriding some of those subliminal cognitive prejudices. But it seems to me that, neurologically speaking, the points of similarity between groups are so much greater than the points of difference. But wherever there's a point of difference between social groups, you will get these automatic mechanisms coming into play. Although I don't think that tells us much about the psychology of national identity or the psychology of race.

*Is it possible to see, at a neurological level, differences between—say—men and women? We interviewed Roz Kaveney, who would describe herself as "trans"—she was a male-to-female transsexual, and she said there was some neurological evidence to suggest that the brains of people who are trans are structured in a slightly different way. Do you think that this is true?*

I think there is some evidence for that. This all goes back to the first part of our conversation about embodiment, unity and continuity. And there are, no doubt, certain things that contribute to our sense of embodiment, and they probably also contribute to our sense of gender and sexual identity. And neurologically, that can go wrong sometimes. There is a strange condition called "apotemnophilia" which is a craving for amputation. So, people who have apotemnophilia will literally seek out surgeons and plead with them to chop off their arms or legs. Now, there is the suggestion that there are parts of the brain that can contain 'programmes' for relating to body parts and accepting and claiming ownership of body parts. And so in cases like this, the problem will, in due course, be shown to map onto those parts of the brain. Now I'm no expert on this, but it seems likely to me that there will also be neurological basis for gender differences, sexual orientation, and people who feel in one way or another that they are in the wrong body.

*Can we draw ethical or moral conclusions from those differences? For instance, if someone has apotemnophilia, if it seems to be that they are genuinely hardwired to believe that their arm should be amputated, does that not raise the question: should a doctor allow that amputation to go ahead or not?*

Well, it may be that as we get to know more about the neurological basis to these states of being, (assuming that we do discover more about them), that will actually inform the clinical decisions. At the moment, no surgeon could ethically chop someone's leg off because they say that it feels alien to them—although, historically, it has happened. But what does happen is that people will self-mutilate—they'll actually try and remove their own limbs. So, there's the other side of the argument, which is: "well, this is a neuropsychiatric condition that is exceptional to most surgical cases." But I think it's one example of where, yes, the neurological knowledge might, in due course, inform clinical practice.

*You have said that it might not be possible to study the self scientifically. Could you unpack that?*

Well, as I said earlier on, you can study the self scientifically, to the extent that we talked about the extended self for instance. So, you might ask "how does the brain construct a sense of self?" or "how does the self respond to the brain when it starts to decay as a result of neurological damage or disease?" Those are perfectly scientifically tractable questions, and we can talk about the minimal self and the extended self, and about how something might fit into one category or another. When it becomes difficult is when one is talking about the personal side of self-awareness, because this inevitably brings into play a first-person perspective. But science can only talk about things in a third-person way. The first-person perspective is opaque to science. Yet consciousness operates in the first person, because we always see things from our own point of view. My experience of me is from my point of view. You can never get into it. You might be able to describe it brilliantly—you might be the world's finest poet and describe my experiences as best as you can, but it's still not my experiences. This is a point, actually, made by the novelist David Lodge, who writes very eloquently about consciousness, I think. He says that science simply doesn't deal in the first person and so maybe this is the point at which art takes over. And he talks about the "dense specificity" of personal experience, and that is a good phrase, I think. His idea is that novels get into the "dense specificity" of personal experience in a way that scientific papers don't, when they get into an extended self. And lyric poetry gets into first-person perception in a way that science doesn't. But lyric poetry obviously isn't science. So, the thing that really interests me, is: what are the boundaries of neuroscience? Are there certain areas of human experience which are not amenable to a neuroscientific approach, but which can be explored in other ways—through other forms of scholarship or through the arts?

*You were talking a minute ago about how the brain might affect our sense of self—so, certain kinds of neurological decay or neurological damage can alter our sense of self. Does that mean, then, that the brain and the self are slightly separate things? Or are they just different ways of talking about the same thing?*

Well, I don't know. Some people would say, "well, of course they're separate things. You have a soul, you have a brain." Or, "you have a mind, you have a brain." And other people would say, "well, no—the mind is the brain in operation." But I've got a slightly different take on that. I would say the mind is what the brain does, but that the self is what the brain does in relation to other minds. So, it takes it on a more social trajectory, so that we can't really make sense of the self in terms of isolated brains.

*So, in a sense, the self can't exist in isolation.*

Absolutely—yes.

*So, in relation to that, is there anything else you could say about us as tribal animals? Do we have much neurological understanding about how that side of our self works?*

This is not my direct area of expertise, but I'm sure that it comes into play. There are all kinds of systems in the brain that regulate social interaction, and there's a whole area of study now called "social neuroscience" which embraces the whole spectrum of how brains interact with one another. And at one level, it's to do with emotional reactions and with perception—what you might call "mind reading" i.e. recognising facial expressions, reading intentions in the eyes and so on. And it is also about how we maintain a continuous, stable, sense of self in relation to other people. I think that's going to be massive as a topic of scientific enquiry. It is already big, but it's going to get bigger, I think. And through those kinds of enquiries, we will find out more about 'in groups' and 'out groups' and that could have an impact on for politics and political decision-making, in ways that we can scarcely conceive of now.

# YASMIN ALIBHAI-BROWN

is a Ugandan born journalist and author. She is a regular columnist for *The Independent* and the *Evening Standard*. Her books include: *Some of My Best Friends Are...*; *Mixed Feelings: The Complex Lives of Mixed Race Britons*; *Who Do We Think We Are? Imagining the New Britain*; and *After Multiculturalism*.

---

*Who are you?*

Well, it's very difficult. I'm writing a memoir at the moment, because hardly anything's written about my people, and we never wrote anything ourselves. Our ancestors were transplanted by the British, as were so many Indians after slavery was abolished. They were just dropped off in unknown countries—Fiji, Trinidad, Guyana, South Africa, East Africa. This was all done quite brutally to a people who were not literate. When I went back to India not so long ago they knew nothing of us. Yet I speak four of their languages and I think of myself as from the subcontinent—that is a part of me. Now, my forebears were taken to East Africa to build the railway. And there are records of the white people who took charge of the bridges there, and there are records of the African side of the history, (and quite rightly, because it was an African story). But there's hardly any record of us. Those Indians transported to Africa, many died, and something like 60 per cent went back to India as kind of broken men really. But a few remained in Africa and very quickly—partly because of famines, partly because of Raj policies, and the lure of new beginnings on a lush continent—an exodus to Africa began. Because it was seen as a paradise, right? People came in boats, dhows. And as numbers grew they very quickly got organised to become the arm of Empire. And it was a very racially structured Empire, where the middle was occupied by browns, blacks were at the bottom and the whites were at the top. You saw it literally on the hills and in the homes—this hierarchy—so the whole thing was completely defined physically. And we never felt African—never. We couldn't really, I mean, there were longings for India. And my lot were converts from Hinduism—very recent converts from Hinduism—so in our mosque there was this kind of compilation, if you like, of worship. So, we are a people of nowhere. We have no place on earth that we can unequivocally call our own. And every single place I've ever lived in, somebody's had the right to say, "fuck off back where you came from".

In terms of a group, I have no single group locale or loyalty at all. And also, my children do not have my identity. And this upsets me sometimes, as it must upset all parents, I guess. But that's okay, because, like I said, I think you have to find your own tribes. I don't think anyone, anyone, even the narrowest of groups up in Oldham has only one tribe. So, I don't think you can have one tribe. What you do have are affiliations of comfort zones where you feel understood without explaining yourself. And I certainly don't feel, for example, that I could ever be English, although I'm married to a very English Englishman. Because I do not feel that I'm easily understood within England.

*How do you define the word "identity"?*

It's internal, like faith is internal. I mean, of course it's external when people see me and tell me, in this country, to "fuck off back where I came from". From their point of view, my identity's external. Physical. But I think identity is an internal drama of one's own life, which is ever-changing and ever-moving.

*And how do you relate to the idea of Britishness?*

I love the concept of Britishness. But it's a false construct. It should be a civic identity which belongs to everyone and not one possessive ethnic group. Which is why so many white people don't want to be British. When blacks began to be British, some white people didn't want to be British any more. It's like not wanting to be in the neighbourhood of certain other people. So, I think there's something quite sinister going on here: that white people are less likely to call themselves British when black people are more likely to call themselves British.

*How do you relate to your home city of London?*

London is my place, yes. London is my place because it belongs to no one. And that's what I mean—it's

hardly a tribe, is it, London? And I'm not even talking specifically about Ealing, although I do love Ealing. In the capital you feel you don't have to answer questions. There are places which don't make you feel like an interloper. There are groups that welcome you in without making too many demands. I know my husband's always saying that he's never, ever, ever felt left on the outside by any of my many circles of black and Asian friends, my family, or the mosque itself. When my mother died, for the first time ever in our history, they allowed white people not only into the private prayers, but to carry the coffin. So, it's all about where you feel safe. Racial and cultural boundaries are artificial enclaves, and I don't care for those at all. I don't feel safe there. I don't think I can be in those places. They feel false, a bit like an ethnic theme park that has been created. And that doesn't mean anything to me.

*What does the idea of "community" mean to you?*

Well, I hate the idea of "community". I don't think there's a white community; I don't think there's a black community. I think again that these are false enclaves that have been created. So I never used the word. Just as I don't use the words "ethnic minority"; I don't use the word "community"—except to criticise it. Because

I think it's an impertinence, really—to claim people in that way, and speak for them without them having elected you. So, I think it is an affirmation of inferiority and infantilism. It was used very successfully during the Raj in particular, and it was an arrangement of the privileged which I just don't care for at all. That said, I can see that people do—more and more—need a sense of collectivity, because the world has become so rampantly individualistic, and in many ways, so frighteningly monocultural.

*Do you mean the world as a whole, or the Western world?*

The world as a whole. I think the world as a whole is going that way. And it's no accident that—just as lots of people think we have reached the end of history, the West has won, there is but one model for economics, and that we all want the same things and so on—this force of resistance to that begins to appear in the twenty-first century. So, I'm not understating the importance to belonging to collectives at some point in your life: when people die, when children are born, when you're in crisis, and so on. But those cannot be fixed and determined in the way people assume they are.

*So why do you think people are so unwilling to let go of those kinds of groupings?*

In some ways, it has been thrust upon them, and now they've claimed it as their own. I mean, it was thrust upon Afro-Caribbeans. What was different about Afro-Caribbeans when they came here in the 1950s? They had the same language, they had the same religion, they were more gentlemanly than English gents, and what was it that kept them on the outside? It was this blackness that was thrust upon them and was used to define them, as unwanted or as a kind of cultural identity. It's very interesting, to consider Notting Hill in the 1950s, and how mixed it was. It is almost impossible to imagine that today. And yet, racism was virulent—one of the biggest race riots we have seen was in 1958 in Notting Hill, and a man was killed, and it was ruthless. That happened, and then the idea became imbibed by the 'outsiders' and later a badge of honour and resistance.

*Does identity relate to an idea of "home"?*

For some. I can't answer that, because I've never had a home, so I don't know. I mean, my identities are very mixed and very movable, but nevertheless, I suppose, they do link to places. They link to things. They link to India because of the ancestral connection, the languages, the songs, the images, the colours. But then, when I go to Africa, I'm completely and utterly lost in that place of my childhood, where I was born, where my mother was born. And I lived there until I was 23. And then I came to London. And I suppose now, if I go to Paris for example, I hate it, and I miss London. I'm a completely unforgiving Britisher when I'm in France, because I hate its open anti-Arab racism so much—it's true! Yes. I no longer go on holiday to France. They will not have my money any more. London gives me the only sense of place I have ever had.

*Can you say something about the multicultural experiment in this country as opposed to the assimilation experiment in France?*

Well, I can't stand France's arrogance. But I don't think either state can take all credit for much of the progress that's been made. Because there was no experiment. There was nobody saying, "we're going to ensure that black and Asian people very soon live in Hampstead". Though there were policies and ideas and anti-discrimination laws. We grew a middle class and some of those policies were in part responsible. The economic obstacles in France to that happening were greater, and it is a scandal, really, that in Germany and France there is no non-white middle class at all. None at all.

*That's interesting, because you are also critical of British ideas of multiculturalism.*

The multicultural model that we now live came in during the Thatcher era. And she was fostering a very narrow idea of a very little Englander, while at the same time she was privatising everything—selling the country, everything, to foreigners. So she had to persuade us that we were still English.

Now, Thatcher's model was actually based on Roy Jenkins' model, which was that everyone had a right to equality and to be different. That was Jenkins' model, and it was embodied in the Race Relations Act. And in that time, 1965, and in that political environment, it was a revolutionary, radical response, and the right response. But, like positive discrimination in America, it overstayed its welcome, and what happened then is that it became a way of emphasising, institutionalising, and rewarding separation and difference. And so it was like we were all playing marbles in the ghetto, in publicly-funded marble playgrounds, you know? And that's where some of the problems came from. There was too much pandering in the UK to cultural protectionism and more assertively universalising policies in France—which in part have been good. The banning of the headscarf is now accepted by most Muslims and welcomed by most of the schoolgirls.

So, in that sense, I think, France did the right thing with the hijab. But it did it in the wrong way and for the wrong reasons, because it's an arrogant little shit of a nation which thinks it's better than everybody else. But you don't find any protests in France now, over the hijab do you? And now we have the burkha issue rising and Britain is again paralysed by it.

But you see, our model served the British political nation—because it meant that there were easily identifiable voting pools: us lot, happy children playing on the edges, and those lot, going to the Royal Opera House, and the Royal Shakespeare Company, and museums and so on. So, it served both sides, until the second and third generations were born, and wanted a larger slice of the cake.

So there was almost a conspiracy here not to let those definitions, those voting communities, break down. And New Labour was complicit in this. No—both old Labour and New Labour were complicit in this. Votes are delivered by people defined into an enclave and by politicians who do not want this pattern disturbed. And the state was, and is, really quite happy with the arrangement, until what's been happening now occured. And that is the Muslim question. The Muslim question is not a unique question. It was the black question in Brixton. It will be another question very soon. Yeah? And people forget the history of it. So I am against this form of multiculturalism. And, in relation to France, now, I do think that prioritising an idea of what is common between us has become

a priority. And I think that there are principles, which are basically human rights principles, from which no community can be excused.

*What kind of response do your opinions receive from people within the Muslim community?*

There is no Muslim community.

*Okay, from other Muslims in general.*

Well, some Muslims hate me so much they want to kill me. You can see the security on my letterbox and everywhere else in the house. And some Muslims completely adore what I do, not necessarily because they agree with what I have to say but because at least I have a voice. Because often, I am not writing about myself. I'm often writing about their views, their lives. It feels like there is always this test you have to pass when you express an opinion. For instance, if I say "we British" in my articles, I get more abuse from white people. If I say I'm a Muslim, that gets me abuse from some other quarters, because I'm married to a white man, and I don't cover my hair. Although I actually do pray, I do fast, I do practice Islam. If I take a very critical line against certain other things then I get abuse from other people. So I've said that black families have got to, like in America, start looking at themselves and ask themselves where they are going wrong in helping to create this culture. We can't keep blaming racism all the time. But then they say, "who's she to talk? She's not even black." So it is always the same thing. Everybody judges your opinion and then decides whether you pass their test. The only way to survive all that is to say, "stuff your test! I decide who I am".

*Do you think that people who share certain aspects of your identity—as a Muslim, an Asian, whatever— might feel that they have some kind of...*

...hold over me? Yeah, but they've learnt it doesn't work. And it doesn't work for any journalist. I know that Muslim woman who went to work for *The Sun* and she found the same pressures there. But I keep saying to these pressure groups, "I'm not your PR person—I'm a journalist and I have to do what I have to do." I think they now have accepted that. They work behind the scenes and they threaten me, but on the whole they know that I cannot be beholden to them. But I'm not the only one—we set up a group called British Muslims for Secular Democracy. A lot of Muslims feel that this hold over our lives actually makes us flee our contemporary identity rather than allowing us to own that part of us.

And I'm very optimistic. I don't share the doom and gloom theories. I really don't. I think this is because of my experience of Muslims that I know personally. But I am very frightened about two things. One: that white liberals, my friends, who all went on anti-apartheid demonstrations with me, are veering to the right when it comes to issues of immigration. And I find their reasons unconvincing. And it's again tied to their identity. And I have no sympathy for that, because they're very powerful people, and what they're doing is rewriting what they think should be the identity of this country, and creating a very excluding identity. And so that worries me: that there is no opposition to this force which is completely convinced that all asylum-seekers are lying bastards that we absolutely have to stop. And these are also the people who want to rewrite the history of imperialism and colonialism. Gordon Brown, for example, stands up in Africa and says, "we have nothing to feel ashamed of with the British Empire, we have everything to be proud of." And there is such a flood of these beliefs now, you know: immigrants are here on sufferance; the idea that all immigrants bring more problems than contributions is gathering strength again, and people are saying "no more, please, but if you're here, you have to adhere to our version of history."

And on the other side, there is, no doubt, primarily among young Muslims, a growing wedge of murderous, stalinist, anti-Western Islam, coming forth. So, those two things are very worrying. But I still think that there's enough there to stop these two sides from taking away what is an extraordinary story, in and of this country. This country has the highest rate of racial intermarriage in the world. Did you know that? And this goes way back. As far back as the sixteenth century there were panicky reports being written about these dirty white women who were polluting the race. But that never stopped anybody, did it? That, to me, signals something deeply important, because

that's a change to the DNA. Mixed race people are the fastest-growing non-white group in this country if you measure the birth rate. So that, to me, is a very positive indication that, at a very human level, people are integrating.

Or look at the coalitions formed against the Iraq War. That wasn't just a Muslim objection, it was from all sorts of people. And the people who objected to this war came together, without anybody commanding them, organising them, or making policies for them, on a platform of human rights and international law, and just knowing the difference between what was acceptable for a modern nation and what was not. So those sorts of things, and there are many of them, actually, give me hope. And I don't think this is only happening in London. I really don't think it's only London. My mother-in-law is a *Daily Mail* reader who voted for Margaret Thatcher, but she now has a granddaughter who's darker-skinned than I am and she loves her insanely. All her attitudes, now, have been filtered through that experience.

It's really interesting. When I was growing up in Uganda, we were Shia Muslims—these very odd ex-Hindus. And next door to us was a very, very powerful woman who was a devout Sunni Muslim—she was very strongly devout. Except, she also smoked, and had dumped four husbands herself! But she was still a real fanatic, and always used to say we were going to go to hell and so on because we were too Western in her eyes. And yet, she loved me, and she supported my mother, and I grew up with all her grandchildren. All of them boys. There were six of them, and they went to live in Bolton, and I went to see them last year, and they're lovely and they've all got sweet, sweet wives, and are very open-minded, but also very Muslim. And when one of them came to pick me up, he said, "you do have to know, we have to tell you something. We've all got white wives too, but our Muslim wives don't know that." All six of them! I mean, what? These are people I've known all my life. So I said, "stop, stop, what?!" And he had told me that, apparently, because he thought it would make him almost socially my equal, because I'm married to a white guy. And I said, "what do you mean?" He said, "well, we've all got second families, and the white wives know about our Muslim wives, but the Muslim wives don't know about the white wives." So

I said, "why?" "Because", he said, "it was just boring. We grew up here, we live in England. And the Muslim wives are all imported. And they're not even from Pakistan—they're from Malawi. And we've just got nothing to say to each other. Nothing." So, they're all running parallel lives—these six brothers! Actually, one is not. So only five of them are doing this. But wait for this: the last one said he's never going to marry a Muslim, and married a white woman, openly, and so all the others don't talk to him. They don't talk to him! So, that's how mixed-up we all are.

*I'm flabbergasted!*

Yes. So was I. I still am! But I've since found out that this is not uncommon. And in a strange and odd way, it probably is a positive thing. Though I'm not sure I like their solution.

But, what I think is, human nature being what it is, you can't live in a country for so long and not become a part of it. In whatever way. I went up to Bradford to do a story on bounty hunters, that is: these young men who were unemployed and vicious, and who'd go around recapturing girls and women who'd gone into refuges in order to escape their families, for £3,000 a shot. I went up to do a story on it, and, of course, as soon as a journalist lands in these places, all the cab drivers pass word around, and it becomes very oppressive. Anyway, eventually I interviewed one of the bounty hunters in a graveyard, and it was very, very frightening at the beginning, and then very funny afterwards, because he started being quite awful to me. And I said, "oi, you, do you know I've got a son who's your age? Would you talk to your mother like that?" And he had a knife in his hand. And he immediately saw a mother. And all the aggression went. And he was completely shame-faced, because mother figures are very important. But during that visit I went and spoke to some truly awful men, who were not bounty hunters themselves, but to whom all these girls were just this, that and the other. Some of them were pimps though they were only pimping white girls of course—not 'our' girls! And they said they hated Britain. So, I said, "well, if you're this unhappy in this country why don't you just go? Go to some perfect Islamic state. You've only got one life, if you're unhappy here then go." So, one guy put his hand up and said, "but miss, we would not be allowed to be talking like this in those countries. They would arrest us!" So, I'm optimistic. I think we dwell too much on the superficialities of separation. But these roots are going in gradually, and they're mingling and nobody's going to be able to stop it.

# JONATHAN FREEDLAND

is an award-winning journalist and broadcaster. He writes a weekly column in *The Guardian*, as well as a monthly piece for *The Jewish Chronicle*. He also presents BBC Radio 4's contemporary history series, The Long View. His books include *Jacob's Gift* and *Bring Home the Revolution—The Case For a British Republic*.

*Who are you?*

I once had a conversation with the Israeli novelist David Grossman who said something which I too had often thought, but it gave it new credibility coming from him. He said that he had three ways of defining himself. And he put being a Jew first; he put being male second; and he put being Israeli, in his case, third. And this was uncanny, because I had, and I don't remember why, once done a similar exercise, and I'd come up with the same thing: the core of my identity, as it seemed to me, was first: being a Jew; second: being male; and third: being British. And I think that still captures, quite well, who I am. But I would add things to that which have arisen since then. Central to who I am now is that I am the father of two sons, and that feels very much like it places me in the world. That is much more important to me now than being the son of my father. It was very central to my identity 20 years ago that I was the son of my father and of my mother. But now, being the father of my two sons is what is important. And you see this in very practical ways—just this morning, I called the school to explain that my youngest was coming in late, and I said, "it's Jonathan Freedland here—Jacob and Sam's dad." That's how I had to explain who I was. And I hope that as I get older, there will be more of that.

*So why choose those three categories: "Jewish, male and British"? Why them above being white, for instance, or being middle-class or being heterosexual or being a journalist?*

Or a Londoner.

*Or a Londoner.*

Well some of those that you suggest are also very appealing. And I would embrace them. But it's funny, I would never mention being white, actually. The only time I would do that was if I had to really explain to someone that I was not black. But I wouldn't cite it as a positive part of my identity. And it's partly because that's when the Jewish kicks in. Because 'white' to me in a British context conveys 'majority'. If you're white, you're not part of an ethnic minority. Whereas, I very much do think of myself as part of an ethnic minority, and I would describe it as that more than as a religious minority. So, whiteness feels to me as if it contains a kind of 'other'. My mother, who is herself an immigrant, will still describe someone as being "very English", as if it was a category that she herself was not part of and which had a very distinct content. She might say "ooh, no, no—he's not Jewish, he's very English." And this goes to a point about class. That designation, "very English", breaks off into two very interesting things. It could either mean very pukka, posh, established, or it could actually mean the very opposite. So, someone who was "very English" was not Jewish because they were salt of the earth, working class, cockney, East Ender. "English" means, for me, either one of those two types. And I grew up with the idea that both of those things are very English and different from us. So, the phrase "British Jewish" feels just right to me, because I feel as if "British" is a really capacious term which allows for hyphenation, and which doesn't have a sort of ethnic content of its own.

How about those other things you mentioned? Well class is interesting. But maybe that is more relevant to how others see me. As for me being a 'journalist', there was a risk that, at one time in my life, I would end up thinking that what I did defined who I was. So quite consciously I tried to not be like that and to think that the essence of a person shouldn't be their job. And so, in a way, maybe I did quite a good job on myself, because that didn't come up in my own head at all when you asked me the question.

You also suggested "heterosexual" and maybe that is slightly like the 'white' thing. I wouldn't offer that as part of my identity, partly because it would seem to be lining up with some majority. But this is a very revealing exercise, because I realise that I could just as easily say I was white or heterosexual. And yet, the identities that matter to me (though perhaps male is in a different category) are those that somehow emphasise the minority status, or the difference from others. And that's quite psychologically interesting. Why would I do that?

*So in that case, why did you list "male" as well?*

I suppose because I think it goes to something quite psychological—the inner voice as it were. My eldest son asked me recently what "soul" meant, and I tried to explain to him that it's that voice that you have in your head when you're not talking to anyone else. It's your inner voice. And that, to me, feels like such a male voice. And this is partly a sexual thing I guess—because obviously the way you look at a woman is different to the way you look at a man. And the sense of responsibility I feel very keenly as a father is wrapped up with that too. It just feels that that heading "male" captures a whole lot of things that I do feel are absolutely part of my inner voice, and how I see the world. I feel that by saying "Jewish, and male, and British", you get 90 per cent there in terms of understanding the laws I've got in my head.

*So who do we think you are? Do you feel that there is a public perception of Jonathan Freedland that is in some way at odds with who you really are? Or do you feel that there are assumptions that you find regularly get made by certain groups of people about you, perhaps because you're Jewish, or because you're white or whatever?*

Yes, I do. The first thing I would definitely say is that one should always be extremely self-aware. I don't really have a public profile, I'm not tremendously well-known—so it's important to establish that. But to the extent that there is any public perception of me, well interestingly, I think some of the things you offered in your second list would come to the fore much more. So, *Guardian* readers, might well see me now as a white, middle-class, and, I fear, middle-aged commentator. And then you could add to that that I was public-school and Oxbridge educated and then, for some people, it would all fit into place—they would see me as a typical part of that whole 'media elite'. So that might be the view that you might hold before you'd read anything I'd written. But then once you'd added in things I'd written, then people would have a perception of me that might be quite different. It's interesting, inside the Jewish community, I'm seen—by a lot of people—as quite dangerously left-wing. There would be some in that community who look down on me as a young and naïve person, because of my politics on the Middle East in particular. But then, among *Guardian* readers, there would be people who see me as quite the opposite—as a kind of apologist, or a defender of the indefensible in terms of Israel. And then there'll be people who are not *Guardian* readers, who are maybe *Telegraph* or *Times* readers, who will see me occasionally pop up on the radio, or on TV, who will think I'm a typical *Guardian* lefty. So, it all depends on their own vantage point. But I guess what this is all getting to is that my identity is quite closely associated with *The Guardian*. At least in terms of my public profile. After all, I've been writing for *The Guardian* for 16 years.

*What does it mean to be a Jew? It seems that one of the core issues here has to do with whether Jewishness is an ethnicity or a religion. Do you have any religious beliefs or engage in any forms of religious practice? And what role does Israel play in contemporary Judaism?*

These are enormous questions. And they're so enormous that they have preoccupied me, really, since I was old enough to think about things like this—so really from my early teenage years up to today. And this all culminated really in the book I wrote in 2005 called *Jacob's Gift*, which was triggered by the arrival of my first son. That was about what it meant to enrol him involuntarily in the Jewish people. He was circumcised eight days into his life, forming the covenant of Abraham, and that was a very powerful moment for me. And what came out of that were a whole set of questions about, "what exactly does it mean to be Jewish and to hand on Jewishness?" So, I have thought about it a lot and still think about it. And the first thing to say about this is: if anybody gives you absolutely firm, monochrome answers to the question of what a Jew is, then they are either kidding, lying to you, or lying to themselves. Most likely they are lying to themselves. It is a complex, shifting and fluid thing and you can spend a lifetime grappling with it.

Now I don't believe it's only a religion, or exclusively a religious designation. I make this point, half jokingly, in *Jacob's Gift*. Nobody would read an interview with Woody Allen in the paper, in which Woody Allen says, "I've been an atheist since I was a teenager", and put the paper down, saying, "that's funny—I could have sworn he was Jewish." Whereas, you *might* feel that about somebody who was a Baptist but then says they are an atheist. But in the Jewish case, we know that these are not mutually exclusive categories—you can be a Jew and an atheist at the same time. So, automatically, it cannot be that the term "religion" captures, at least wholly, what it is to be Jewish. "Ethnicity" gets you much closer to it. Because you're Jewish the moment your mother is Jewish, and anything which goes through the blood line like that has to do with ethnicity. But it's not like any other ethnicity, because you can have black Jews and white Jews and Chinese Jews and all that. And the trouble with the Jewish case, and the reason why our enemies have spoken over the years about a "Jewish problem", is that it really doesn't fit neatly into any of the other categories. In the early Zionist years there was this idea of "Jewish nationhood". But this is very difficult, because there is a multiplicity of different languages and different histories, and most nations in the world tend to have just one language rather than lots, and have a single or continuous history. By contrast, Jewish history is like a family tree, where there are whole branches which have gone off into other directions. And religion only provides the roots of that tree. And so just as you would never judge a tree only by its roots—you'd look at the whole thing, including the fruit that has come from it—I would say the same about Jews. Jews are an entire civilisation, a people. You can speak meaningfully of the Jewish people, whose culture, civilisation, sprung originally from religion. But while there is a close—even inseparable—relationship to religion, religion is by no means the sum total of it.

*And how important is religion to you personally?*

Well if you and I were having an intellectual or theological argument, I would have to define myself as an atheist. But I suppose I have this belief—which is half cute, but true—that: I'm not sure if God exists, but I'm pretty confident that, if he does, he wants us to believe that he doesn't exist. Because I believe that atheism is a better way of living. And I think it's very interesting, even religious Judaism is constructed on that basis—with the idea that God isn't going to help you. So you can't say, "we'll deal with this in the next world." Religious Judaism is very specific about the here and now—you have to act, really, as if, in effect, God didn't exist. Everything is up to you. And there is this beautiful image in the Jewish tradition of humanity as being in partnership with the divine in the process of creation, and if anything, humanity is the senior partner. And I find that as a humanist—which is a word that I prefer to "atheist"—that is very liberating. I attempted to argue in *Jacob's Gift*, that the reason why are there so many Jewish radicals throughout history was because, in a way, Judaism was the first humanism. You see this from the minute that Abraham is bartering and arguing with God over saving the people of Sodom. When he asks, "well, if you'll accept 100, what about 80? What's the difference?" then immediately, you're into a completely different notion of theism, in which God actually allows himself to be dictated by Abraham. And so it's as if God is telling us: "guys—it's up to you. You're in the driving seat here. I did the creation bit. Now, it's your show, from here on in." So, I think it's a humanist creed, and I would want to call myself a humanist.

That said, I'm a very proud cultural Jew, and I don't believe you can be a proud cultural Jew if you entirely cut yourself off from religious tradition. So, therefore, my family do stay home every Friday night, and we light the candles, we have wine and the two loaves of bread, and we say the prayers and so on. My children go to a Jewish faith school. And I would like them both—though it would be partly up to them—to have a Bar Mitzvah, and to learn Hebrew. To me, this is a great ethnic heritage, it's a great cultural heritage, and so why would I want to deprive them of that? And so, it's very hard for me to separate those things from their cultural heritage and see them as acts that require literally, a leap of faith. I don't think they do.

*Obviously, contemporary Judaism is incredibly wide—you've got everyone from Woody Allen to the very hardcore fundamentalist settlers in Hebron and elsewhere. How do you see your relationship to Judaism worldwide, both in terms of the diaspora, and Israel? After all, you're very critical of a great deal of what Israel's done.*

Well, the first thing is to say is that I really do relate to the rest of the Jews around the world. I mean, there is this whole post 9/11 discussion about how everyone fears the notion of a global Muslim brotherhood, or Umma. People often speak as if it's the most terrifying thing. But I don't find that terrifying, because I understand it, and I feel myself part of the Jewish equivalent of that. I don't find the notion of an international peoplehood frightening. I very much feel myself to be part of a global Jewish conversation. So, I write a monthly column in *The Jewish Chronicle*. And now, in the internet age, that is discussed and picked up elsewhere. And it seems to me, that just as there is a British national conversation, there is also a Jewish national conversation, and within that there's a sub-conversation about Britain, and about British Jewry. And I want to be a participant in that discussion about where the Jewish people collectively, across the world, are going wrong. And believe me, I do think that the Jewish people are going wrong—particularly in Israel. Let me fall back on one specific point in regard to this. I wrote recently about Avigdor Lieberman, the very right-wing new Foreign Minister of Israel. I covered his party and his campaign in the Israeli elections. I spent a lot of time with them and even went to their victory party. And the penny dropped for me when I thought, "the trouble with this lot, who style themselves as Jewish nationalists, is that they've forgotten what it actually is to be Jewish." Now what did I mean by that? Well, they had really forgotten how it is to live as a minority in majority cultures. In the past minority living was inseparable from Jewish living. Now I'm not one of the people who makes a fetish of that and who thinks we were all much more noble and pure back then. We were just powerless so we didn't have the chance to behave badly. It doesn't mean we were inherently better people, we just didn't occupy any land so we couldn't behave brutally. But you cannot escape the fact that minority-ness has been intertwined with the Jewish experience. And there are 36 times in our holiest books, when it says: "treat the stranger justly, because you too were a stranger in a strange land." That is inherent in Judaism—it's bound up in what we are. But it struck me that Lieberman and his folks had forgotten that. If they were able to say to others: "your citizenship will be contingent on the swearing of the oath of loyalty", then they have clearly forgotten what it was like to be a Jew in Spain being told "get to your knees and profess your faith, otherwise you will lose your rights in this country." And I feel that's a microcosm of something larger that's happened in Israel, Jews seem, somehow, to have forgotten themselves. They are drunk on national empowerment. They suddenly have the tools of nationhood and statecraft that they were denied for two millennia. Now, it's only been 60 years, and I do think this rush of blood to the head will recede. But right now, in my lifetime, and I believe it will go on for most of my lifetime, the Jews have got themselves into a place where we have forgotten too much of our own history. And we are heading down a path that is ultimately self-destructive—even putting aside the impact it's having on everyone else. So, in my own *incredibly* small way, and I don't kid myself that one voice in the British Jewish context is going to have any impact on the freight train that is Israel, I am trying to do something about that.

*Many defenders of Israel would focus on the fact that it is one very small country surrounded by much larger, more threatening ones. In that context there might still seem to be a sense of minority-hood.*

This is very deep water, so let's just unpack all this because it is very good stuff. I suppose, first of all, you have to say that: "it all depends on what your lens is, both in terms of time and space." So, the typical *Guardian* reader, sees Israel and says, "it's been the occupier for 40 years, and the dispossessor for 61 years, and it is the mighty superpower in the region, lording it over, governing, ruling over these Palestinians." That's what it sees.

Now, your *average* Jewish Israeli, *and*, I have to say, most of the Jewish supporters of Israel in the world don't see that. Their lens is different. They see how we've been the victim for 2,000 years, and that what's going on now is a blip, but that basically we're still the victim. And then, in terms of the land itself, they pull the camera back, and whereas *Guardian* readers have been focusing on Israel and the West Bank, they see tiny little Israel, the size of New Jersey or Wales, surrounded by 22 huge Arab states. I mean, Iran alone is four times the size of France—

and that's a *non*-Arab state. So then you've got 22 Arab states on top of that. So, it *all* depends what you look at. So, in my more provocative moments, I would say that the rest of the world looks at Israel and sees a guy in a tank commander's uniform with a helmet and huge, bulky equipment. And the Israeli, or Jew, looks in the mirror and sees the skeletally thin victim, in striped pyjamas, coming out of Auschwitz. And Operation Cast Lead in January was a great example of that. And I made myself very unpopular writing a piece in *The Jewish Chronicle*, where I said, "if somebody came down from Mars, and looked through the ads and the fundraising appeal letters that were appearing in *The Jewish Chronicle*, they would have said, 'well, clearly what's happened is, in the last three weeks, 1400 Israeli civilians have been killed, and perhaps a maximum of ten Palestinian fighters have been killed. And the Palestinians must be using the full might of the Palestinian air force to bombard Israelis in their homes." If you look at those appeal letters in *The Jewish Chronicle*, with one Jewish charity after another, describing how "our people are under bombardment", you would realise something very deep, which is that we can only see ourselves, because of this longer view of history, as victims. And I understand that, and I think it would be naïve and incredibly callous for people to say, as they sometimes do: "the Holocaust happened. We get it. Get over it." It's too soon for that, it will be hundreds of years before those wounds have healed. But with understanding and with care and concern for Israel's future, I still think it's possible, and, in fact, incumbent on other Jews to say to Israel, "you're on a path at the moment which even putting aside the impact it's going to have on Palestinians, is just going to end in disaster for Israel itself."

Now this is a very hard message for Israelis and for Jews outside of Israel to hear, because so often, they question the motives of the speaker. They will ask "why are you saying this? You're saying this because fundamentally you want us to disappear." It's very hard for them to believe that I'm somebody who actually does not want Israel to disappear. I want Israel to survive and thrive. I'm not a Jewish anti-Zionist. If "Zionist" means that you believe in the Jews' right to self-determination and national fulfilment, then I'm a Zionist. And so, I am somebody who wants this project to succeed, and wants the State of Israel to survive and thrive and flourish, but I despair for it at the moment. I really do despair for it.

*Do you ever hear yourself described as a "self-hating Jew"?*

I've had that description put to me in hate mail. But I don't think anybody credible has ever said that to me in any formal way. I hope, (and some people have said that this is the case), that within the Jewish community I'm seen as somebody who, yes, is fiercely critical of Israel, but is doing it absolutely from within. It's like a conversation around the family table. You care about this family; you love it; but you're also a fierce critic of it. I think the key question is: do you share in the joys and sorrows of your people and, in this case, of Israel? And I think that most people would say that was true of me. And it is the truth. I do share in Israel's joys and sorrows. I desperately want things to work out with that country, I'm bound up with it. My mother was born there; I have family who live there; I spent formative years there; I travel there at least twice a year. My criticism is not about hostility or a desire to gloat.

And this is something that I try and explain to people who are fiercely critical of Israel. When they say, "I'm only being anti-Zionist, I'm not being anti-Semitic", it's difficult because as Howard Jacobson put it: "Jews see in Israel a version of themselves, so to attack Israel is to attack a version of themselves." It's so important that people understand that. It isn't, for us, like hearing somebody criticise Burma. It is about criticising something to do with our essence. So it's a very complicated issue, and it's a hugely burdensome thing to carry. And this is really what I was grappling with in the book I was writing about my son Jacob. It felt like I was enlisting him into this battle where, you spend your life around the family table, haranguing and arguing with your relatives, saying, "why is Israel doing this? Avidgor Lieberman is a fascist, how can we do this?" And then, around other people you're having to suddenly defend Israel because you're worried that they're not really attacking Israel, they're attacking something else. And you can tie yourself up in such knots about it all.

*Would you ever consider making aliyah—moving out to live in Israel?*

Well, I did consider it quite seriously. When I was 18 or 19, I was full of idealism, and I spent a year in Israel. But I never actually took any steps to do it. I had a whole lot of friends who did make that move in their 20s, but then a lot of them came back to Britain. Some stayed, but a lot came back. But what's interesting is: that all happened in their 20s. That was the age before settling down, before marriage, and it was in that period that I went to Washington. So, it was almost like my urge to be away, in the end, wasn't channelled towards Israel. That was partly a language thing—my career and my living is made in the English language—but it also had to do with my home and my family and other things. While I feel bound up with Israel and everything else, I'm very much not an Israeli. My temperament and personality could not be more British. There is no place in the world I feel more British than when I'm in Israel. People think that might be true of any country when you're abroad, but it's *specifically* and *intensely* true when I'm in Israel, because euphemism does not exist there, politeness does not exist there! The brusqueness, the rudeness, the constant assumption they have that somebody's about to con you is so alien to how I am. And I find myself becoming this diffident, Hugh Laurie or Stephen Fry character by contrast with them! So, when you ask "who are you?" and "how are you seen?" well the minute I set foot on Israeli soil, I'm seen as "that British guy" by anyone who would meet me.

*So, what is Britishness, then? And what is Britain? You wrote a book called* Bring Home the Revolution *about the need for reform of the British constitution—why is that important?*

Well that came out of my time living and working in America where I felt tremendously liberated. This was partly because I'm Jewish, actually, and I liked the fact that in America, anybody could be whoever they want, and still be fully American. It's that basic thing of the hyphenation—you can be Italian-American, Jewish-American and so on. And when I came back to Britain I just could not see any logical reason why the same couldn't be true here. Now that was back in 1997, and I think as the years have gone on that has become truer and truer. So people can be Scottish-British or British-Asian, or anything else. Now, whilst that is true of America and true of Britain, it's not true of everywhere else. It's not true of France or Spain or other places. We have an identity which builds hybridity into it. America has that for all kinds of reasons to do with its immigrant history. And Britain has it because it's four nations merged into one crypto-federal structure. So, that's partly why I believe that Britishness is something valuable and worth holding on to.

*So, what is the core of Britishness? Some people might look to institutions like the monarchy.*

It's certainly not the monarchy. It's not any institution. And I also resist these attempts to offer lists of values and qualities which are meant to be British—like 'fair play', or 'tolerance' or whatever.

*That is Gordon Brown's approach to Britishness.*

Yes. But I think that is very mistaken. Because it implies that those values are unique to Britain. But it's not as if the Swedes, for example, don't believe in fair play. Do the Swedes believe in unfair play and intolerance as being fundamental to their national ethos? Of course not. I don't think Americans sit down and say, "well, what is American-ness? It's all about the entrepreneurial spirit." I just don't really think they do that. So it's not really that there's an essence to Britishness that can be identified. I don't think it is about specific institutions. I mean, we're stuck with this clunking and archaic, nineteenth century political machinery, and I think people's mistake in the past was to think, "well, we can't change any of that, because we'll be left without any identity." I just don't feel that for a minute. There's so much about Britishness which is absolutely not based on these institutions.

I mean, maybe it has something to do with this land, the physical landscape of this country. I didn't travel around much when I was a child, but I have done so much more since I was a teenager and it's an absolutely physically beautiful country.

We're also an island, and there is a lot which comes from that. Yes, that can result in a certain inward-looking-ness, but it also means that we face the rest of the world and you see this in the internationalism of a city like London. London is a very big part of my identity—the diversity of it. So, I know there is a temptation to create a list of attributes, but, ultimately, when I think about it, there's a sort of freedom to Britishness, actually, which says, "once you're here you can do your own thing." It's very, very open to you to form your own identity. I don't think it's a coincidence that your Karl Marxes and all the other dissenters throughout history came here and came specifically to London. I think there's a tolerance about Britain which says, "now that you're here you can get on and be whoever you want to be." And it doesn't come with the 'ra-ra-opportunity-American-dream' stuff of America. But we Brits are almost embarrassed to spell all of this out. But then that's also part of its charm in a way. Andrew Marr has written quite well about this. He points out that there is no explanation for why these small, cramp, damp islands have produced bands like Oasis and Blur and all the world's best actors and so on. It's just that there's something in the atmosphere here that allows people to flourish creatively.

But I also think the whole notion of Britishness has been really hijacked by the heritage industry. And there is a focus on certain institutions which seems to me to be entirely about power. We have an elite who've done very well out of this. And when they say "we can't possibly change the House of Lords—that's 1,000 years of British history", I want to say, "well, it's 1,000 years of *your* history—it's not 1,000 years of *my* history." And similarly, when, in the book, I called for us to elect our own Head of State, some people said: "well, we couldn't do that—there wouldn't be any continuity with our past." And I think, "well, there's continuity between the family of Windsor, and the aristocracy. But a republic would have huge continuity with the people's history—the Tolpuddle Martyrs, the Peasants revolt and so on." So, I think there is a radical, dissenting, questioning culture that is actually central to what Britishness is to me. But that has been pushed aside in a kind of heritage monarchist vision of Britain, which says, "That's what Britishness is, and you mustn't touch it." And recently I've been feeling the same kind of the despair and panic about Britain that I feel about Israel which is: "this political machinery here is so clunky and old that if we do not update it we are also heading off a cliff." You see this absolute *lack* of democratic legitimacy exposed by the expenses scandal and the financial crisis, and yet the establishment just wants to say, "business as usual". I find the inability of this country to change itself is tremendously frustrating and it comes partly from this view of, "well, this is what Britain is, and it's locked in stone." Yet in some respects that is very un-British given the country's huge history of revolution and change.

*What is "multiculturalism"?*

Well, I think multiculturalism is one of these things that has been hugely misunderstood. It should be quite a positive thing. After all, what is the opposite of multiculturalism? It's monoculturalism. It's saying, "there is only one culture here. Anything else has to be driven underground and become a subculture." Whereas multiculturalism says: "no, there are actually lots of cultures going on here." And essentially, that is nothing more than a recognition of a reality. And if you go back 100 years, *before* there were any of the groups that would now be understood as minority group, Britain was a multicultural place even then. There was Scottish culture, Welsh culture, Irish culture, and English culture and there was diversity within regions, so Cornwall had its own language and so on. So we have *never* been some homogenous island, ethnically and linguistically. Britain was multicultural even in the golden age of Victorians. So in one sense, all the term "multicultural" says is that those things are valid and validated.

I'm hugely influenced, in all of this, by those four years I spent in America. It was incredibly affirming. I mention in *Bring Home the Revolution* that I went to a welcoming ceremony for newcomers, and the official there was saying, "you're from Vietnam—welcome. Don't lose your heritage. You're from Afghanistan. Welcome. You're part of our American family." An immigration official made this speech to these 25 people in this holding room at the heart of some bureaucratic office. That is their official message, and

that is what multiculturalism should be. We should be saying to Poles living in Holloway, "you're part of our mosaic now. Welcome. You're part of this. You don't have to lose your Polishness."

But where multiculturalism was misunderstood was that it was assumed to *only* mean that people should hold on to their heritage and original identity. Whereas, what it actually means is: "yes, you're all those different things, but you're also part of this larger group." People forget, when they talk about a mosaic that while it's made of lots of individual pieces, there's also a glue there which sticks them all together. Otherwise, it's not a mosaic—it's just a lot of chips and shards on the floor. And that mosaic forms a pattern, collectively, which is larger than any of the pieces. This is beautifully captured in the American slogan *E Pluribus Unum*. You will never lose the "*pluribus*"—there will always be many groups. But in the end there is one society. And the left-liberal multiculturalist mistake was that it put so much emphasis on diversity and so on, that it forgot the glue which holds the mosaic together. It forgot about the ties that bind. And you have to focus on that, too. So, I think that *because* you're a multiculturalist you *have* to focus on the Britishness side of it too. Otherwise, everyone's just going to fracture off from each other and balkanise and people will resent newcomers. So, if you want this thing to work, you've got to emphasise the things that we all have in common.

So how do you then do that? My view is: that it has to be an act of seduction rather than coercion. After all, you can't force somebody to love you. And this is where America is so effective. It is a collective act of seduction. The aspiration to be American—to learn English and so on—is analogous, really, to falling in love—people there really want, desperately, nothing more than to belong. You *cannot* scold people into becoming more British. The whole Norman Tebbit, cricket-test approach, which *scolds* people into being British, is not going to work. You catch a fly with honey, not with vinegar—and so we have to make Britishness seem appealing. And it did seem like this to members of my own family. In *Jacob's Gift*, I tell the story of one Jewish immigrant who came over at around the same time as my mother did and of how it meant the world to him the day he was naturalised. He enlisted in the cadets because he wanted to wear the uniform of King George. And I have to say that even as a third- or fourth-generation Jew in this country, I actually still do understand that. And I felt a little *frisson* within myself when I arrived at my Oxford college for the first time. I had an awe, and reverence, and joy, at being part of this society. So that's a good thing. We should be proud of it and encourage it. It's nothing to be ashamed of. But you do it by making it seem appealing. You do not do it by scolding those people who have not yet reached that point.

*Where is home? What does that word mean?*

That's a profound question, isn't it? And I suppose initially I do picture the house I live in—home is where my family is, really. There would have been a time when that would have meant my extended family, but now, home is where my wife, my two sons and me are. But that, it's inseparable, really, from London and from Britain. I did for a while consider very seriously moving to America, and ultimately I couldn't do it because it wasn't home. And so, the connection I feel to this country and to London and to where my family is, is very profound. Whereas I couldn't, in all honesty, say that Israel was home. It's complicated, because it does feel like the spiritual homeland or centre for one very large part of my identity. And I have a feeling of connection to that place that I don't feel to anywhere else. But I wouldn't call it "home" in the sense of that deep comfort which I think you feel in your home. In a way, this brings together the two halves of our conversation. If there is a thread through everything I say, really, it is that the more you love something and identify with it, the more you care about its future and therefore feel the urge, and sometimes the desperate, aching need for it to change. And it's only because I care about Israel deeply, and worry about it, that I've written what I have about its policies and why I have denounced its settlements and all that. And it's similar with Britain. If I didn't care about Britain, I wouldn't have bothered banging on and on, week in and week out, about the changes we've got to make. It's a sign, really, of love. So if there's one thing that runs through all the stuff I've written about Britain or about Israel, it is probably that: love.

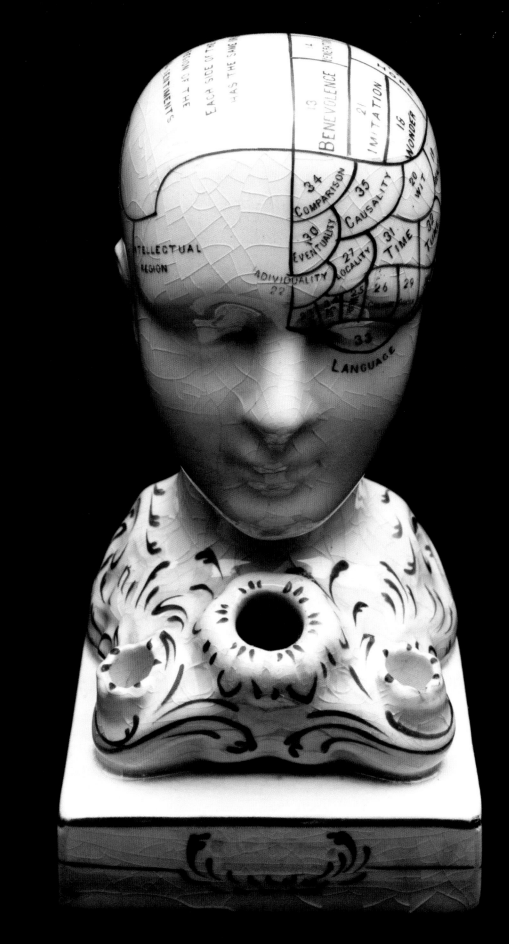

# FRANZ JOSEPH GALL

Ruth Garde

> *We expected to see a charlatan with his hair finely frizzed, and his manner full*
> *of impudence and conceit, and were pleased to meet a good-looking man with the*
> *air, gait and manners of a philosopher. As the doctor walked about the rooms,*
> *many eyes were gazing on him—some were so fortunate as to be introduced*
> *to him—others crowded round him to catch the words that fell from his lips.*
> Henry Reeve, physician, 1805

The polarity of these reactions—suspicion, respect, worshipful admiration—to Franz Joseph Gall, the originator of phrenology exemplifies the standing he held both in his own epoch and thereafter. Personally reviled by many as a greedy mountebank, repudiated professionally and ridiculed for quackery, by others he and his doctrines were admired, respected and proved greatly influential.

Trained as a physician and widely regarded as a skilled anatomist, Gall came to public attention (and is still best known) for his theory of brain localisation, which he termed the "doctrine of the skull" or "organology". This is the field that became known later through his disciples and popularisers as "phrenology". The theory held that moral and intellectual qualities are innate; that they function through organs located in the brain, the size of which indicates their prevalence; and that these are reflected in and can be identified through the shape and size of the cranium. His system was founded on the observation of the skulls of individuals exhibiting extremes in behaviour or intellect, from lunatics and criminals to renowned geniuses. Gall's taxonomy identified 27 organs controlling psychological and moral faculties, whose categories were deliberately generalised and without defined anatomical boundaries. Gall stated that his categories could only indicate propensities and he distanced himself from the more specific and detailed brain maps developed by his erstwhile assistant and collaborator Johann Spurzheim, as well as Spurzheim's application of phrenology in prognosticating character and aptitudes.

The apparent materialism of Gall's doctrine caused his public lectures to be banned in his adopted city of Vienna. He then embarked on a lecture tour of Northern Europe before settling for good in Paris in 1807. It was in Britain that his theory—modified and successfully promoted primarily by Spurzheim and Scottish phrenology devotee George Combe—enjoyed its first widespread acclaim. However, even in its heyday in the 1820s–1840s, it was under constant attack by opponents both scientific and lay. Whilst its fashionable appeal is attested by the mass manufacture of phrenologically-themed objects (such as marked heads, ladies' fans and snuff boxes), the many scientific and popular satirical attacks demonstrate the widespread ridicule and opprobrium which it elicited.

The progressive adulteration of Gall's doctrine into more extreme forms by subsequent practitioners and phrenology's deterioration into a seaside entertainment has robbed Gall of a wider recognition of his merit and influence. Whilst he was not the first to propose a doctrine of cerebral localisation, his work was the most developed attempt to map moral and intellectual character. His belief in cerebral division of labour was propounded in a climate where the holistic tradition (a belief in the brain's homogeneity) was ascendant. Though his organology and its correlation to skull features is now wholly discredited, the general principle of cerebral localisation has nonetheless become commonplace and the effort to map certain propensities and abilities within the brain is a thriving area of contemporary neuroscientific research.

This small bust was designed as a penholder and produced in glazed earthenware by Frederick Bridges in the 1830s or 1840s. Such items show the popular reach of the science that became known as phrenology, which was launched by the doctrine of the German anatomist Franz Joseph Gall that moral and intellectual faculties could be associated with particular regions of the brain.
Courtesy Science and Society Picture Library.

*Below* Gioachino Rossini was one of many notable figures illustrated in Joseph Marriott's *Phrenological album*, which he produced in 1850. The numbers 31 and 32 inked on to the temples are said to correspond to the composer's large organs of "Time" and "Tune".

*Opposite* This image is taken from Marriott's *Phrenological album*. Its subjects—ranging from Queen Victoria to Shakespeare, from Martin Luther to Heidegger—were chosen for their remarkable moral sentiments or intellectual faculties. Each has a number marked on their head locating their particularly noteworthy brain organ. This drawing showing George Bidder, a mathematical child prodigy, has the number 28 beside his right eye, indicating a large organ of "Number".

Courtesy Wellcome Library, London.

G. ROSSINI.

# GEORGE BIDDER,

*The calculating phenomenon of England.*

*Who at eight years of age & having received no instruction in arithmetic possessed the power of resolving
difficult arithmetical questions without hesitating or shewing any appearance of mental operation,
Which power continues & improves.*

He was born at Morton Hampstead in Devonshire June 14th 1806.

Engraved July 1815. by Freeman. from a picture by John King.

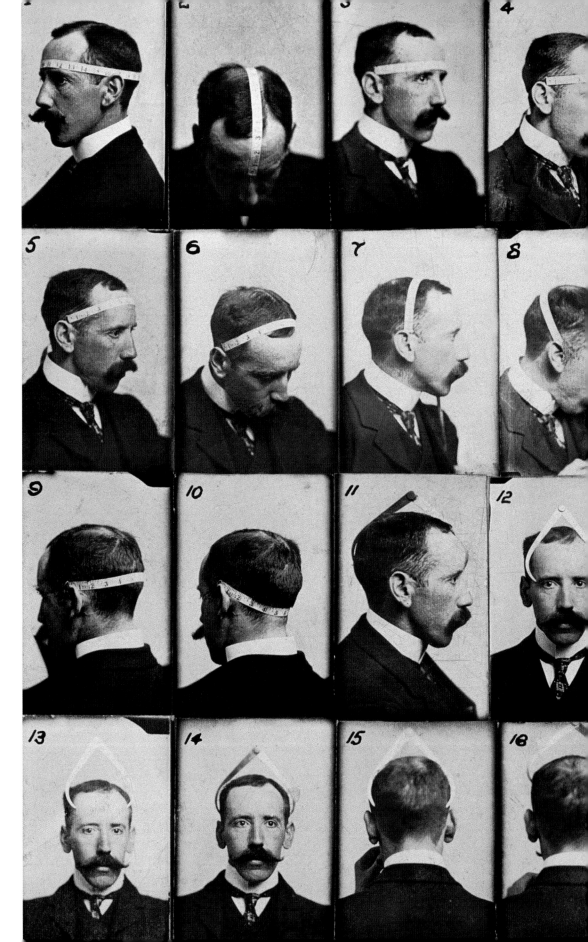

F. JOS. GALL,
Docteur en Medicine, à Vienne.

*Opposite* Bernard Hollander was a Vienna-born psychiatrist who studied and worked in London from the late nineteenth century. He sought to revive interest in phrenology, but with a focus on its original Gallian, scientific concerns. He is shown here demonstrating his own method of cranial measurement.

*Above* This 1803 portrait of Franz Joseph Gall is a mezzotint by Franz Wrenk after Catharina Escherich.

Courtesy Wellcome Library, London.

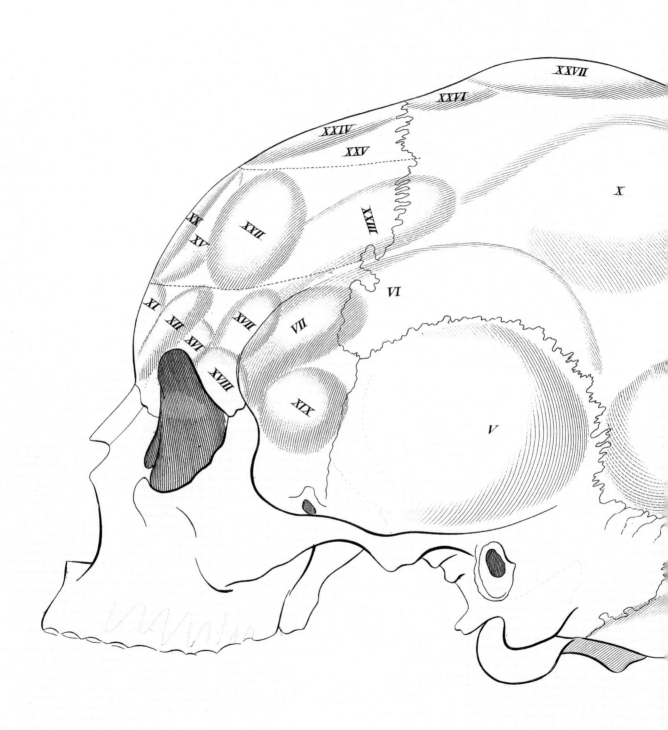

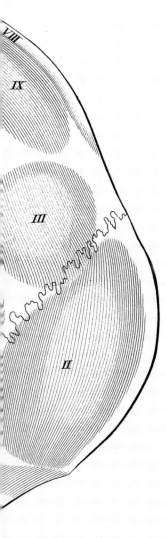

This illustration of the skull, showing the "seat and form of the organs", is taken from the volume of plates that accompanied Gall's six-volume magnum opus on the functions of the brain, published between 1810–1819. It shows most of the 27 organs identified by Gall, including Cunning (VI) and Cautiousness (X).

Courtesy Wellcome Library, London.

This set of 60 miniature phrenological heads, made in Manchester in 1831, may have been produced as a teaching aid or a reference collection. Each specimen is analysed according to the system of Johann Kaspar Spurzheim, Gall's assistant who later modified his taxonomy in a way that Gall rejected. The heads demonstrate a wide variety of talents and dispositions. Head No. 31 is that of a "born Astronomer", whose organs of "configuration, size, locality, order, calculation, marvellousness, cautiousness, firmness and self-esteem predominate". The organs of No. 23, on the other hand, reveal "the head of a dangerous bigot when in power".

This humorous pastiche demonstrates the sustained mockery to which phrenology continued to be subjected in the twentieth century, even as its popularity began seriously to dwindle. This advertisement for Hudson's Soap, dating from around 1910, combines authentic phrenological faculties such as acquisitiveness and destructiveness with invented ones more suited to the claims of the product.

Courtesy Wellcome Library, London.

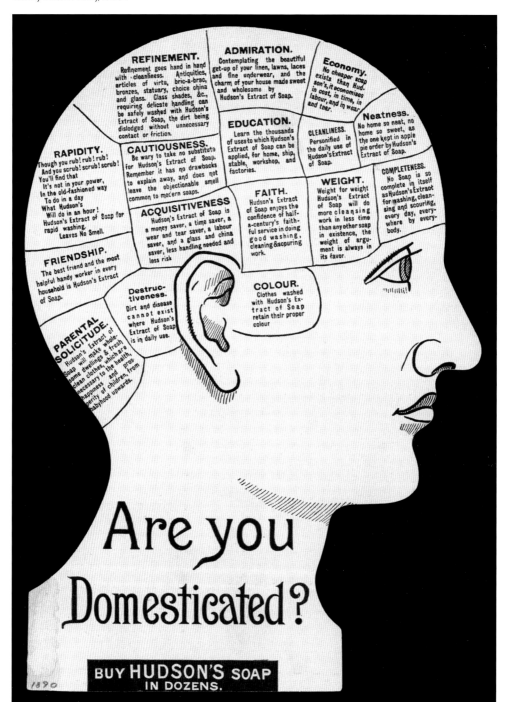

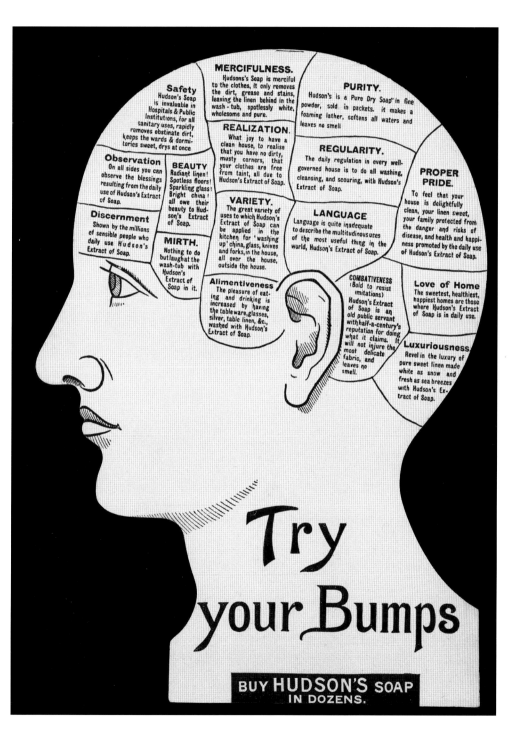

This plate from Gall's *Atlas of the Brain* represents the "female brain".
Courtesy Wellcome Library, London.

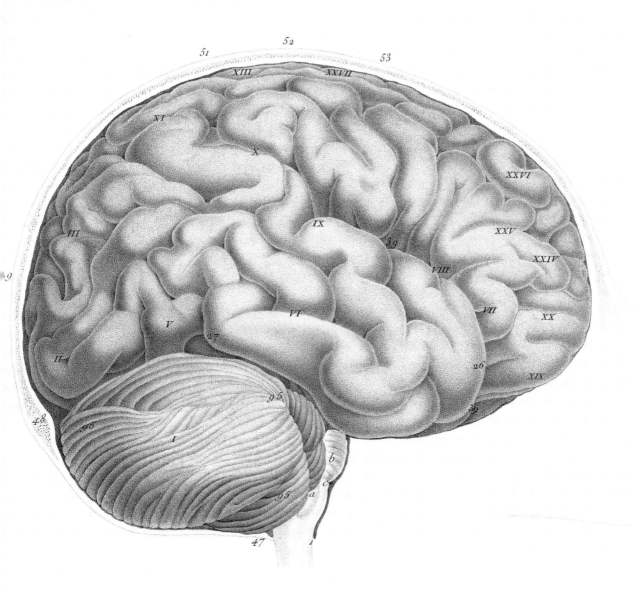

## Craniological Gall

I sing of the organs and fibres
That ramble about in the brains
Avaunt – ye irreverent Gibers
Or come and be wise for your pains.
All heads were of yore on a level,
You could not tell clever from dull
Until I, like Le Sage's lame Devil
Unroofed with a touch every Skull.
Oh! I am the mental dissector
I fathom the wits of you all
So come in a crowd to the Lecture
Of Craniological Gall

The passions, or active or passive,
When touched by my magical spells
As busy as bees in a glass Hive,
Appear in their separate cells.
Old Momus who wanted a casement
Whence all in the heart might be read
If living would stare with amazement
To find what he wants in the head.
Oh! I am the mental dissector
&c &c

*Opposite* In this poem, the unknown writer lampoons the practice of phrenology and its claims to discern the character by feeling the skull. He goes on to manufacture ridiculously specific and frivolous faculties, such as one "for driving a Tilbury gig", or "giving booksellers a lift", and predicts that henceforth love matches should be decided not on the feelings in one's heart but by analysing a prospective partner's cranium instead. Indeed, some practitioners did suggest using phrenological analyses as a way of vetting potential marriage partners.

*Below* This coloured wood engraving made around 1845 by Henri Bushea depicts the location of the mental faculties that is a hybrid of the theories of Spurzheim, George Combe of Edinburgh and the American Fowler brothers. The Fowlers, whose system was seen as a vulgarisation of the science by traditional phrenologists, were highly successful practising phrenologists in the late nineteenth century.
Courtesy Wellcome Library, London.

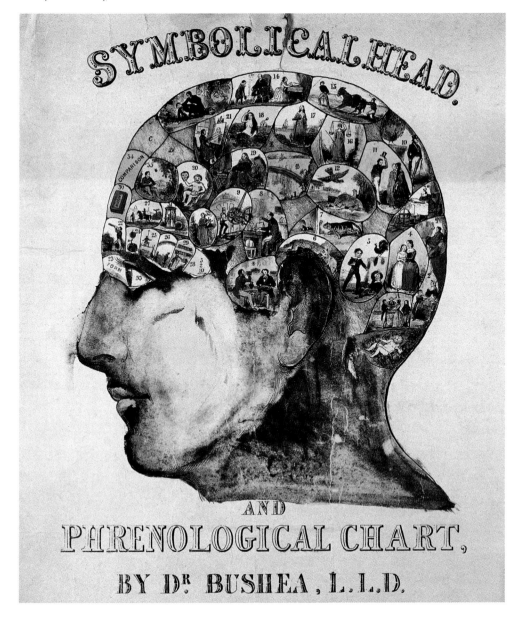

*If this Science be cultivated, I doubt not but the time will come when on hiring a servant, an examination of the organick manifestations of the mental faculties as developed on the superficies of the pericranium, will supersede the necessity of further enquiry into character.*
see Colon on Phrenology.

*Published by W. Taylor, 5 Mount Street Walworth.*

*Above* Many caricaturists found phrenology impossible to resist. This print shows a servants' employment agency where applicants are screened by having the (conveniently exposed and exaggerated) bumps felt on their heads. The author supposes that this scientific method might "supersede the necessity of further enquiry into character".
Courtesy Wellcome Library, London.

*Ladies and Gentlemen*
*Having thus concluded the hundred and thir*
*Talkativeness with Gulling, standing*
*Under Evident Contradictions, Stands*

*Below* The animated lecturer represents the Edinburgh phrenologist George Combe. Behind him are his inspirations, Spurzheim as a bust standing on the floor, Gall in a jar on the shelf. The creators of this coloured lithograph of 1826 style themselves as L Bump and J Lump.
Courtesy Wellcome Library, London.

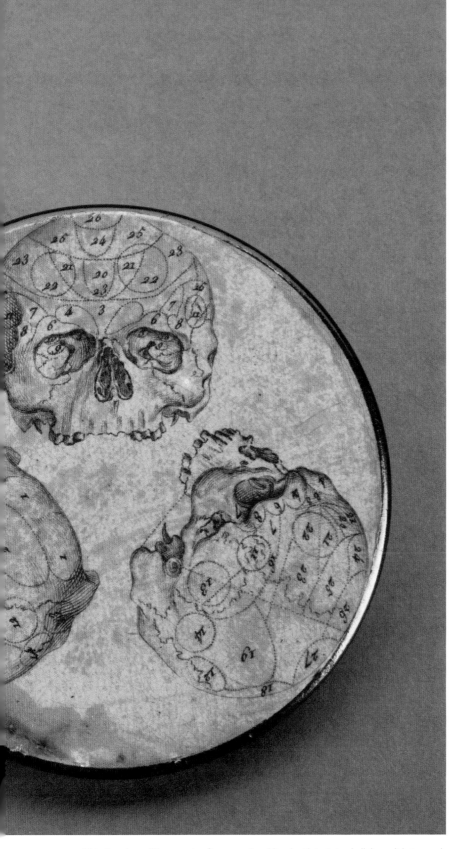

This French snuff box, made of pearwood and lined with tortoiseshell, has a lid stamped with three views of a skull with organs numbered according to Gall's scheme. The key is given on the base of the box.

Courtesy Wellcome Library, London.

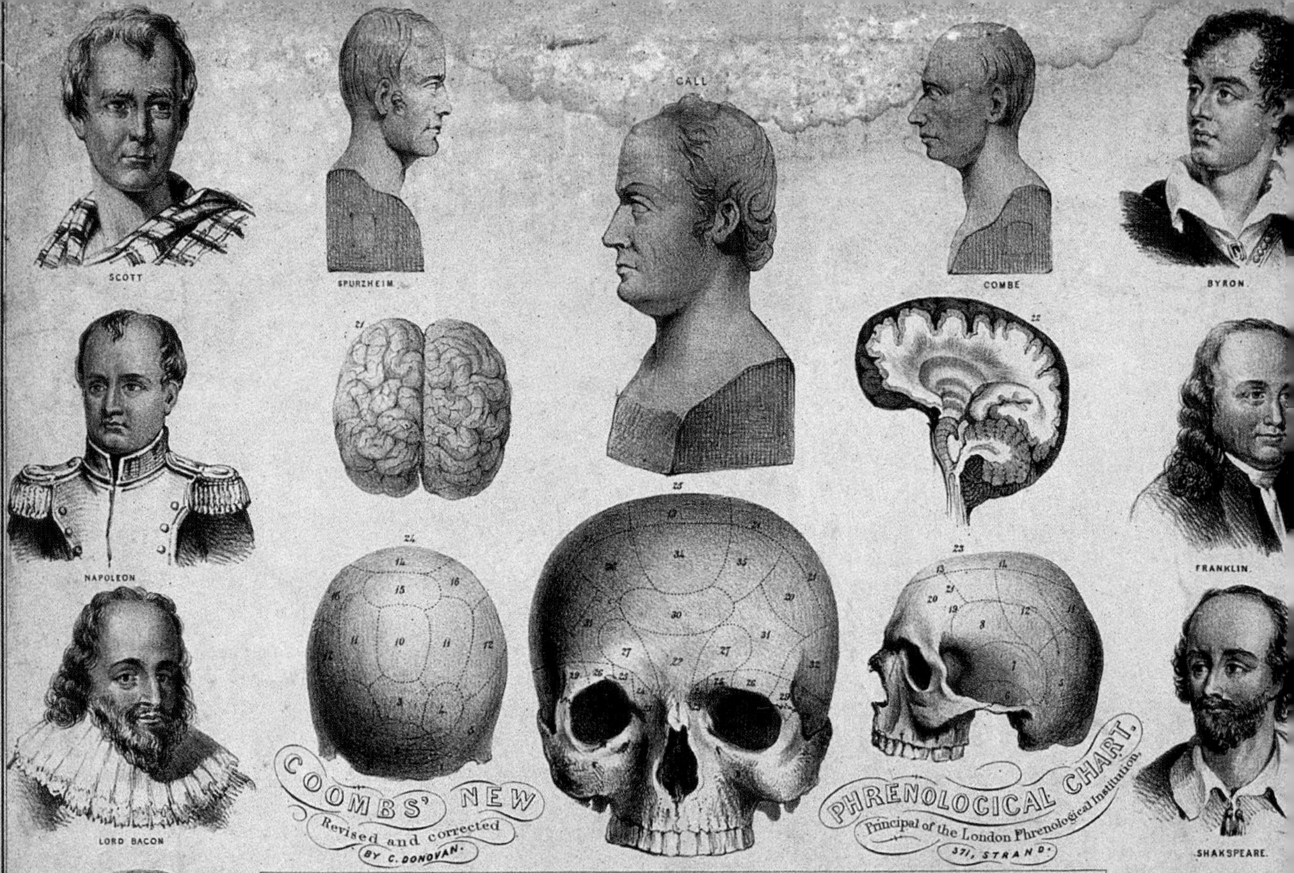

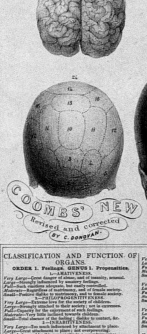

GALL
SCOTT
SPURZHEIM
COMBE
BYRON
NAPOLEON
FRANKLIN
LORD BACON
SHAKSPEARE
COOMBS' NEW
Revised and corrected
BY C. DONOVAN.
PHRENOLOGICAL CHART.
Principal of the London Phrenological Institution,
371, STRAND.


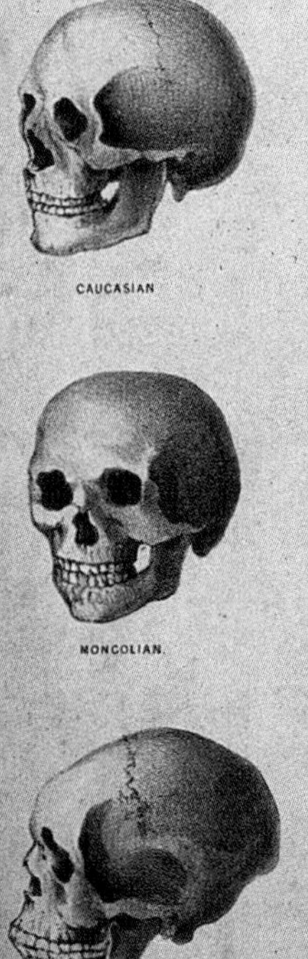

CAUCASIAN
MONGOLIAN
NEGRO


## CLASSIFICATION AND FUNCTION OF ORGANS.

### ORDER 1. Feelings. GENUS 1. Propensities.

**1.—AMATIVENESS.**

*Very Large*—Great danger of abuse, and of insanity, sensual.
*Large*—Strongly influenced by amatory feelings.
*Full*—Such emotions adequate, but easily controlled.
*Moderate*—Regardless of matrimony, and of female society.
*Small*—Positive dislike to matrimony, and to female society.

**2.—PHILOPROGENITIVENESS.**

*Very Large*—Extreme love for the society of children.
*Large*—Strongly attached to their society; not in extremes.
*Full*—Capacity for the enjoyment of such feelings.
*Moderate*—Very little inclined towards children.
*Small*—Total absence of the feeling; dislike to contact, &c.

**3.—INHABITIVENESS.**

*Very Large*—Too much influenced by attachment to place.
*Large*—Great attachment to place; not overpowering.
*Full*—Influenced by this propensity in a secondary sense.
*Moderate*—Regardlessness of particular places, residences, &c.
*Small*—Total inability to form such attachments.

**4.—ADHESIVENESS.**

*Very Large*—Frequent and ardent friendships; too fond of society.
*Large*—Inability to dispense with friendships.
*Full*—Friendly, but under prudent restrictions.
*Moderate*—Regardless of individuals; no attachments.
*Small*—Positive dislike to society; solitary.

**5.—COMBATIVENESS.**

*Very Large*—An absolute passion for contention.
*Large*—Proneness to fighting; martial; quick to strike.
*Full*—An adequate degree of self-defensive feeling.
*Moderate*—Dislike to contention and quarrelling; peaceable.
*Small*—Actual inability to raise an arm in self-defence.

**6.—DESTRUCTIVENESS.**

*Very Large*—Extreme liability to anger; bloodthirsty; cruel.
*Large*—Energetic, forcible, fond of field sports.
*Full*—Not liable to bursts of anger; "Suaviter in modo, fortiter in re."
*Moderate*—Wanting ardour and energy; dislike to bloodshed.
*Small*—Abhorrence to the functions of this faculty.

**7.—SECRETIVENESS.**

*Very Large*—Resorting, on all occasions, to deceit and manœuvring.
*Large*—Danger of being tainted by cunning and trickery.
*Full*—Ability to be secret, and to oppose cunning to cunning.
*Moderate*—Great openness, plain speaking, and directness.
*Small*—Inability to conceal or hoard; blabbing; too communicative.

**8.—ACQUISITIVENESS.**

*Very Large*—Inordinate desire to obtain property; covetous.
*Large*—Inclined to traffic; desirous of gain.
*Full*—Sufficiently regardful of gain; adapted for trade so far.
*Moderate*—Not fond of traffic; regardless of gain; wasteful.
*Small*—Total inability to acquire property.

**9.—CONSTRUCTIVENESS.**

*Very Large*—Genius for architecture; bricks and mortar mania.
*Large*—Talent for architecture and engineering; handy.
*Full*—Capacity for acquiring constructive arts; not genius.
*Moderate*—Unsuited to architecture; unable to use tools.
*Small*—Total inability to perform any handiwork; dislike for such.

**ALIMENTIVENESS.**

*Very Large*—Voraciousness; gluttonousness; inordinate hunger and thirst.
*Large*—Strong tendency to the abuse of food and drink.
*Full*—A due regard towards diet; sufficient appetite.
*Moderate*—Delicacy of appetite, regardless of eating.
*Small*—Loathing of food; not discerning flavours.

### GENUS 2. Moral Sentiments.

**10.—SELF ESTEEM.**

*Very Large*—Extreme pride; self-exaggeration; contempt for others.
*Large*—Desire of command; self-confidence; pride.
*Full*—Adequate self-reliance; readiness to compete.
*Moderate*—Diffidence; want of self-confidence; humility.
*Small*—Extreme undervaluing of self; "Mauvaise honte."

**11.—LOVE OF APPROBATION.**

*Very Large*—Total dependence on opinion; greedy of praise.
*Large*—Ambitious to excel; full of emulation.
*Full*—Not over sensitive to praise and blame; sufficiently so.
*Moderate*—Not stimulated either by applause or disapprobation.
*Small*—Prone to defy and despise public or private opinion.

**12.—CAUTION.**

*Very Large*—Extreme timidity; incapacity to face danger.
*Large*—Not courageous; anxious to avoid risk.
*Full*—Circumspect; provident against danger, but not timid.
*Moderate*—Venturesome; imprudent; senseless of hazard.
*Small*—Totally wanting in circumspection; foolhardy.

**13.—BENEVOLENCE.**

*Very Large*—Entire devotion to philanthropy and sympathy.
*Large*—Sensitively alive to humanity.
*Full*—Capability of feeling, in obvious cases.
*Moderate*—Regardless of the sufferings of others.
*Small*—Positive dislike to mankind; misanthropic.

**14.—VENERATION.**

*Very Large*—Liability to fanaticism, and extremes in religion.
*Large*—Reverential to superiors and authorities; religious.
*Full*—Duly affected by the functions of this faculty.
*Moderate*—Not easily susceptible of respect to authorities, &c.
*Small*—Great danger of irreligion; disrespectful; rebellious.

**15.—FIRMNESS.**

*Very Large*—Obstinate; unyielding; positive, to a fault.
*Large*—Enduring; patient; calm; resolute.
*Full*—Ability to exercise the faculty; not unyielding.
*Moderate*—Wanting due resolution and presence of mind.
*Small*—Vacillating; "To one thing constant never."

**16.—CONSCIENTIOUSNESS.**

*Very Large*—Scrupulous, and self-accusing beyond reason.
*Large*—Love of abstract justice and integrity.
*Full*—Fond of the right, but liable to be swayed.
*Moderate*—Preferring expediency to truth and honesty.
*Small*—Acting dishonestly, without compunction.

**17.—HOPE.**

*Very Large*—Irrational reliance on future events.
*Large*—Prone to clothe the future in brightness.
*Full*—Rational expectation of favourable results.
*Moderate*—Not relying sufficiently on the future.
*Small*—Gloomy; desponding; despairing.

**18.—WONDER OR BELIEF.**

*Very Large*—Credulity; credence without enquiry; gullibility.
*Large*—Readiness to believe; easily convinced.
*Full*—Accessible to conviction on reasonable evidence.
*Moderate*—Incredulous; difficult to convince on demonstration.
*Small*—Absolute scepticism; irrational incredulity.

**19.—IDEALITY.**

*Very Large*—Forsaking the real for the imaginative.
*Large*—Poetic; fanciful; flowery; figurative.
*Full*—An active conception of the sublime and beautiful.
*Moderate*—Absence of poetic taste; "matter of fact."
*Small*—Totally devoid of elevating emotions.

**20.—GAIETY.**

*Very Large*—Liable to bursts of extreme hilarity and laughter.
*Large*; Gay; fond of humour and the ludicrous.
*Full*—Susceptible of these emotions in moderation.
*Moderate*—Difficult to excite laughter; "sombre."
*Small*—Impatient of gaiety and cheerfulness; grave.

**21.—IMITATION.**

*Very Large*—Inability to refrain from copying others.
*Large*—Possessing a talent for imitative arts.
*Full*—Not incapable of imitating, yet original.
*Moderate*—Slow in catching manner; unable to copy.
*Small*—This inability in an extreme degree.

### ORDER 2. GENUS 1. Intellectual Faculties,

*Which perceive Existence and Physical Qualities.*

**22.—INDIVIDUALITY.**

*Very Large*—Microscopic clearness, and accuracy of observation.
*Large*—Talent for chemistry and other physical sciences.
*Full*—A modified desire and power for the study of objects.
*Moderate*—Want of sufficient observation; inattention to facts.
*Small*—Actual inability to notice realities; perceptive blindness.

**23.—FORM.**

*Very Large*—Genius for drawing; composing forms with ease.
*Large*—Power to discern and remember forms and persons.
*Full*—Discernment of forms in a medium degree.
*Moderate*—No talent for drawing; regardless of outline.
*Small*—Extreme liability to forget persons and objects.

**24.—SIZE.**

*Very Large*—Very accurate perception of space, dimensions, &c.
*Large*—Power to estimate sizes and distances correctly.
*Full*—Not liable to make great errors in such estimates.
*Moderate*—Necessity for frequent reference to measurements.
*Small*—Inattention and dislike to the observation of sizes, &c.

**25.—WEIGHT.**

*Very Large*—Extreme accuracy in estimating momentum, balancing, &c.
*Large*—Fond of dynamics, delicate in touch and manual operations.
*Full*—Capable of accuracy when the attention is directed to weight and force.
*Moderate*—Apt to make false estimates of forces and weights.
*Small*—Incapable of dexterity in delicate manual arts.

**26.—COLOUR.**

*Very Large*—Ardent imaginativeness in painting; liability to abuse.
*Large*—Talent for painting; accurate discernment of shades.
*Full*—Correctness in discerning simple colours.
*Moderate*—Devoid of talent for painting, &c.
*Small*—Actual inability to discern colours; distortion of colours.

**27.—LOCALITY.**

*Very Large*—Genius for travelling and exploring; fond of travelling and brief sojourns.
*Large*—Good memory of places; pleased with travelling.
*Full*—A medium state of this power.
*Moderate*—Forgetful of places and positions; regardless of exploring.
*Small*—Inability to traverse cities, &c., without a guide.

**28.—NUMBER.**

*Very Large*—Instinctive talent for mental arithmetic.
*Large*—Capacity for numerical calculations.
*Full*—Ability to study and acquire the numerical art.
*Moderate*—Stupid at figures; bad accountant.
*Small*—Great dislike to arithmetic; no power in numericals.

**29.—ORDER.**

*Very Large*—Rendered unhappy by all departures from regularity.
*Large*—Love for order; everything in its place.
*Full*—Capable of observing order; not a victim to it.
*Moderate*—Content amidst confusion; irregular.
*Small*—Nothing it its place; moral and physical confusion.

**30.—EVENTUALITY.**

*Very Large*—Extraordinary memory of events, history, &c.
*Large*—Talent for history; fond of recording.
*Full*—Power to record important occurrences; not minutiæ.
*Moderate*—Forgetful; requiring memoranda; inaccurate in history.
*Small*—Totally regardless of incidents; incapacity for business.

**31.—TIME.**

*Very Large*—Tendency to record periods, and to "take note of time."
*Large*—Accurate in dates; fond of the philosophy of time.
*Full*—Not forgetful of periods relating to important affairs.
*Moderate*—Incorrect in dates; oblivious of passing hours.
*Small*—Incapacity for music irrespective of tune; no sense of time.

**32.—TUNE.**

*Very Large*—Genius for music; passion for composing.
*Large*—Good capacity for music; sensitive to melody.
*Full*—Not regardless of, nor unaffected by melody.
*Moderate*—But a slight appreciation of tune and harmony.
*Small*—Positive inability to perceive tune; dislike for music.

**33.—LANGUAGE.**

*Very Large*—" Leprosy of eloquence; "flux of speech."
*Large*—A good command of language; capacity for oratory.
*Full*—Not deficient in words to express the ideas.
*Moderate*—Barrenness of words; trite and common place in speech.
*Small*—Total inability to speak with ease and clearness; taciturn.

### GENUS 2. Reflective Faculties.

**34.—COMPARISON.**

*Very Large*—Irresistible tendency to use metaphors and similes.
*Large*—Great ability to illustrate by such figures.
*Full*—Power to explain and teach by the aid of similitudes.
*Moderate*—Inability to discern mutual relations and connexions.
*Small*—Dislike to similes; no conception of their use.

**35.—CAUSALITY.**

*Very Large*—Genius for metaphysics; fond of deep reflection.
*Large*—Quick in seeing the relation between cause and effect.
*Full*—Open to conviction by reasoning; not profound.
*Moderate*—Illogical; difficult to convince by argument.
*Small*—Inability to comprehend causation and induction; irrational.

⁂ The student must remember that, in no case, is the state of the entire mind to be inferred from the state of one organ. In single organs, or even groups of organs, "'Tis but a part we view, and not the whole."

### TEMPERAMENT.

There are four main temperaments acknowledged by all physiologists—viz.,

THE SANGUINE—Indicated by a full development of the muscles and vessels; by a ruddy, glowing, and healthful complexion; a love for bodily exercise; by fair skin and hair.

THE LYMPHATIC—Prevalent in lazy and fat persons; gives a disinclination to exertion; is often accompanied by beauty of the languishing order—never by active energy and strength of the nervous system; unfavourable to mental exertion.

THE BILIOUS is discerned by the darkness of complexion, firmness of texture, absence of obesity, emphasis of muscular development, endurance, and mental activity and continuity.

THE NERVOUS—Quickness, activity, thinness of skin, absence of fatness, sharpness and delicacy of features, smallness of bone, excitability without endurance, are the leading indications of a nervous temperament.

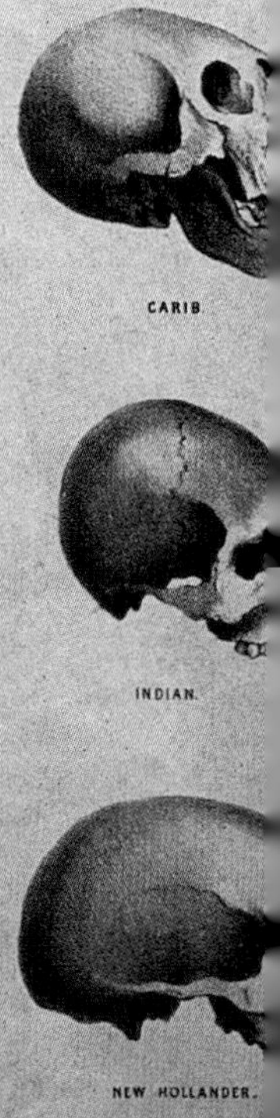

CARIB.
INDIAN.
NEW HOLLANDER.


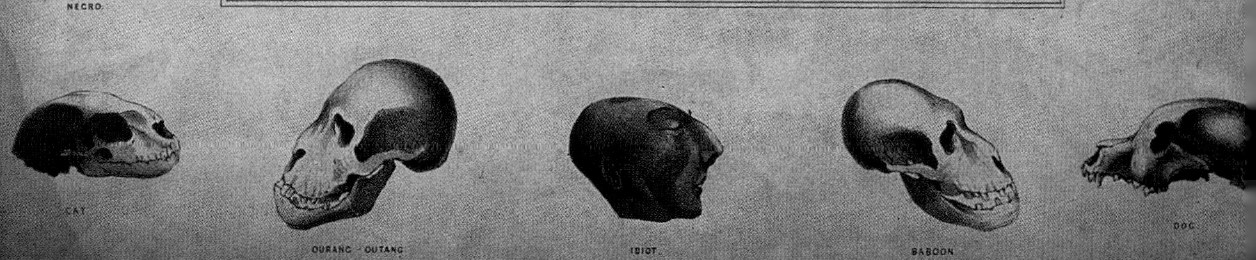

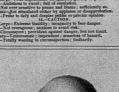

CAT.
OURANG - OUTANG.
IDIOT.
BABOON.
DOG.

This chart by George Edward Madeley and Cornelius Donovan dates from the mid-nineteenth century. It largely follows the system of George Combe, then the most prolific advocate of phrenology in Britain. As the variety of skulls indicate, phrenology had ambitions to measure brain differences on a racial basis. Combe wrote that the phrenologist "has observed that a particular size and form of brain is the invariable concomitant of particular dispositions and talents, and that this fact holds good in the case of nations as well as of individuals".

Courtesy Wellcome Library, London.

# DAVID GOODHART

is the founder and editor of *Prospect* magazine. He was a senior correspondent for the *Financial Times*.

---

*Who are you?*

Well I'm known by my name, first of all, which is David Goodhart. I'm a journalist; I'm a husband; I'm a father; I edit a magazine; I'm British; I'm middle-aged, I suppose, I'm 52—though I feel rather younger! What else? I'm male; I'm middle-class or upper-middle-class. I guess that'll do for now!

*Are there any elements within what you have said there which you feel are predominant? Or are there groups within society or the wider world that you particularly identify with?*

Well, it's situational, isn't it? When I'm at home, I'm a husband and father. When I'm at work, I'm the editor of *Prospect*. When you are doing different things then different aspects of your self emerge as prominent.

*Ziauddin Sardar, in his book,* Balti Britain, *says that he has a very complex relationship with a word like "Asian" but nonetheless he does see himself in some ways as a British Asian, and that seems to be a very prominent part of his persona. Would you say you had an element in your self-identity to parallel that, or do you feel that the relationship to ethnicity or race is something that is not of significance?*

It's not something I think about every day. I suppose you think about it when you go abroad, or you meet a foreigner, or whatever. And I guess if you're a member of a minority, then you're presented with the issue more often. Although, if you're not well integrated at all—if you live entirely amongst your own kind—then you might not be presented with that. But it's a relatively abstract thing, unlike being a man or a father or having any particular occupation. Nationality or ethnicity is real, but it's also more abstract. So, it's not something you really think about the whole time. It

is in you the whole time and you express it the whole time, you're just not aware of it.

*And do you think perhaps the reason for not being aware of it is because, at a personal level, that aspect of you doesn't feel under threat in this country in this context?*

Yes. You live in Britain and you're British—so it's like walking or reading, you don't think about it.

*In relation to that, if we go back to the earlier question, do you have a particular sense of how other people see you, either in your personal life or in your professional life, or in a wider context? Do you feel that your public profile is at odds with how you see yourself?*

Well, I hope not. I suppose part of the aim of leading a good life is to make sure that gap isn't too large. But I guess that most people really don't have sufficient self-awareness to be able to measure that gap. But of course we wander around every day with illusory ideas about ourselves, which, I guess, are a sort of aspiration of what we'd like to be. So we might hold these ideas in our heads, but it's easier for other people to see the gap between that aspiration and the walking, talking, person that we are.

*I suppose the other side to that question is whether you feel that other people might misunderstand you in a way that you think is false. So, for instance, you described yourself as upper-middle-class earlier, and someone might choose to see that particular element of you as the dominant feature of your identity. Do you ever get a sense that you are being seen in a way that is unfair?*

Well we're said to be a very class-conscious society. And I went to Eton, so that represents the pinnacle of being upper-class, or upper-middle-class. And I've often been aware of that, and I've spent a lot of my life trying to come to terms with it, trying to live it down—trying to pretend I didn't go to Eton. But I think I've come to terms with it now. Though perhaps it's just that one becomes more confident in oneself as one gets older. In your teens or even into your 20s and 30s you can still be quite unsure of who you are. Not that I'd necessarily be able to write down very precisely who I am now, but you just get used to yourself. And I suppose in my case, class is one of the bits of me that stands out from the crowd most. The fact that I'm six foot four and a half is another!

*It's interesting that you said that you gained a stronger sense of your own identity as you got older. Does that suggest that identity is something that emerges or is fluid over time? Do you get a sense of your own identity as something that is in flux, or something that is open to further change?*

Oh yes—definitely. One's idea of oneself certainly changes over the years. One grows and changes. I'm quite a different person to the person I was when I was 20. But then if I got to know somebody again who knew me when I was 20, they might see much more continuity than I would see. I'd feel much more different than they would see me, I suppose, because the things that make me different to my 20-year-old self are hard for another person to detect.

*So there is a difference then between how we see our identity internally and how other people might see it?*

Yes. Again, there's a common pattern. I feel a lot more comfortable in my own skin now than I did when I was 20, but then I probably made a bigger effort to *appear* confident in my own skin when I was 20. So unless one knew me very well one might not see the difference.

*You described yourself earlier as "British". What is Britain? What is Britishness?*

Well, technically, it just means being a British citizen. That is, to have British citizenship, which I acquired automatically through being born here and having British parents. Though actually, both my parents are half-American, although they're also British. But that's obviously just a bureaucratic definition. So what is Britain? Well, Britain is its history and its institutions and everyone who's wandering around the streets of Britain today and everything that's going on in their heads. That's what Britain is. And historically, I think, it's a country that has had a rather complicated sense of itself for a number of reasons: it is four nations in one state; it had an Empire which came to an end; there was mass immigration; and there was the turmoil and upheaval of the 1960s and 70s. And I think it's only recently that some of these questions have been looked at more confidently and more straightforwardly. We sort of moved from having a kind of implicit understanding of Britishness, or perhaps one should say Englishness, to suddenly having to be more self-conscious about it. And that self-consciousness, I think, created a great deal of anxiety.

*Why do you think that that shift happened?*

I guess that, certainly amongst the liberal elite, it was because of the really quite dominant anti-national sentiment that came out of what sociologists then called the "universalist shift" in the mid-century. This was embodied in the UN Declaration of Human Rights, which suddenly made liberal universalism the political norm in Western liberal democracies. This is a movement which arose in response to the horrors of the first half of the twentieth century: two world wars, the holocaust, colonialism and so on. And through things like the end of colonialism, and the civil rights movement in America, the idea of the moral equality of all human beings arose. This was a very powerful and simple thought, but it was one that had been a utopian and a religious idea until the mid-twentieth century, when suddenly it became a reality—at least in terms of our constitutions and on our banners as it were. And it was very much taken up by liberals, and even by liberal conservatives, all over Europe in particular, where some of the worst horrors of the first half of the twentieth century had taken place. And I think that was a mistake in many ways, but I think that led to the easy association that, the phrase "liberal universalism" was 'good', human rights were 'good', and the nation was 'bad'. That the nation was blamed, wrongly I think, for Nazism and many of the other horrors of the first half of the twentieth century and indeed the nineteenth century.

So there was a challenge to many kinds of hierarchies. Racial, ethnic, gender, even social hierarchies were challenged by the moral equality of all humans. And that obviously allowed for a huge step forward. But that's just something that we all just take for granted now, and anyone who's remotely liberal embraces it, as I do. But I think the category error of many liberals, particularly in the 1960s and the 70s, and particularly in Britain, because of the extra complications that I mentioned before is that we have embraced liberal universalism as if it was something that made the nation-state impossible. And my argument is that that's a very big mistake and that it's possible to embrace the 'universal shift'—to believe in the moral equality of all human beings—but also to believe that we have special obligations to fellow citizens, and that if we don't, then the system simply doesn't work. I mean, why do we pay 25 times more for the NHS than we pay in development aid every year? Well the obvious analogy is to the way families work. We don't think our families are morally superior to other families, but we will, nonetheless, put our own families first. Equally, the nation-state doesn't work unless you have a degree of fellow-citizen favouritism. And I think the nation-state has to be made to work, because all the things that liberals like actually stems from the nation-state—democratic accountability, the welfare state, redistribution and so on. These things only work, or have so far only worked, at the level of the nation-state. It's also a pragmatic argument in a sense—in order for the nation-state

to produce those good things, we have to have some degree of fellow feeling for each other. And this obviously becomes more attenuated in our more individualistic, postmodern era. This is particularly the case when many different people from different countries come and live here. Because then we may no longer have the implicit mutual understandings that are vital. This is why, in their clumsy way, New Labour have been trying to create a kind of American or French, or Canadian-style civic patriotism that we've never had to have before. It may sound very clunky and 1950s, but I think it's important. And although Gordon Brown's not necessarily the most articulate exponent of it, I think his heart is in the right place on this.

*Can we define a British citizen as opposed to French citizen or an American citizen? Is there something about citizenship in Britain that is unique or unusual or particular to this country?*

Well, merely the fact that it is British. British citizenship is attached to this particular plot of land and these sets of institutions. And all countries have their own particular histories and institutions. It doesn't mean to say that every individual British person is unique and if you sliced them open then they would look different to an American citizen— obviously they wouldn't, we're all human beings. We have all grown up in particular places, with particular languages and institutions and the social psychologies that go with them. And obviously, we all have our own histories, our own identities, our own journeys. But these journeys have just taken place in a wider context—in a particular society, in a particular nation, in a particular political community. And being a good citizen is broadly the same in any country, I suspect—looking after your fellow citizens, paying your taxes, obeying the law, perhaps giving more to the common weal than you take out of it. These are, I suppose, straightforwardly religious ideas that many of the world religions would endorse—that's probably where they come from.

*Could you perhaps, in the context of the question "how do we decide who should get to be a citizen?" unpack your thoughts on immigration?*

As in "who should be given citizenship?" Well, I suppose, anyone who asks for it should be considered for citizenship. But I do think there should be more visible hurdles for a new citizen to cross. In order to cohere, a political community has to have walls around it. Not anybody can become a member of it. Most people become members of it through living here over a period of time and therefore, we hope and assume, they absorb the norms of behaviour, and they learn to speak the language and so on. And I do think there are very big questions about how much immigration is required. Liberals obviously tend to assume immigration is somehow an inherently good thing. I don't think that is always necessarily true. Immigration is actually a very difficult thing both for immigrants and for the receiving communities. And I think part of the universalist shift has been that we've deracinated the idea of the individual human being, in some ways, and so we've undermined the idea of community. The idea seems to have become that there is no such thing as community, we're all just rational individual human beings, and therefore a larger number of them makes no difference. But actually, that's not true, is it? There are such things as human communities although the left has tended to be very hypocritical about this. It perceives human communities very strongly when it comes to social class. But when it comes to nation or even region, it becomes almost Thatcherite in its individualism.

It's funny, in the 1950s and 60s, a lot of people on the conservative right felt that the great family of the Empire should continue within Britain, and that it was right and proper that people from the West Indies and Asia should be automatically British citizens. As indeed they were—it's extraordinary, the 1948 Citizenship Act actually made six hundred million people citizens of Britain. But that was at a time when mass travel was very expensive and only a tiny number of people could do it. Nehru could come here and go to the LSE, but the average Indian peasant certainly couldn't get on a plane and fly to Britain. But now, at a time when someone not far above a peasant, can get on a plane and travel, the equation has entirely changed. And it's also been entirely changed by the development of the welfare state. When you have all sorts of resources that are free to anyone who is within the state and you don't even have to be a British citizen to get free healthcare and free education then it becomes pretty hard to distinguish between people who are citizens and people who aren't citizens. And so as soon as that happens, then, I think, mass immigration becomes very much more problematic. And we didn't give it enough thought, really, when it was all starting in the 1950s and 60s and 70s. But now we are giving it more thought because immigration is happening on an unprecedented scale.

*Is that why we're giving it more thought now?*

Partly yes. There is less guilt about talking about it now. I think we've seen through the universalist myth, to some extent. And most of the time, in any country, immigration is very unpopular, because people do have a sense of being disrupted by it. And it's the people who have the keenest sense of community, the white working classes and so on, who are often on the receiving end of it. And their voices have been listened to more in recent years. They were usually caricatured as nativists and xenophobic and I don't think that's any longer the case. It has often been the case that all of our public attention is on the celebration of minority ethnicities and so they would feel written out of the script. It's what one might call "asymmetrical multiculturalism"—the idea that it's fine for minorities to express their sense of tradition but it's not fine for the majority. And I think one can exaggerate it—one doesn't want to end up sounding too much like the *Daily Mail*! But I think it has happened. It has been going on. And I think that a powerful democratic voice has emerged to say, "hold on. There are things happening here that are not good." And you can now say that without being accused of being a racist. Whereas I think that was not so easy 20 years ago.

*There is a left-wing critique of multiculturalism which says that it entrenches difference, and sees minority communities particularly, as being static and unable to change. Is that something that you would agree with?*

Well I don't think that is a "left-wing critique", I think it's just a sensible critique. There is a soft and then there's a hard multiculturalism. The soft multiculturalism is about treating everybody equally and all of that. It's about equal rights, it perhaps includes some degree of positive discrimination here and there and it acknowledges that people can find it difficult, initially, to break into society and so it wants to help them out. That is sensible and mainstream. But then there's a hard multiculturalism which involves a sort of fetishisation of difference. This says that ethnicity is actually the most important thing about people, particularly with minority communities. And it's a denial of equal human rights, and so the public sphere becomes one of competing ethnicities, rather than being a liberal political community which we are all members of. And I don't think that sits well with democracy, basically, as everything ends up being a battle between groups—either ethnic or religious. And lots of societies are condemned to that. Just look at India and places like that, they are hugely diverse. People often say that diversity's good, but often it is not. There's a great deal to be said for homogeneity. And we have a relatively homogeneous political culture that has come from a thousand years of melding between Anglo-Saxons and Celts and so on and we've created something relatively homogeneous out of that. Okay, we have different social classes, of course, and plenty of different regional interests, but generally our homogeneity is what's allowed us to have a liberal democracy in some ways. We don't have a focus on group rights—but rather on individual rights.

*So, how does that relate, then, to the situation for recent migrants? For instance, you mentioned language earlier, and you said that part of being within this community is the willingness to speak the language. Some multiculturalists would say, "well, actually, no. Preserving languages of a migrant community is a very important thing to do." And on the other side, there are some politicians and others who have talked about legally obliging migrants to learn a language. Where do you stand on that?*

Well learning the language is part of the citizenship test now, which I think is absolutely right. But the two things are not in contradiction. And of course, minority languages should be preserved. And unless people are coming from somewhere that ceases to exist when they move here, then the things will be preserved in their own country. So we don't have to worry about global languages. But otherwise the language thing seems to me to be a complete no brainer. And I would hope people's mother tongue becomes English after a generation. Unless people can speak good English as well as their mother tongue, then they can't play a full role in the community that they have chosen to be part of. And that's bad for them and it's bad for the British people they live amongst. I just can't understand why anyone would have a problem with that. Unless they really don't believe in nations at all, but that's just a death wish on everything decent, it seems to me!

*In his book* Balti Britain *Ziauddin Sardar defends the idea of encouraging and protecting diversity through multiculturalism. He is very aware of the problems that exist amongst Muslims in this country, with rising fundamentalism and so on, but he argues that much of the current critique of multiculturalism is a form of Islamophobia in disguise.*

Well, I just think that's nonsense. I actually think the response to Islamist terrorism has been remarkably liberal. You remember the days after 7/7—everybody, but everybody, was saying, "this is just a tiny minority, they are unrepresentative extremists". So I think there was a fantastic response to that and I just think that people like Zia are wrong, really. Islamophobia is largely an invention in my opinion. Of course, people are suspicious of those they don't understand and there is some prejudice. But one of the problems is that the universal shift in the twentieth century raised all sorts of unrealisable expectations. And I think that from the best of motives we gave people the impression that coming here was easy, that transporting yourself from one culture to another was easy. And we encouraged people in the belief that they would just slot in—everything would be fine. But that was a very terrible mistake. Because of course, if there are, suddenly, lots of people around who look very different to you and behave very differently to you and cook very different food to you then that is going to generate some hostility. So we had, in the past, a very childish view of all of this.

*What's your attitude to the relationship between religion, particularly Christianity, and contemporary British identity, or the notion of identity in general? Is it something that is just falling away naturally? Is it something that should be actively avoided? Is the idea of defining oneself in a religious sense, an intrinsically bad thing?*

Oh, I think Christianity's a very important part of British history and British traditions. We have a largely secular culture now, but we have some residual Christian beliefs and holidays and I think that's fine. Should we disestablish the Church? Perhaps we should. Although, there's actually some resistance to that from other minorities, who feel that if we disestablish the Church then religion in general will start to play a smaller part in public life. I think that probably the time has come to disestablish the Church, but either way we will remain a majority Christian country. I'm not a believer myself, but I think Christianity's a pretty decent religion compared to some of the others. The point is, it's our religion—it's deeply ingrained in our language and our heritage and that's fine. I sometimes think, "the more practising Christians, the better". They tend to be serious people who think about how they behave.

*Where does the idea of the nation state, in terms both of our identity as individuals and as a community, fit into an idea of a wider international community? Britain is, after all, part of Europe. How important do you think those kinds of international relationships are? Are they a good thing for our national identity, or do they potentially undermine it?*

Well I think they are obviously necessary. In a very interconnected world we need to be part of alliances and institutions like the EU and NATO and there's nothing really too problematic about that. Though there is still quite a powerful anti-national impulse, particularly amongst people on the left, amongst liberals, that wants to dissolve the nation-state into those entities. I think that moment has probably passed for the EU, which is going through a wobbly patch currently, but of course, you can be a nation-state and you can give up some of your sovereignty.

Part of the point of being a nation state is that we have a sovereignty to give up. And we can do that where it makes the best sense—whether that means sharing military functions or in negotiations on world trade and so on. Where the EU's gone slightly wrong is with its own faux nationalism, with things like a flag, a national anthem and so on. All of that stuff just frightens the horses and is completely unnecessary. I mean the EU saved the nation-states of Europe really. But there's this conspiracy between Europhiles and Eurosceptics, who argue that the nation-state is being squeezed out of existence by the European project but that is nonsense.

*In terms of your views on immigration, some have described you as "the Enoch Powell of the left". How do you respond to that? Is the logical consequence of your argument that at some point it might be necessary for us to have no immigration, either permanently or for an extended period of time?*

Oh, I don't think it's really possible to close borders any longer, and it's certainly not desirable. But I do think immigration is too high—we have net immigration of 200,000 to 250,000 a year which is extremely high. And as a liberal society we can absorb it most of the time, but I think there are a lot of very specious arguments about the economic necessity of immigration. I don't think it is economically necessary—immigrants grow old too and all of that. So I think we should pause now and absorb the very large number of people who have come in within the last 15 or 20 years, so we can sort it out. We need to make people feel confident again, we need to create a feeling that we are in control of immigration, and that people come here because it's in the interest of the existing society, the British community. That should be the test, really. Immigration's always almost in the interests of the immigrants, otherwise they wouldn't be coming here. It's not always necessarily in the interest of the people that are here already.

*And so is that the core ethical shift in terms of how we should look at it? Should the primary question be: is it in the interests of our society, rather than the immigrant? Should society take precedent over the immigrant?*

Absolutely, yes. How else can you look at it? Unless you have a completely cosmopolitan view, which I think is incoherent. Because so many things that make the world good require nation-states.

*I suppose the response to that is that it entrenches and accepts the brute fact that our lives are based to a large extent on the luck of the draw. The lottery of birth means that you and I are very lucky to be born in this country but someone might be much less lucky and be born in Somalia where there is virtually no functioning state at all.*

Yes, it does accept that. But there are lots of people from Somalia who are here. They're lucky enough to be British citizens. And they, on the whole, probably don't want other people from black Africa to come. Recent immigrants are often the people most hostile to mass immigration. Because they're the poorest, they're the people who rely on housing and welfare and so on. And we should listen to them. And don't forget, black Americans have been the most hostile to mass immigration in America. The left, and the trade unions and black America used to be very hostile to mass immigration in America. However a degree of political correctness has crept into the unions, I think, so it's not quite so clear as it once was.

*If we accept this kind of 'luck of the draw' approach to nationality, does that then have a knock-on effect in terms of our relationship to other nations with things like international aid and so on? Does that increase our moral responsibility to other, particularly poorer, countries?*

It probably increases it. I think we have a responsibility, as a rich country, to do that. And particularly as a former colonial country, I think we have a particular responsibility to our former colonies. I'd far prefer for us to send money there, to open our markets to their products, than for their people to come here. After all, usually the people that will come here will be the brightest and the best—doctors and scientists and so on. And we're screwing up all these countries by allowing them to come here—we're sucking them in here while actually they should be building their own nations and we should be helping them to build their own nations. This should be an absolute no-brainer. Yet, of course, the most desirable immigrants are the people who are actually most needed at home.

# AC GRAYLING

is Professor of Philosophy at Birkbeck College, University of London, and a Supernumerary Fellow of St Anne's College, Oxford. He is the author of numerous philosophical books and is also a distinguished literary journalist and broadcaster. He is a contributing editor of *Prospect* magazine and writes a weekly column for *The Times Saturday Review*. His most recent book is *Liberty in the Age of Terror: A Defence of Civil Society and Enlightenment Values*.

---

*Who are you?*

Before I talk about myself, let me begin by looking a little at the philosophy that lies behind our thinking about social, religious, and other forms of identity. There is a distinction to be drawn between what is called "numerical identity"—that is, when putatively two or more things, *x* and *y*, are in fact one and the same thing—and qualitative identity, which means that two things are so alike that it's very hard to tell them apart, but actually there are two or more of them despite their similarities. The idea of trying to find a principle for explaining numerical identity over time is something that John Locke was confronted with in his *Essay Concerning Human Understanding*. In the second edition of the *Essay* he included a new chapter (Chapter 27 of Book Two) on the question of what makes a person the same person over time—from birth to age 90. Prior to his time nobody had bothered to think about this problem because they believed that people have immortal souls and the substance of the immortal soul is what makes persons the same over time.

But this idea was being called into doubt at that time. William Molyneux, the Irish correspondent of Locke, prompted him to consider the question of numerical identity over time. Locke's response was to say that what constitutes identity of a thing depends on the kind of thing in question. In the case of something like a stone, it consists in the continuity of the same matter. In the case of an oak tree as it grows from an acorn into a mighty specimen, it is the same continuous organisation of matter, as light, water and nutrients are used by the living organism to build itself over time. But in the case of a person it is insufficient to think in the same terms as a tree, that is, in terms of solely physical or bodily criteria. To see why, note that the idea of a person is not the same as the idea of a human individual, because (to take just one reason) a human individual could become so severely brain damaged as to have no personality associated with it, no memory, no capacity to reason or make choices or be expected to meet responsibilities. As this shows, the concept of a person is a forensic concept, that is, a moral and legal one. The Shell Oil Company is a person in the sense that it can be sued, and it has responsibilities, in just the same way that an individual human person can be. Conversely, a one-day-old baby is not a person, and neither is a demented and senile individual, for neither can be regarded as having responsibilities or owing duties. So, the identity of a person cannot be the same as that of a stone or an oak tree.

There therefore, said Locke, must be a psychological principle involved. He described this as "consciousness of self"—indeed he was the coiner of the term "consciousness"—from *con-scire*—to explain the idea of being self-aware of one's continuity as the same person over time. So, for Locke, memory is the criterion. If you remember your past, then you are continuous with the person you remember.

But, of course, the *immediate* criticism was that it meant that if a brick fell on your head and you lost all your memories, you would not be the same person as you were before the accident. And, indeed, Locke said that in such a case you would not be the same person; there can indeed be discontinuity of personhood. Moreover, he allowed that you could also be more than one person, because you might have a split personality—Locke acknowledged all these possibilities.

His successors in the debate such as Bishop Butler and Thomas Reid were very critical of this suggestion. Reid's argument was this: suppose a boy steals an apple and then, some years later, becomes a subaltern in the army and wins a medal for leading the troops on to victory. Now that young subaltern might remember stealing the apple, but the ageing major-general into whom that subaltern ages might remember getting the medal but have forgotten stealing the apple. By Locke's criterion he is not continuous with the boy who stole the apple. Yet surely, if the subaltern is continuous with the apple-stealing boy, and the major-general is continuous with the subaltern, then the idea of transitivity of identity comes into play: if *x* is identical to *y*, and *y* to *z*, then *x* is identical to *z*. But Locke's theory violates this principle.

This gives rise to the following interesting thought: supposing you have two things, *x* and *y*. *x* is a small, round, pink, soft thing. *y* is a large, brown, square, hard thing. Suppose these two things travel through successive worlds in which they swap a property each time. In the first world, they swap a colour—so, the thing small, round, pink and soft becomes small, round, brown and soft. And so on. At the end of their journey through these worlds the thing that was large, brown, square and hard will have become small, round, pink and soft. It is the same but in reverse for the thing that was small, round, pink and soft in the first world; it is now, of course, large, brown, square and hard.

So now we have a problem. According to the principle of the transitivity of identity, the thing that was large, brown, square and hard in the fourth world is identical with the thing that was small, round, pink and soft in the first world. The problem is that in addition to the principle of the transitivity of identity there is another principle, that of the indiscernibility of identical things (if two or more things are genuinely numerically identical you cannot, obviously, tell them apart), and it conflicts with the transitivity principle in this example. The only way that you can overcome the conflict is by saying, "there is something *essential* to *x*'s being *x*, and something else *essential* to *y*'s being *y*, which is quite independent of the accidental properties of smallness, pinkness, brownness, softness or hardness that they happen to have. So, *x* remains *x* through all these worlds, despite changing all its accidental properties, because it's got some essential property of being *x*."

*It sounds like we're running the risk of talking about a soul there.*

Not necessarily. This might be a non-animate object which is changing its properties, as when a lump of wax melts, ceasing to be white and solid and becoming translucent and liquid. Rather, what we're doing is we are introducing a distinction between essence and accident. These notions of essence and accident are crucial to Aristotelian and Scholastic philosophy, and remained an important part of the debate right up into modern times—even into twentieth century philosophy. Saul Kripke made a case for invoking the notions to make sense of talk about "possible worlds". This idea is that there could be another possible world, not this actual one but which is exactly the same as this one, except that in it, for example, AC Grayling smokes. Then the question is, "how do you know that that's AC Grayling in that other world? AC Grayling is not as healthy in that world as he is in this world, so how can he be the same person? There is at least one property he doesn't share with the non-smoking AC Grayling in the actual world, so how can that be the same person?" One answer is, "there must be something essential to the AC-ness, or Grayling-ness, of AC Grayling that makes him mappable across different possible worlds." This was how Kripke came up with his semantics for "possible worlds" theory. This version of the idea of "possible worlds" involves having to commit yourself to a form of essentialism. Now you can say, the idea of identity, and especially of identity over time, seems to make best sense if you invoke an idea of essence. Because if there is no such thing as essence—if all properties are accidental properties—then if you change one of them, the thing in question becomes something different from what it was before.

Well, that is some of the philosophical background to this. It explains, I think, why people who are rather uncertain about what they are, or who are not given possibilities of making themselves what they choose to be, are so eager to clutch at *single* identities, because they think it gives them an essence. So, for example, by covering yourself completely with a burqa you say to the rest of the world, "I am one thing: I am a Muslim woman." This stands in sharp contrast to Amartya Sen's view, which I think is completely right and very well put, when he observes that every individual is a multiplicity of identities: you are a father, a Professor, a friend, an Englishman, a rugby fan—you are all sorts of things, and you express yourself in these different ways according to context. It is quite wrong to try to make any one of them the overriding thing, or expect other people to treat you according to one interpretation of yourself. So when people think about their own

identity, in answer to the question, "what am I? who am I?" they do something quasi-Kripkean, that is, they seek for an essence—something that would identify them constitutively; and this might quite typically be their sense of nationality or their religious commitment, or what football team they support, or anything else that would do the job of assigning them to a tribe or group, an affiliation of some kind.

But remember what Oscar Wilde said: "everybody is somebody else"—everybody is living somebody else's opinions and choices, without much sense of who or what they themselves really are. That is why they assume the cloak of an identity; putting on a burqa, a crucifix on a chain, a yarmulke, or whatever it might be, is an effort to have something of which they can say, "this describes me, this is what I am." The contrasting view, the view that Amartya Sen so eloquently articulates, is that in fact none of your identities is essential to you. They might be important to you, but that's a very different thing from their being essential to you. And it's the very multiplicity of them which makes it possible for us to live in a pluralistic world and to relate to lots of people in many different ways. If you do not recognise the multiplicity of your identities, and you only have one, you have *immediately* made it impossible to relate to most other people.

*So in that context, can you relate this to who you are personally?*

Well, I'm a British academic, a writer, a man married with children, with lots of lovely friends, a holder of left-liberal political views, many likes and some dislikes, and so on—one could go endlessly on listing things one is or takes oneself to be. And, in fact, the longer one goes on, the more complex one's persona would seem to be. The more we would find that what is characteristic of our personae is that they have inconsistencies and contradictions in them. It is from these that we to try to construct a narrative of our own lives as we work out our inconsistencies and deal with them, and try to make ourselves more integrated. People are multiple, they have multiple identities, and because in some of those identities they fail, it is important that they should realise that that does not mean they fail in their other identities. So, somebody who has had a bad marriage, let us say, might think "oh I'm a terrible human being, I'm never going to be able to relate well to another person." But the answer to that is, "no, just because you and that particular other person did not work out together, it does not follow that you are a bad philosopher, a bad playwright, a bad father, or a bad anything else." This is a mistake that people make too readily. They fail to recognise their own multiplicity, and the variability of that multiplicity. But, of course, we also have to organise and integrate that multiplicity into a satisfying, overall personality which has a uniform direction. This idea of imposing some kind of integrity onto the variety that is oneself is the central task of making an overall, workable and settled self-identity.

*Could you define "integrity"?*

Yes. "Integrity", the word, has the same etymology, obviously enough, as "integration". Integration is about bringing things together and making them cohere: in the moral sense, bringing together one's character traits, talents, aspirations, values, and efforts. So living a life of integrity is living a life which has a well-combined purpose and directionality, in which inconsistencies are resolved or at least governed, and directed fruitfully. A well-integrated personality is one which could incorporate its flaws and foibles and manage them well. I suppose, to take an illustrative example of an endeavour in this direction, that psychotherapists seek to help people find ways of integrating themselves.

*Do you have any sense of how you're perceived by the outside world? Of who other people think you are?*

To a certain extent, yes. Obviously for the majority of people their profile exists largely among friends. The way friends react to one, how they tease one, what they ask of one, what they do for one, what they accept from one, gives one a sense of how one appears to them. It is a different thing wondering how one is perceived by strangers or, if a person is to any extent in the public eye, what his or her public persona is perceived to be. One thing that is obvious about people with a public reputation of any kind is

that they quickly learn how very few people are able to please everybody. Some people might think a given celebrity is great while other people think he is terrible, and he will soon learn of both sorts of view in the blogosphere of the internet. Any well-known actor, writer or politician quickly learns that he has an appearance in the public domain which is as if it has been reflected in the eye of a fly. There is not one but dozens of images he has in the minds of onlookers, they are fragmented, and they all exist simultaneously. But that celebrity or politician will feel that he is none of those things in actuality. The tabloid newspapers go on and on about celebrities, but you can be pretty sure that the celebrity in question does not recognise himself in those caricatures. It is inevitable that that should be the case, because, of course, anyone who does not know that celebrity personally is only ever going to be able to get a two-dimensional and partial grip on what he is really like. This is because the depth of someone's identity, and the way that he integrates that in his personal life, is orthogonal to how they appear in the public domain. Someone's public persona in this sense is a bit like a two-dimensional representation of a three-dimensional thing.

*It seems to me that, in contemporary discourse, the two most significant ways that people's identities in everyday life are defined—I'm not talking about celebrities now—are either by their religion or by their race. Could you talk a little bit about that in a context of a sort of multicultural society? Is it fair to say that multiculturalism is very much about emphasising difference and specific differences? What's your attitude towards that?*

You are right to say, of course, that race and religion are big markers of difference. But they are expressions of a certain practical need that people have to locate themselves vis-à-vis people they encounter in their social environments. Almost anyone, meeting somebody else, would instantly begin to make some judgments about what sort of person that other person is, on the basis of how they speak, what they wear, where they met, as well as their skin colour and any self-chosen marks of differentiation such as religious symbols or clothing. We taxonomise and classify all the time, in order to know how to deal with the people we meet, how to respond to them. It may very well be that having ways of taxonomising others is important, useful and right—we should be able to do this so that we can treat other people appropriately. In order to be responsive and sensitive in our dealings with other people, it is important that we should encounter them appropriately. But, of course, the best way to do that is to engage with them and talk to them and find out what they think, and not to do this on the basis of stereotypes, which are far too readily imposed on things like accents and skin colour. It's very hard for people to do this, because people are naturally tribal and we have learned through bad experiences to be defensive. So you might get, for example, an East Ender being hostile, contemptuous or defensive when meeting somebody with a posh accent for instance. People often have the wrong kinds of default positions. Therefore a focus on identity can help us to engage with other people in a way which we think appropriate, but it can also have the negative effect of making people operate on the basis of unfair assumptions about others and can put up barriers between them.

This kind of thing can happen both on the large scale and the small scale. The large scale is prejudice and xenophobia directed at foreigners in general. An example of a much smaller scale instance is something I remember from when I was a young lad: I was speaking to somebody who had moved into a village in Sussex, who said, "we're just beginning to be accepted here now, because we only came to the village after my husband retired." I asked, "how long have you been here?" and she said, "18 years"! That was a classic example of the problem on the small scale, where it is sometimes more intense than it is on the large scale.

*It's interesting that you talk about tribalism, because it seems to me that the word "identity" can exist in two mutually bound, but contrasting settings—that of the group and that of the individual. We are tribal animals, but also, particularly in Western society, there's at least a nominal focus on the importance of the individual and the ego, as it were. Can you talk a little bit about that distinction, and how you think they*

*relate, and whether one is more important than the other?*

Generally speaking feelings of anxiety about and hostility to other groups are prompted by general characteristics that those groups display (skin colour is a classic case in point). These characteristics become much less significant when people get to know individual members of the other group, and once they become friendly with two or three people from the other group, it's hard to think in group terms any longer. This is one reason why promoting integration, community and mutual understanding worldwide and within one's own community is *so* important, and why anything that 'ghettoises' or divides, such as for example faith-based schooling, is a bad thing.

But, as with everything, there's a positive side to the identity issue as well, in this way: feeling an identification with one's group, one's community, one's nation, ties into the point we made earlier about humans being essentially social beings. We need connections with other people, we need something to identify with, we need to be part of a team in some way, to have a family and friends: we need something shared in the way of social experience and setting. Now of course strong community bonds can then have a negative impact on how groups relate to other groups, and you can see that expressed in a somewhat primitive way in football fans when they fight one another.

Given that group identities can have positive and negative aspects, we need to develop an understanding that while a feeling of group cohesion and common cause is desirable, it does not mean that we must automatically dislike other and different groups for having their own sense of cohesion. Although tragically, of course, the classic case of group or tribal identities and the need to find enemies to be hostile to so as to cement one's own group identity, is the gangs that teenage boys form. Look at Los Angeles or Chicago for a tragic example of how that can work.

*Do you have any thoughts on why we place so much emphasis on the face in our culture, as opposed to the rest of the body? How do you see this in light of recent medical developments with face transplants?*

There is an obvious reason why the face is important, and that is because it's the most individuating part of the human body. I suppose there are some people who might have strangely shaped abdomens by which they could be picked out by others, but usually the face is the most instantly recognisable and individual thing. It's also the part which is carried at the highest point of the body, and so when you meet someone, that is the bit you identify. We seem to be hardwired not just for facial recognition but for interpretation of facial expressions. Day-old babies can mimic expressions on the faces of their mothers, because of the operation of their mirror neurones. This is an entirely non-conscious computation in the baby's brain, yet the fact that it can mimic facial expressions is intimately tied to our ability to recognise what other people are feeling, and to our being able to empathise with them. In the jungle of our social environment, being able to do these things is crucial. The face is the most labile, most mobile, most expressive part of us. It is true that there are other parts of our physicality which are very expressive too—voice, cues from body position and hand gestures; but facial cues are the most important.

So, when the whole thing about facial transplants was mooted, two things emerged. The first was the instinctive question: what would it be like to see the face of somebody you know, but who is dead, on somebody else's head? This thought was just a bad mistake, because if the whole of your face were transplanted on to someone else's skull, the latter would not look anything like you, because underlying bone structure and—just as importantly—personality has a huge influence on facial appearance. Even if the surgeons managed to connect all the nerve endings well, the facial expressions would still be very different. You only have to compare the photograph of a person to actually seeing that person in real life, to see how dissimilar they can be.

The second point is to ask what it must be like for a face-transplant patient when he looks at his new face in the mirror. Well, we know exactly what that's like already, because through the experience of ageing, or losing your hair, you can get to a position where, for a while, when you look at yourself in the bathroom mirror in the morning, you think, "who on earth is that?" But, if you think about it, that might happen to you for a week or two weeks or a month, but you are not going to keep having that reaction for ever. You are going to come to accommodate that sense of yourself. It's like putting on weight and seeing an old, fat man walking towards you in a shop window, and then you recognise it as yourself reflected there. You adjust—you may not like it, but you certainly do.

So, there is a lot of misapprehension about face transplants in those two respects. Behind it is the sense that somehow the face is so intimately connected with who the person is, it is such a marker of individuality as the main focus of recognition for other people and for the person himself, that to move a face from one person to another, from one body to another, from one life to another, seems to be a massively disruptive transition. But this is the fear of ignorance. And if somebody has had a horribly disfiguring accident, or has suffered terrible burns, they have already been massively disrupted. So if they are able to get a new face, whoever's face that is, and are able to walk down the street without people staring at them, that is a great good.

*Could you relate your thoughts on identity to the proposed scheme to introduce identity cards for all British citizens?*

This is an interesting issue! Historically identity cards have been simple, highly forgeable documents with a photograph, a signature, and a name and address. What is being proposed now is different: identity cards bearing biometric data, annexed to a central "national identity register" on computer. The scheme for this Orwellian system is driven by two agencies—one is the security services, who want individual human beings to have a number plate, as on a car, so that they can be readily and easily tracked; the other is the biometric data companies who can see billions of pounds of recurrent revenue pouring into their pockets, those billions from the pockets of those who will thus be numbered and monitored.

As envisioned by the scheme, an identity card will be something that encodes biometric information about individuals, such as fingerprints, DNA, iris or retinal patterns (though it has been discovered that these are insufficiently stable for secure identification), so that any individual can, allegedly, be securely identified as that individual. This is the idea. But, of course, a small plastic card with this information encoded on it could be stolen, lost or, for enough purposes enough of the time, forged. And because the risk of that is too great, it's obvious that an identity card will cease to be a card, and will become an implant in your earlobe or under the skin of your wrist. It is already the case that one can encode all that information in a device the size of a full stop—the biometric data companies state this proudly on their websites. So, that is where we are headed: we are going to have the modern equivalent of the number branded on a Jewish arm in the concentration camp, so that the authorities can track us everywhere and always establish who we are.

One of the deepest objections to this, if not *the* deepest objection, is that it completely changes the relationship of the individual to society. At the moment, we as individuals have the status of volunteers in society. But when identity cards or devices become compulsory, we become conscripts of the system. Everywhere we go, and everything we do will leave a trail right the way along, through which we can be traced and monitored.

Now, it is true that we already have passports, driving licenses, credit cards, bank cards, library cards, supermarket loyalty cards, membership cards, indeed quite a number of such things. Some people say, "well, I've got so many cards already—why not just have one, which is my identity card, that I can use for everything?" But that misses a vital point. That point is that all those cards are voluntary. You enter into voluntary relationships with banks and the immigration authorities and whoever it might be, for certain specific purposes. Even though it would be extremely inconvenient not to have a driving license or a passport, nevertheless you could choose not to have one. But in the case of an identity card or device which eventually becomes compulsory, it will be something without which you cannot get any of the goods of citizenship, or claim any of your rights or entitlements as a citizen.

One of the many shifting reasons that politicians give for wanting to introduce identity cards was to stop illegal immigration. Because if you're an illegal immigrant and you do not have an identity device, then you do not eat, you cannot get a job, you cannot get medical help—you are excluded. You become, literally, an outlaw, outside the recognised domain. This illustrates the effect of the proposed scheme: you are only a citizen with access and rights if you are a numbered conscript of the state.

*Is it important, for our sense of identity that we are able to keep things private?*

Absolutely. Privacy is a great good, and a vitally important one. So much so that even in the most intimate of relationships and of joint enterprises in life, such as marriage, it matters that individuals should have an arena of life which is private to them, some reserved psychological (and I would add, physical) space where they can be alone and inviolate with themselves. That is tremendously important. I would guess that even those rather unthinking teenagers who put "all" their private information on the internet, undoubtedly still keep some things private. There is always going to be something that they are not telling, because it is too tender, too personal and vulnerable, to share. But the risk of putting so much information on the internet is that it can never be expunged. And in five, ten, 20 years' time, people are going to ask themselves, "why the hell did I put all that out there?" It could come back to haunt them. Employers will look for information about people on the internet, as will security services and others.

I suspect that there will be a backlash against all this as people begin to see what effect it is having on their lives. But of course, technology and the internet will still significantly change things. For example, you can wear a lapel camera which supplies a direct feed to your internet site, so people can see where you are going and what you are doing all day. You become a walk-in CCTV version of your own life.

So for some people, particularly of a younger generation, technology like this will mean that their sense both of themselves and their identities could end up being very different.

132/133
134/135
136/137
**138/139**

# JOHANN HARI

is an award-winning journalist and columnist for *The Independent*. He also contributes regularly to *Attitude* magazine and the *Huffington Post* and has been published by many newspapers and magazines around the world. In 2008 he became the youngest person ever to be awarded the George Orwell Prize, which *The Observer* newspaper calls "Britain's pre-eminent award for political writing". And in 2007 he was named Newspaper Journalist of the Year by Amnesty International for his reporting on the war in Congo.

---

*Who are you?*

I'm a journalist who lives in London and writes about the world. But I guess like everyone, my identity, would be like the layers of an onion. So, I'm from North London, I'm from England, which I suppose is an intermediate stage that I would have to acknowledge, I'm from Britain, I'm European, I'm English-speaking. And from another point of view, I believe in all sorts of causes—I believe in universal human rights, I believe in opposing anthropogenic global warming and I believe in various other transnational causes. I guess that's who I am.

*Who do we think you are? How are you seen by outsiders?*

Well, it depends on which outsiders you mean. It just completely depends where you are. When I report from Congo, for instance, I go with all the baggage of a white European. But to be honest I don't spend a lot of time thinking about how people see me. Though obviously I belong to certain groups, and people make assumptions about me on the basis of those groups—whether it's being British or being a liberal, a left-liberal, or being gay, or whatever. People ascribe certain things to you on the basis of those groups.

*You said you were English, but you dismissed it as an intermediate thing. Why doesn't that aspect of your identity interest you particularly?*

Well there is a whole range of reasons for that. It's partly because of my mother, who is a militant Scottish person. The only time she's ever shouted at me about anything I've ever written was when I was reporting on the Republican National Convention in New York City in 2004, and for the sake of a pun I referred to myself as "an Englishman in New York". And she phoned me the next day and said, "No son of mine is an *Englishman*!" Even now, she'll occasionally ring me up and harangue me, saying: "Oh, is that my *English* son? Is it?!" But I've lived in England virtually all my life, so obviously I have some sense of it. Though it is difficult in other ways because Englishness has *generally* been claimed by the right, and is generally associated with an antediluvian white ethnicity. Whereas Britishness is already more relaxed in that sense because it is made up of three nations and a province, and encompasses a whole range of different people.

*You have said very little, so far, about being gay or working-class or lower-middle-class or however you might want to define it. Why are those things not something that you would mention in response to the question of who you are? They often seem to be very much a part of your writing, or your public persona as a writer.*

Well I'm not working-class or lower-middle-class. I'm rich. I'm in the richest one per cent of people in Britain. People always forget this. Take the median wage in this country—so that is the wage which half the population will earn less than and half will earn more than. If you ask most journalists, "oh, what's the median wage in Britain?" *Invariably*, they will guess, "oh, £45,000". But when you point out that if you earn £45,000, you're in the richest ten per cent, they just won't believe you. You can prove it to them and they don't believe you.

*So what is the median wage in Britain?*

It's £24,000 a year. But part of the whole problem with class in Britain is that we have a very unhelpful vocabulary about it. You'll always get *The Daily Mail* describing things as "an attack on the middle classes". Yet often what is meant by middle class in that context are people with two cars, their kids in private schools and a big house. But those kinds of people will be in the richest one per cent or certainly the richest five per cent. That's not the middle. But the problem is that the language of 'upper-class' is associated with the landed aristocracy, which of course is a real thing. So in a way, it's more helpful to use the advertising terminology of classifying people as *a*s, *b*s, *c*s, *d*s and *e*s, but that doesn't have emotional resonance with people yet.

*You talk very passionately and very knowledgeably about the issues of class, and that surely comes from your own family background. Your sister lives in a council estate for example.*

I hope I would believe the things I do even if I had been born in a family of millionaires. I don't like an approach to identity that is about saying "I believe this because I'm part of this group." I mean, I'm not black, but I believe very strongly in opposing racism; I'm not a woman yet I believe very strongly in equality for women. Some of the best defenders of gay rights have been heterosexual. The American president who did most for the American poor was Franklin Roosevelt who was born into a family of multi-millionaires. So I don't like this idea that the "group you happen to have been born into defines the causes you believe in." Of course, to some degree, the position you're in will shape you, but it's not a simple, transparent causal relationship. And I wouldn't want it to be—it would actually be a very depressing, balkanised world if we couldn't show solidarity with the people who are in slightly or even very different positions to us.

But it's true that both of my parents came from very poor backgrounds and my father's not even from this country, and didn't really speak English when I was growing up. So, I had that classic immigrant experience of writing things and translating things for him and so on. And my mother was from a very poor part of Scotland, and lived in a very poor family. All four of my grandparents left school at 14 and had just unimaginably different lives to me and so obviously those memories and your awareness of that does affect you. I guess it has a visceral effect on me when I hear snobbery. When people are talking about "chavs" or whatever, I think about my grandparents, who would have been classified that way and I feel emotional disgust. But I'd like to think that I would feel that anyway. I feel emotional disgust when I hear abuse of black people, but I don't have black grandparents.

*How does your homosexuality affect the way you see things?*

My view of homosexuality is that it is an extremely boring, genetic quirk which should be irrelevant. Sadly it's not, because there are some fools and bigots who choose to think it's more important than that. But in every single human society that's ever been, between two and four per cent of people have happened to want to have sex with people of the same gender. It doesn't mean anything, it doesn't ascribe other values to you, and it's not interesting. It should be profoundly trivial. But it's not, because some really foolish people have tried to ascribe superstitious or moral categories to a completely harmless, natural thing that occurs in the animal kingdom, and that occurs in all human societies. Now, obviously, I'm happy to identify myself as gay. I'm very happy with it. But, I don't think it's an interesting or salient thing about me.

*But those stupid fools often tend to be quite powerful people in society and in history. Doesn't that create a context which can then enforce an identity upon gay people to which they then respond? Can that not radicalise someone's sense of their identity? And if being gay is a boring quirk, how does that relate to this?*

It *should* be a boring quirk. But obviously, if you're being herded into a gas chamber at Auschwitz then, as you say, it's not a boring quirk—it's the thing that's going to cause your death. Or rather, it's the thing that's caused lunatics to cause your death. So, obviously, a huge amount of identity is thrust upon you without your choice and if you are persecuted for identifying as gay then your identity is going to be shaped by that. But for me, personally, I don't experience any persecution. I'm in the incredibly rare and fortunate position of it not making a huge difference to my life, so I don't see it as a big thing. Now, obviously, I believe in showing solidarity with gay people who are being treated very badly, whether they're a kid at a school five minutes up the road, or someone in Jamaica or in Gaza who's going to be killed because of it. But I expect you think that, and you're not gay.

*Yes. But I guess the difference between you and me is in the emotional experience of that position. I'm not gay and so I don't have the same kind of connection to the issue as you might.*

Yes, but I don't feel threatened as such. I've sat with Islamic fundamentalists or Christian fundamentalists who say gay people should be killed. But you can have a slightly different perspective on it when you know that you live in a country where they're not going to come to power. And really, it's no different to how I feel when I hear people making horrible comments about women. I don't feel a more visceral reaction to it than that.

*So is it the case that our values and beliefs, then, are the most useful way of defining who somebody is?*

No, they're a dimension of it. And it varies from person to person. You are the sum total of all sorts of things—where you live and where you come from, and so on. And there is a very complex interconnection with your values. One of the interesting things about the nature of identification, is that it can shift over time, because of the technologies that prevail in society. So, for example, European nationalism only really took off with the printing press. That's when you get someone like Mazzini making the case for Italy—because you have a linguistically-sealed population which can communicate with itself. And we've seen another shift in our lifetime with the internet. The internet can make transnational identifications much more feasible. 20 years ago, if you were a lad living in Southend, and you thought you had more in common with someone in Gaza than with the white guy up the road, you would have been bonkers. But today, you really can spend all day talking to that guy in Gaza on Skype, and you can read all the same things as him, and so on. So you really can have a closer identificatory bond with him. Also, the nature of technology can shape the nature of the identity. So, if you look, for example, at Jihadism or—if you go to the opposite end of the moral scale—at the anti-globalisation movement, they are shaped like the internet—there is no central organising structure. This is one of the things that is generally misunderstood about al-Qaida. Rather, there are inspirational figures within the movement, and everything is organised through diffuse webs. They're not structured like national armies or like the IRA was. They're like swarms of bees rather than a defined hierarchy with somebody at the top. So, that's an example of how advances in technology can shape our identity.

It is also interesting to see how quickly certain identities can take hold. Just look at the development of European nationalism. There's this amazing fact that Dennis Max Smith who is an historian of the

*Risorgimento*, the Italian unification movement, gives: in 1870, the year Italy is unified, only five per cent of Italians have heard the word "Italy". And as Massimo D'Azeglio one of the first Italian Prime Ministers said, "We've made Italy. Now we need to make Italians." Now most identities create a foundation myth, which says that they've existed for ever and that they're based on something primal and innate. Yet in reality, they are almost always based on things that are mutable and historically contingent and actually very recent. So they create what you might call an imagined community in which an imagined identification with other people emerges that is based on what you choose to privilege at that time. And that's determined by technology and all sorts of other things.

*So this can lead toward an idea of identity as something which is fluid rather than static.*

Of course. Anyone who believes in static identity is in denial of history. When amoebas emerged from the swamps in Cornwall, or in Central Africa, or in the places where they were emerging, which of them was English and working-class, or gay or whatever, then? None of them, obviously.

*What is multiculturalism and what are the problems with it?*

Well, multiculturalism's a theory that was invented in the 1950s in the Netherlands, by the Dutch right, with a very specific purpose. They did not want immigrants, they were inviting in guest workers because they needed them, but they did not want them to stay and they did not want them to integrate. They wanted them to come for a temporary period and then leave. So, they developed this idea of multiculturalism, which said: "they are a different culture. They are not going to become Dutch. They will never become Dutch. We will warehouse them in this separate culture, where they will continue practising whatever they practise in Turkey or Algeria or wherever they come from, and then they'll go back home." But of course many of them didn't go back. Yet the theory remained. And interestingly, although the theory didn't change very much, it actually migrated across

the political spectrum. And it went from being a theory of the anti-immigrant right to being a theory of the pro-immigration left. And it became defined by the manners of the time, which, to a much more limited degree, still exist today, and where the idea was: "immigrants aren't like us. They're different. We'll be polite to them by respecting the culture, as defined by their leaders, who we will find."

There are many problems with this theory. Firstly, it defines immigrant communities through, basically, a static model of identity, which is exactly what we were saying just now is so wrong. It thinks the identity of a group of people is determined by who it was at a particular point in history, when they happened to make a migratory journey. And then it gives power to self-appointed community leaders, who are invariably reactionary old men, to decide what that culture is, and how it should be perpetuated. And that's bullshit. For example, there's a school ten minutes up the road from here, which is overwhelmingly Muslim. And every day the Muslim girls are brought to the school gates by their brothers or by their fathers, wearing the full jilbab. And then they get in, take it all off, and start snogging their boyfriends. Then, come three o'clock, they put it all back on and go to the mosque. Well, whose culture is that? It's not their culture. They're as British as I am. It's not their culture to believe in some Wahhabi desert doctrine that means nothing to them.

So if you think of all the defences that people offer for multiculturalism: it's about welcoming people, and respecting their different ways and so on. Well these are actually much better fulfilled through the paradigm of liberalism. In a liberal society, you can do whatever you want, as long as you're not harming anyone else. And I passionately believe in that. If you want to wear a hijab or PVC hotpants, it's fine by me, as long as you are genuinely choosing it and are not being forced into doing it. Liberalism privileges the autonomy of the individual. Multiculturalism privileges the autonomy of the group. The problem with that is: there will always be individuals within the group who want to oppress others within the group. So, for example, among British Muslims, there will be elderly men who want to stop women having any form of sexual or social freedom, and who want to stop gay people from having any sexual or social freedom. So, you can't simply side with that culture as a whole—there is conflict within that culture, as there is conflict within any culture. And therefore you have to take a side. Now, I think we should take the side of people who want to have individual personal freedom and don't want to harm anyone else, rather than the people who want to restrict other people's harmless personal freedom and treat them like shit. But you have to make that choice. You can't just say, "there's a homogenous block, and I'm going to side with that homogenous block." Because there is no such thing as an homogenous block. And there never has been, there's always been conflict within cultures. For example, look at the debate about female genital mutilation. I've reported from Kenya, where there are some amazing women who have organised against this. But you'll get some people who'll say that "female genital mutilation is a cultural practice in Africa, and we should respect it, and it's not our job to oppose it." Well Agnes Pareiyo, who I interviewed in Kenya, is a woman who runs a charity called the Tasaru Ntomonok Rescue Centre to stop this. She's a Masai women who was pinned down when she was 12 and had her vagina hacked out with a knife. And she says, "I didn't find that unpleasant because a white woman told me to. I found that unpleasant because it was my body being mutilated. So don't tell me I'm not African."

Whenever people talk about feminism being culturally relative, I always think about a girl I met in Bangladesh, who was living in a hostel for kids who had run away. When I met her she was about 15, but she told me that when she was 11 she loved singing—she'd always loved singing, it was her favourite thing. But when she turned 11 and went through puberty, her parents, who were Islamic fundamentalists, banned her from singing again, and said to her: "you're acting like a prostitute, singing is wrong." Now, bearing in mind that this is rural Bangladesh, she said to me: "well, I just didn't think that was right, because my brother was allowed to sing. And I wasn't allowed to sing just because I was a girl. And that seemed stupid to me. What does it matter if you're a boy or a girl?" And she thought of that all by herself in a village in the middle of Bangladesh. So, you've got to be a bit careful when you're talking about ascribing qualities to groups, particularly when those qualities

are defined by really horrendous fundamentalist or reactionary agendas. Because individuals within those groups will always naturally rebel against vile restrictions.

*Ziauddin Sardar, in his book* Balti Britain *argues that the kind of critique that you've offered of multiculturalism is often little more than a veiled attack on Muslims and allows for that group to be targeted in a more extreme way than others.*

Well it's an attack on some Muslims in defence of other Muslims. Look, no mullah is going to stop me being gay. No mullah is going to take my sister and stop her leaving her house. But they can do that to Muslim women. Now, if you just don't give a damn about Muslims, you can simply say, "Fine. That's their way, it's none of our business what they do." But I think it would be a profoundly racist attitude, or certainly a very bigoted attitude, to say, "I don't give a toss about Muslim women or Muslim gay people." Now, it's true that there is a hard core of unreformed Islam which is more problematic than a hard core of unreformed Christianity within Britain. But this is partly because there's been a longer battle against Christian fundamentalism by Christians and atheists and secularists. You've also got to be aware, that the critique of multiculturalism is often rolled into a whole load of other things. For example, you'll often hear the right confusing multiculturalism and mass immigration. But those things must be separated. I'm passionately in favour of immigration. I'm the child of an immigrant; I believe in more immigration to this country, not less. But the best way to welcome people to Britain is not to say, "hello, member of *x* group. We have a box for you here called 'your group' and you will now live there." That's not why people come to Britain. It's certainly not why my father came to this country and it's not why most immigrants come. That can actually be very offensive and unhelpful to the immigrant themselves.

When you take this doctrine of multiculturalism very literally, as opposed to being a liberal, you can actually end up terribly harming people from within immigrant communities. The strongest example of this is what happened in Germany with Muslim women's rights. Following the Second World War, for obvious reasons, it was written into the German constitution that the state should have respect for religious rights. And there was a case of a woman who was a German but of Algerian descent. Her parents had been Algerian—though she had lived in Germany all her life. And she married a guy who was horrifically violent. There was no dispute about this, he went to prison for it, and there was lots of police evidence to prove it. He went to prison for, I think, three months because he'd beaten her, and he'd beaten their child. Now in Germany, you have to have been separated for two years before you get a divorce. But she just wanted him out of her life so she applied for an earlier divorce due to extenuating circumstances. And she went to court and the female German judge comes back and says, "well, I've looked at this case, and clearly you were being violently abused. But the constitution also requires for me to look at your religious rights. And so, I went and looked at the Koran." And she then read out the passages from the Koran which recommend beating your wife if she's disobedient, and she said, "well, this is your culture. You should have expected this. So, in the light of this, I can't annul your marriage." And there were a series of findings by judges that were very similar. There have been a number of so-called "honour" killings, where young Muslim women have been murdered for being sexually independent—for having sex with men. And in several instances, the charge was lowered to manslaughter, even though it was plainly premeditated murder, on the grounds that, as one judge put it, "I understand this woman offended your moral precepts." There was another case where a 14 year-old girl wanted to go on a school trip and her parents forbade her because the school trip was further than a camel can travel in a day, which was the criterion in the Koran, as laid out in Mecca in the seventh century. But the girl wanted to go. And the school, to their credit—a British school wouldn't do this—went to court to take her on the school trip. Yet the judge came back and said, "well, I've looked at the law and there's a good precedent for this." This is how he put it: "retarded people have to have a chaperone when they go on school trips. I don't see why Muslim girls should be any different." Now I'm sure they all felt they were being very culturally sensitive. But in the name of cultural sensitivity,

they ended up telling these people that their human rights were negated. They had the best of intentions, but they come out with these abhorrent views. And there's a much easier way to deal with people who are immigrants. You say, "welcome. We have a liberal rule of law. You are now one of us. We will now treat you exactly the same as everyone else." And I think that's what most immigrants want. They don't come here to have a mini-Turkey or a mini-Pakistan. And if Zia is saying, "oh, this is a particular problem for Muslims", well, then he should be going to the imams and the fanatics who are abusing ordinary Muslims' rights and saying, "you are creating problems for us." He shouldn't be complaining to the people who are trying to deal with it or show solidarity with Muslim women or Muslim gay people.

*Well immigrants do often choose to live in their own communities and amongst their own people—could that be seen as ghettoisation?*

I don't have a problem with people living together. In a liberal society, you can associate with whoever you want. But I guarantee the majority of people who live here come here because they wanted what Britain had to offer. When they were burning Monica Ali's book, *Brick Lane*, just over the road from where I live, I went and interviewed people up and down Brick Lane in restaurants, who said, "they're nutters. We came here to get away from them." I went to lots of the restaurants there and I've got 20 people on the record saying, "they want to come and film here? They're very welcome. Come and film in my restaurant." Now, of course some people are maniacs, if you walk past the mosque up the road from here you will get some people handing you leaflets, saying "death to democracy", but equally, the majority of people will look at those leaflets and laugh. In a liberal society, you can associate with whoever you want. There are no more problems with the Bengali community focusing on Brick Lane than there are with the gay community focusing on Old Compton Street. But the question is: do you obey the law and do you respect other people's freedoms?

*So what's the problem with David Goodhart's critique of immigration, then? He argues that mass immigration actually undermines a lot of the progressive traditions, because it doesn't allow for a sense of community or...*

... social solidarity. Sure. It depends how effectively you assimilate immigrants. When people have a sense of group identity and rights within the group which are ascribed because everyone contributes something in and everyone gets something out, then that can be diluted if there's a feeling that there's another group coexisting alongside you who are not making the same contributions. So, if you see society as a range of groups—what Amartya Sen calls "plural monoculturalism"—then it's true, that it would be weakened. But if you see immigration as being about expanding the group—because that's how most people understand the arrival of immigrants—and if those immigrants contribute to society, as overwhelmingly immigrants do, then I think people are generally happy with it. It's only when a sense arises that there are different groups with different structures, who are not contributing anything, that people become begrudging, and say, "well, why should I pay for that?" But if immigrants are prepared to be part of society, then I think most people don't have a problem with it. And if you look at the polling you see that the majority of British people are supportive of immigration. Virtually no one is in favour of repatriation. Virtually no one is in favour of turning immigrants away. When people say they're in favour of multiculturalism, what they mean is: they're in favour of immigrants.

*Can we go back to the debate around gay identity. You are a gay man who is very pro gay rights, but you're also very critical of the radical side of the gay movement. Could you unpack some of that?*

Well, I think the gay rights debate is one where you can see how identities that were at one point liberatory can become confining. So, the self-identification of people as gay is relatively recent. Michel Foucault famously said that "there were no homosexuals before the twentieth century." Now he didn't mean by that that in the past there weren't men who wanted to fuck men and women who wanted to fuck women. He meant that there were no

people who self-identified with that as their primary sexual identity, because there wasn't the vocabulary to describe it. Now I slightly disagree with him. Because he thinks it's all socially constructed—and I don't think that's true. I think that's empirically wrong. I don't think in a different social structure I'd be currently performing cunnilingus! I think these things are, to some degree, determined at birth or at an early stage of development. But it's very interesting, if you look at the formation of gay identity in the early twentieth century, it became very important for people to ascribe positive qualities to homosexuality to countervail the widespread perception that there were all sorts of negative connotations with homosexuality. So they would describe the positive qualities of homosexuality, and would venerate those positive qualities. So gays were seen as being more stylish or whatever and you can see that this began to cause a shift in attitudes in the 1970s. But I've always found, the identity that says, "we're more stylish, we're very good with clothes, we're aesthetes, and so on" quite baffling. It is true that when I was growing up, I was a beneficiary of the people who had fought that fight. Because of them I wasn't going to go to prison or anything like that. But I can't connect with that kind of identification, because I obviously have no style or ability with clothes. I was always more interested in war zones! The nicest thing anyone has ever written about me is: "when Johann Hari talks about Jordan, you know he's talking about the country in the Middle East, not the wife of Peter Andre."

I wrote an article about this a while ago and I was surprised that it got such a backlash. I was talking about Queer Eye for the Straight Guy, which is a programme on TV where a load of shrieking gays go and live with a straight person to give them a sense of style. And I said, well, imagine a programme called Black Eye for the White Guy, in which a group of whooping and hollering black people go and live with a white person to give them a sense of rhythm. Or imagine Jewish Eye for the Gentile Guy, in which a group of Jews go and live with a gentile to give him a sense of cunning and financial prowess. Now these things are all things that we would think were reifying completely repulsive, negative stereotypes about people. So, we haven't quite got to that stage with gay people yet. And I remember having a gay friend, who appeared to be very straight, saying to me, "well, I can't be gay, because I don't want to listen to Abba and wear a dress and do all those kinds of things." So, this is an example of how an identity that is liberating at one point in history can harden and solidify into an identity that's actually alienating for the next generation. But I think now there has been a really helpful shift in gay identity, from saying, "I am what I am", which is a proud assertion of difference, to saying "I am what you are" which is an assertion of sameness. Now it's true that there are some gay people who are going to be very camp and effeminate, and I'm absolutely okay with their right to be as camp and effeminate as they want, and if anyone wants to pick on them they have to get past me. But equally there are straight people who are camp and effeminate, and there are gay people who are not at all camp. So the danger with sticking to the old stereotype is that actually it is confining and unhelpful, and can become condescending. Because it says: "you gays, you're very good with clothes and shopping but don't worry your head about the army." So, there's been a shift in that. And you can see that in the shift in the paradigms of the gay rights movement. If you look at the 1960s and 70s, the dominant goal of the gay rights movement was firstly "just leave us alone, stop persecuting us", which was absolutely the right one. But there was also a lot of separatism—there was a very popular lesbian separatist movement. Whereas now, everything is very much about integration. It's about saying, "we want the right to get married, we want the same rights as everyone else." And that's what I believe. I mean if you look at people like my friend, Andrew Sullivan, he was, in the early 1990s, one of the first gay people to call for marriage and he got the most unbelievably vicious abuse. There were other gay people, saying, he was a sell-out, he was a trainee heterosexual, he was an assimilationist and so on. But now, I think the gay rights movement is broadly where it should be in Britain. And this means that they are saying, "we're the same as everyone else and that means we should be treated the same as everyone else as well so our relationships should be accorded the same respect." And there is still a long way to go—gay teenagers are six times more likely than heterosexual teenagers to commit suicide for

example. But we're making progress on that, and we've got a lot more to do. But, in a lot of places in the world, they're at a much earlier stage. If you're a gay person in Saudi Arabia, your job is simply to try and stay alive.

*Where is home for you?*

Well, in relation to this, I think there's been a problem with the way we've debated nationalism. There was a really interesting row in the early twentieth century between GK Chesterton and Rudyard Kipling. Chesterton said to Kipling, "your problem Rudyard is that you don't really love your country." And Kipling of course was furious and said, "how dare you I am the great imperial bard". But Chesterton replied, "yeah, you write all these nationalistic anthems and these nationalistic poems. But you always say you love Britain by saying, "It's the best at *x, y* and *z*." But that's not why you should love your country. I don't love my mother because she's the best cook in the world, the fastest runner or the best cleaner. I love her because she's mine. And you shouldn't love your country because it is the best. You should love your country simply because it's yours." And that's how I feel. I love my country the way I love my flat. That doesn't mean I want to go and smash up the next flat down. And it doesn't mean that I think other flats are rubbish. It's just that my flat has the things I like in it. In the same way, when I get out of the Eurostar at Saint Pancras, and I'm back in Britain, I feel, "Oh, I'm home." But it doesn't mean that I think Britain is better than anywhere else I've been. It just means it's mine, it's my familiar place. And so home to me is Britain, and particularly London, because that is where I've always lived. But I'd expect someone from Paris or Kinshasa or Sydney to feel the same about where they're from.

| | Oreille dr. 1e | Long$^r$ | | Pied g. | | Coul$^r$ de l'iris g. | N° de cl. | |
|---|---|---|---|---|---|---|---|---|
| | | Larg$^r$ | | Médius g. | | | Aur$^{le}$ | |
| 1$^m$ | | Long$^r$ | | Auric$^{re}$ g. | | | Pér$^{ie}$ | |
| | | Larg$^r$ | | Coudée g. | | | Part$^{es}$ | |

M$^r$ Galton 19.4.93

277

| | | Nez. | Racine (cavité) | | Oreille droite. | Bord o. | s. | p. | f. | | Barbe |
|---|---|---|---|---|---|---|---|---|---|---|---|
| lin$^o$ | | | Dos | Base | | Lob. c. | a. | m. | d. | | Cheveu |
| ut$^r$ | | | Haut$^r$ Saillie. Larg$^r$ | | | A. trg. i. | p. | r. | d. | | Car |
| g$^r$ | | | l | l | | Pli. f. | s. | h. | E. | | Aut |
| t$^{es}$ | | | Part$^{es}$ | | | Part. | | | | | Sig$^t$ dr |

# FRANCIS GALTON

Hugh Aldersey-Williams

Francis Galton was the archetype of the Victorian scientist—self-assured, all-curious and indefatigable in his mission to order the world. He was a polymath and a prolific innovator whose notions were often far ahead of his time, but on other occasions proved spectacularly wrong-headed. He popularised weather maps, proposed a decimal currency, and made periscopes to afford a good view at Queen Victoria's Diamond Jubilee. His principal concern however was the measurement of things, and more especially of qualities relating to people. In meetings of the Royal Geographical Society he even counted the rate of fidgeting among the audience to gain a quantitative measure of boredom. He became a pioneer in the field of anthropometry which sought to classify human populations according to physical measurements.

Galton always regarded his older cousin Charles Darwin with "the utmost veneration"—one of Galton's major publications was *Hereditary Genius*, a book whose title, it is clear now, owes more to wishful thinking than to science. In *The Origin of Species* published in 1859, Darwin had speculated about the variation of animals under domestication, and this fuelled Galton's interest in variation among the human population.

At the International Health Exhibition of 1884, Galton set up a laboratory to measure the 'family faculties' of volunteers, recording "Keenness of Sight and of Hearing; Colour Sense, Judgment of Eye; Breathing Power; Reaction Time; Strength of Pull and of Squeeze; Force of Blow; Span of Arms; Height, both standing and sitting; and Weight."

Though he was not the first to record fingerprints, he was instrumental in seeing that the technique was adopted as an official means of proving identity. His own studies illustrate the fundamental confusion under which Galton laboured. For while fingerprints might be a key to the identity of individuals, they were no guide as to types. Galton exhaustively measured the fingerprints of "Jews, Basques, Red Indians, East Indians of various origins, Negroes, and a fair number of Chinese" as well as "students of science, Quakers, notabilities of various kinds, and a considerable number of idiots at Earlswood Asylum" but, as he was ultimately forced to admit, "without finding any pattern that was characteristic of any of them".

Similar difficulties beset his efforts to pin down "types" according to facial appearance (his sample populations were another social, professional and geographical ragbag). He tried "composite photography", layering facial images to find a representative average, and its reverse, "analytical photography" to reveal differences.

All this data was of little real use unless, like cattle, humans could be improved. In 1883, Galton coined the word eugenics to describe this ominous project.

Galton's unlucky propensity for turning his sophisticated objective methods onto impossibly subjective topics is illustrated by an attempt to survey "British beauty" (London came out top, Aberdeen bottom). His most significant legacy is not the results he obtained from any of his massive studies, but the methods he developed for analysing them, especially the use of statistics to make sense of large volumes of data.

Born in 1822, the youngest of nine children, Galton was idolised by his mother and undoubtedly held at least as high an opinion of himself as others did. He died in 1911 at the age of 88, having remained busy to the end, if not always up to speed on the latest science. In his autobiography he contrives not to mention his wife by name at all; ironically for a man obsessed with heredity, they had no children.

These photographs of Francis Galton at the age of 71 appear on a French anthropometric identity card of a type promoted by Galton's colleague and rival Alphonse Bertillon.
Courtesy UCL Library Services Special Collections, Galton Papers.

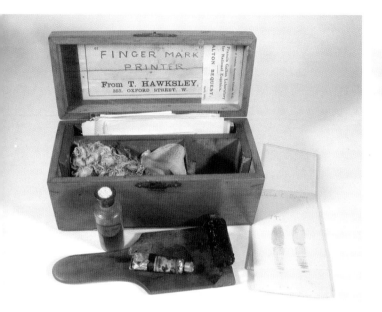

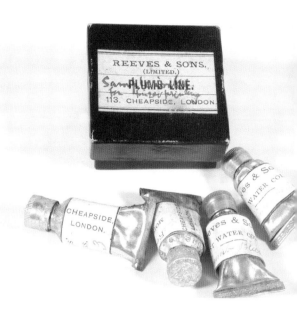

*Left* Francis Galton took this portable fingerprinting kit with him on his travels so that he might be prepared to record the prints of interesting people he met. The Prime Minister William Gladstone and the philosopher Herbert Spencer were among his subjects.

*Right* Black watercolour artists' paint was rolled out on a palette onto which subjects carefully placed their fingers and thumbs. "All this is rather dirty work, but people do not seem to object to it", Galton wrote.
Courtesy UCL Galton Collection.

Excellently defined prints have been made with their very rude travelling apparatus. It was smoked over a wax lucifer match (carried in the pocket inside the brass tube). The finger was blackened, and impressed on paper simply wetted with the tongue when nothing better was at hand. Usually it was rolled inside luggage labels

*Left* When it was not practical to take his full fingerprint kit and paints, Galton improvised other methods, such as using a film of lamp black as described here.

*Right* Galton developed a variety of whistles with which to test the sensitivity of humans and animals to high-pitched tones. Galton whistles are still used to test hearing today.
Courtesy UCL Galton Collection.

Galton believed that composites assembled from photographs of people of one supposed type might produce a kind of average that would reveal some essential feature of that type. The inclusion of family composites such as this is a reminder of Galton's abiding interest in hereditary characteristics.
Courtesy UCL Library Services Special Collections, Galton Papers.

# APPLICATION OF COMPOSITE PHOTOGRAPHIC PORTRAITURE

TO THE PRODUCTION OF

## IDEAL FAMILY LIKENESSES.

### By FRANCIS GALTON, F.R.S.

SPECIMEN

OF A

Composite Photographic
Portrait.

———◆———

It is, of course, best that
the individual portraits should
be those of persons of the same
sex, and nearly of the same
age; but this specimen shows
these conditions to be nowise
essential.

This Portrait is
composed of those of
six members of the
same family, viz., the
father, mother, two
sons, and two daugh-
ters.

*The letter overleaf is addressed to Amateur Photographers, and contains a request for Photographic Portraits for the purpose of experiment.*

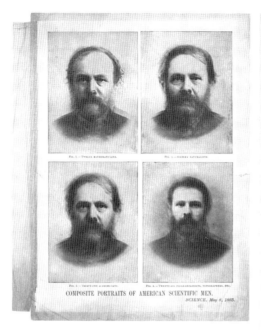

COMPOSITE PORTRAITS OF AMERICAN SCIENTIFIC MEN.
*SCIENCE, May 8, 1885.*

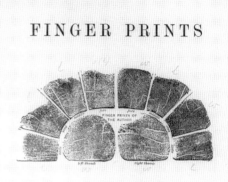

# FINGER PRINTS

BY

FRANCIS GALTON, F.R.S., ETC.

London
MACMILLAN AND CO.
AND NEW YORK
1892

*All rights reserved*

Like many a scientist before and since, Galton used himself as a subject in early demonstrations of his fingerprinting technique.

Galton eventually recorded the fingerprints of some 8,000 people, many of them selected for their membership of various social and professional groups, in the vain hope that some pattern might emerge that would reveal a key to personality types. Galton collected fingerprints and body measurements from well known figures of his acquaintance and from volunteers at public events such as the International Health Exhibition held in South Kensington in 1884.

Courtesy UCL Library Services Special Collections, Galton Papers.

The International Health Exhibition.
1884.

| Taille 1ᵐ | Tête. { Longʳ | Pied g. | Nᵒ de cl. |
| Voûte | Largʳ | Médius g. | Coulʳ de l'iris { **Aurⁱᵉ** |
| Enverg 1ᵐ | Oreille dr. { Longʳ | Auricʳᵉ g. | Pérⁱᵉ |
| Buste 0, | Largʳ | Coudée g. | Partᵉˢ |

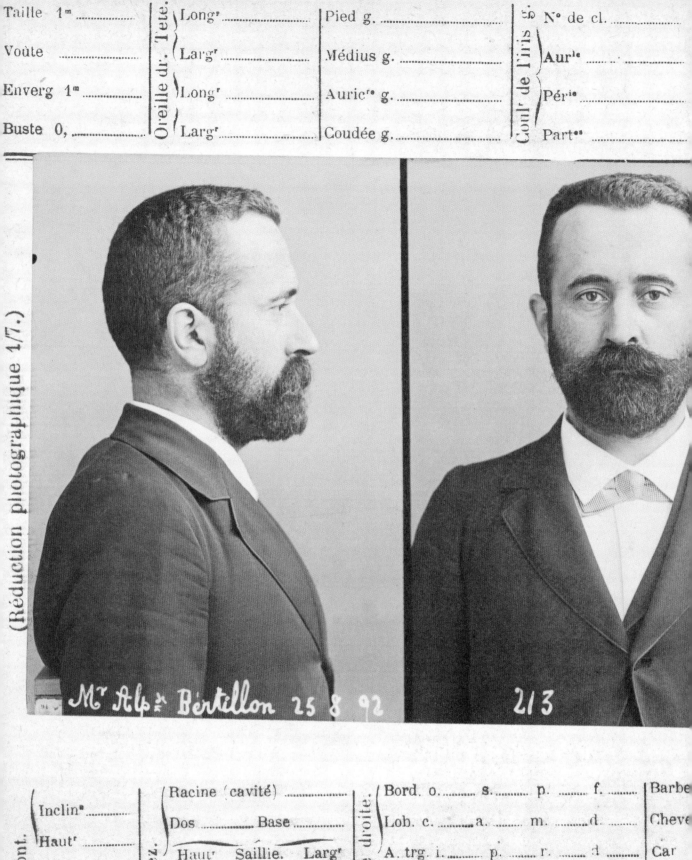

Mᵣ Alpᵉ Bertillon 25 8 92        213

| Front. { Inclinⁿ | Nez. { Racine (cavité) | Oreille droite. { Bord. o. s. p. f. | Barbe |
| Hautʳ | Dos ___ Base | Lob. c. a. m. d. | Cheve |
| Largʳ | Hautʳ Saillie. Largʳ | A. trg. i. p. r. d | Car |
| Partᵉˢ | ___ l ___ l | Pli. f. s. h. E | Au |
| | Pontes | Part. | Sigᵗ |

The use of anthropometric data to establish identity was pioneered by Alphonse Bertillon who established the Judicial Identity Service of the Paris Police in 1988. Here Bertillon, at the age 39, is recorded on one of his own anthropometric identity cards.
Courtesy UCL Library Services Special Collections, Galton Papers.

Galton believed that the new science of photography could help him in his mission to identify human types. He took individual photographs of people of representative types, from "Ph. D's" and "Baptist ministers" to mental patients; the shifty-looking fellows here are six "Millbank murderers".

Courtesy UCL Library Services Special Collections, Galton Papers.

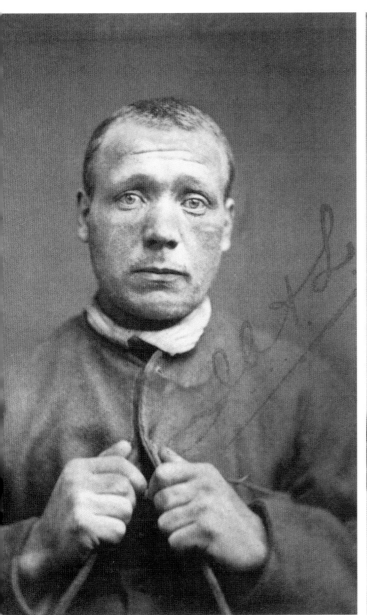

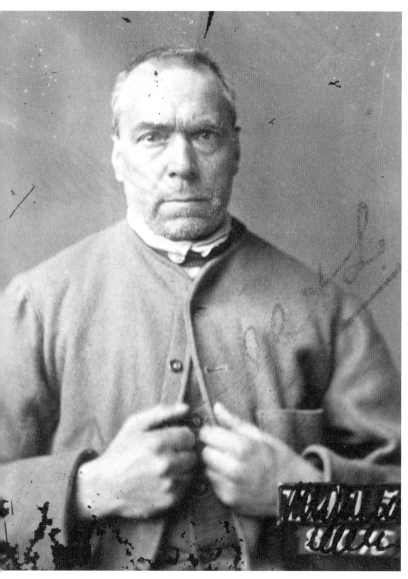

Four "Chatham privates".
Courtesy UCL Library Services Special Collections, Galton Papers.

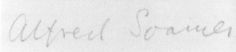

Six "Westminster schoolboys".
Courtesy UCL Library Services Special Collections, Galton Papers.

# ALEC JEFFREYS

is a British geneticist, who developed techniques for DNA fingerprinting and DNA profiling which are now used all over the world in forensic science to assist police detective work, and also to resolve paternity and immigration disputes. He graduated from Merton College, Oxford and is the recipient of numerous awards including the Royal Medal of the Royal Society and the Stokes Medal.

*Who are you?*

Right, who am I? I'm a very ordinary guy. I was born in Oxford, though on the wrong side of the tracks maybe—I was raised in a council house. My interest in science was stimulated by my father when I was eight—he gave me the most fantastic chemistry set and a microscope, which I still have in my office. I was then educated at Oxford University, initially as a biochemist and then as a geneticist. And I guess I'm best known for the development of DNA fingerprinting—which was an entirely accidental discovery. But I'm still very much a bench scientist. What drives me in life is getting out there to the lab bench and exploring the world. It's a tremendous privilege and very, very exciting—you never know what you're going to stumble upon. DNA fingerprinting is a very good example of that So, that's who I am—this perfectly ordinary person who enjoys what he's doing. This is basically my hobby—it's not a job.

*Who do we think you are?*

Well, other people often see a very different creature. I've been mythologised over the years into this genetic titan who doesn't bear any connection with me whatsoever! It's always a bit of a comedown when people come to meet me in the flesh and see a perfectly ordinary guy. I've had people come through my door who were literally quaking! It's just ridiculous. So, I've seen the bizarre divergence that's happened over years and years, between the real me—the person that my colleagues and my family know—and this sort of mythical me, that strides like a colossus across the world doing amazing things. But I don't do that, I just enjoy the science. So, that's a very simple answer to a very easy question. There are two me's. And I know the one I prefer—the real one.

*In terms of your identity, can you take us through your personal journey of scientific interest and into your current work?*

Sure. As I say, it all started when I was a small kid. My chemistry set got me into chemistry, and my microscope got me into biology. And it was pretty obvious by the time I was in my teens that what I wanted to do was biochemistry, which is the union of the two. It is using chemistry to explore biological systems. And so, I went to Oxford and studied that for four years. It was a great course, and the lecturers were fantastic, but it didn't quite hit the spot for me. And then, I suddenly realised it was genetics I wanted to do because that involved asking some of the most fundamental questions that you can ask about life.

*What are those questions?*

Well: "who are we?"; "where did we come from?"; "how did life originate in the first place on this planet?"; "how is genetic or heritable information stored and how is it transmitted between generations?" These are all questions where the answers are written, to a large part but not completely, in our DNA. So, it was very obvious, by the time I'd finished my PhD on human genetics, that DNA was where I wanted to go. But there was a horrible challenge at the time. The human genome, the totality of human genetic material, was an impenetrable tangle. We didn't have the technology to break into it. It was rather like having a million tons of spaghetti, and someone saying, "okay, I would like you to give me a very detailed description of one particular bit of the spaghetti, even though it looks exactly the same as all the rest of the spaghetti."

But it was what we call the "recombinant DNA revolution", which kicked off around 1974, that really opened the door. Imagine this huge pile of spaghetti which is the totality of our DNA. What you can do with recombinant DNA technology is to split it up, pick pieces out at random and then propagate them in bacteria. So, instead of having one bit, you've got millions, billions, trillions of copies—enough to start doing analysis. That paved the way, not only for understanding how genetic information is stored in human DNA, it also enabled us to start asking questions such as "do these bits of human DNA vary between people?" And this is what I got very excited by when I first arrived here in 1977. Now, up to that point we knew that we were all unique, and that a great deal of that uniqueness was due to genetics. But our understanding was very limited. We could only look at things like hair or eye colour. In those days the main tools that geneticists used to distinguish between people were blood groups

and the natural variations in proteins that you find in blood. It only allowed for a very limited perspective on the uniqueness of humans.

So when I arrived in Leicester in 1977, the first question we asked was: "can we use these new techniques that I and others had developed to directly pick up variation, right at the most fundamental level of all—the DNA sequence?" And we did it. In fact, the very first person we ever saw a variant in, using this very primitive technology as it was at the time, was my technician, who still works with me in the lab today.

*So you found a variant in her. What does that mean, specifically?*

Well, the region of DNA that I was particularly interested in contained a little cluster of genes that code for haemoglobin. So, that's where we started looking. Now DNA is made up of different combinations of four bases, each given a code letter—A, C, G and T. Each human inherits three billion bases or letters from mum, and three billion from dad, so there is a lot of information there. So, what we were looking at was not the full three billion. That can be done now, but not in those days. We were looking at a bit of DNA that was only about ten thousand bases long. We were systematically trying to screen it, using *very* primitive technology, for places where you had variation of a particular base. It turns out that most DNA doesn't vary between humans, but as you go along the DNA, every few hundred bases or so you're going to find a base that does vary. So, I might have an A in a particular place which means that I've inherited an A from both my mum and my dad. But I might find in you, that you've got an A from your mum, but, say, a G from your dad. So, it's almost like there is a little typographical error in the human DNA, and that, in fact, is the most common class of human genetic variation. These are what we call SNPs—Single Nucleotide Polymorphisms. So, we were amongst the first groups to report on this kind of variation, and we also made the first attempt to try and estimate, over the entire human genome, in how many places this variation occurred—we estimated around 15 million. As it turned out, we weren't far off, because we now have a full catalogue of most of this variation thanks to the human genome project.

So, suddenly, we went from this very blinkered, myopic view of human variation, to having this *fantastic* new resource of potentially millions upon millions of types of variation. We still didn't have the technology to get at them all, by any means, but nevertheless, the principle had been established. So, that was very exciting. But it was also a bit depressing, because these were very, very subtle variants, and they weren't genetically very informative. For example, if I had an A and an A, then any of my children must inherit an A from me, and that doesn't tell me whether my kids have inherited the A that I've got from my mother or from my father. You need what we call "segregation"—tracing genetic variants through generations—to do any genetics at all.

So the bottom line was that this discovery opened up an entirely new field of human genetics. It led to the first tools that enabled others to create maps of the human genome. But these weren't very informative markers. So, I just felt intuitively there had to be bits of the human genome that were a lot more variable than these rather boring little single-letter typos. I felt that the way forward would be to look at what we call "repeated DNA", or more specifically, the regions we'd later call "minisatellites". These are bits of DNA, typically about 30 bases long, where the sequence is repeated, head to tail, over and over again. So, from about 1980, the quest was to find these highly variable sequences of human DNA which didn't show simply a 'two-state' variation between people, but which rather allowed for an indefinite number of states. So, for instance, you might have a minisatellite with 15 repeats from your mum, and 23 from your dad, but I might have 196 repeats from my mum, and 492 from my dad, and so on—the potential for variation is enormous.

And to cut a *very* long story short, we totally accidentally stumbled upon methods for getting at these minisatellites generically in the human genome. The discovery was based on the observation that many minisatellites did exist in the genome, and that they often shared a patch of sequence in common. It's a sequence that we think promotes stuttering—so, in the same way that a person might stutter over a given sound, such as "p", so DNA might have that same propensity, with a specific chemical sequence promoting the stuttering. So, the

quest then was to isolate these minisatellites and use them as very informative genetic markers for basic genetic analysis such as mapping chromosomes and tracking disease genes. So, having discovered this little shared sequence motif, the prediction was that if you used it as a probe, it should be able to bind, through base pairing, to a lot of minisatellites at the same time.

Before we started trying to isolate any minisatellites detected by that approach, we had to do a simple key experiment, asking whether the probe would react with human DNA to detect multiple variable bits of DNA. And that's what we did and that's exactly what we found. That experiment, purely by accident, generated what proved to be the world's first DNA fingerprint. And I can tell you *exactly* when I got that result. It was at five minutes past nine on a Monday morning—the 10th of September 1984. And my life literally changed in a flash.

*So you immediately realised the significance of what you had discovered?*

It took about 30 seconds for the penny to drop. Here was a bit of x-ray film with each person's DNA looking a bit like a barcode. We had my technician, and her mum and dad on it, giving us a family group. We could tell them all apart very easily, and we could also see how the technician's DNA fingerprint was a composite of characters inherited from mum and from dad. You could trace it all back very simply, it was very visual. So it was immediately obvious to us that, if we could improve the technology, this might provide a basis not only for the biological identification of individuals but also for sorting out family relationships. We could also see, potentially, its use in criminal investigation—if DNA could be recovered from crime scene samples, which simply was not known at the time. And on that very first bit of film, we didn't just have humans, we also by chance had a bunch of other species' DNAs as well, including a cow, a seal, a mouse, a rat and some tobacco DNA. All the samples seemed to produce DNA fingerprints. So here was a new DNA-based approach to identification that seemed to yield fingerprints from absolutely everything. It was *astonishing*. So, that was a real eureka moment—these very rarely happen in science.

The first case in which this technique was used in a practical way was with an immigration dispute. And this happened only a few months after our initial discovery. First we improved our technology and began to get these amazingly rich, informative patterns. Then we published our first scientific paper in March, 1985, which was reported by *The Guardian*. This was then read by Sheona York, a lawyer at the Hammersmith and Fulham Community Law Centre who'd been handling a really tricky immigration dispute that had been dragging on for about two years. Basically this revolved around a family of Ghanaian origin who were UK citizens living in London. The youngest boy in that family had gone back to Ghana, and then returned ten years later with an expired British passport and a current Ghanaian passport. The immigration authorities, I think understandably, took the view that this boy was not guaranteed to be genuine. Their worry was that the boy coming back was not the son of the mother in London, but one of her nephews—the offspring of one of her sisters in Ghana. Now the boy had been subjected to blood group testing as available at the time. And those tests said that, yeah, there probably was some sort of relationship between the mother and the boy, but as to whether it was a mother-son or an aunt-nephew relationship, there was no way of telling. So, anyway, we were asked to take on the case and it was a really tricky one because we didn't have the father, and we didn't have access to any of the sisters in Ghana. All we had was mum, the boy in dispute who was facing deportation, and the three undisputed children in the family. But their DNA fingerprints just blew me away. The answer was just so blindingly obvious—every single genetic character that you could see in this boy was either present in the mum, or if it wasn't present in her, it was present in at least one of the other undisputed children, and so must have come from the missing father. So, you could actually rebuild the DNA fingerprint of the missing father from the undisputed children, and then just check that this boy matched mum and dad all the way through. And that was absolutely consistent with this boy being a full member of the family.

*So he was the same boy that left ten years ago.*

That's exactly right. So we were round about 99.999 per cent certain that this was the genuine son, not a nephew. This was evidence the like of which we'd never seen before in genetics.

*And this boy was therefore allowed to stay in the country?*

Yes. We provided the evidence to the Home Office, and although they'd probably never heard of DNA, and certainly hadn't heard of DNA fingerprinting, they decided to drop the case against the boy. They did this rather than coming to a decision based on the DNA evidence because that might have established some kind of quasi-legal precedent for it. I think my happiest moment in the whole story was being there, at the tribunal, hearing that the case had been dropped, and then going to the mother—who had been fighting this for two years which had done her health absolutely no good—and looking into her eyes as she was told "you're okay, your boy's back, we've won". That was fantastic. That was the moment when suddenly I realised that this wasn't straight science any more.

Then, of course, everything went completely insane. We had *literally* hundreds, if not thousands, of people phoning us up or arriving in person, embroiled in an immigration dispute, and wanting to get themselves tested. A few months later, we'd taken on the first paternity case, which saw DNA evidence being accepted in a magistrate's court—the first time ever in the world that DNA had gone to court. And that, then, led to another avalanche of enquiries from people who were involved in paternity disputes.

In terms of criminal investigation, we knew that DNA fingerprints would be too complex, so we then simplified the technology down to what we call "DNA profiles". Instead of there being lots of bands in the barcode, there would be just two bands per person. We first started employing that, I think it was late 1985 or early 1986, in a local, and singularly dreadful murder case in which two young girls had both been raped and murdered, three years apart. Following the second murder, a young man who seemed to know far too much about the case was arrested, and confessed to the second murder, but denied any knowledge of the first. But the police wanted to tie him in to the first murder, because the pattern of the two murders was so similar. So they approached me because they'd heard through the press about the DNA work that we were doing. Initially we assumed that we wouldn't get anywhere because nobody had ever attempted a crime-scene analysis. But we managed to get semen DNA profiles from both victims, along with the victims' profiles, and lo and behold, the semen DNA profile was indeed indistinguishable from the two victims. So, the police were right—the same man had raped and presumably murdered both of the girls. But the semen DNA profile was a complete and utter mismatch with the blood DNA profile from the guy who had confessed to the second murder. Now I didn't believe this result and the police didn't believe this; and so we did more testing; eventually, we came to the conclusion that the science was reliable and this was a false confession. So, this guy was released. Had it not been for the DNA evidence, I'm fairly sure he would have been convicted and jailed for the rest of his life and the true murderer would have gone undetected.

So, the police then launched what proved to be the world's first DNA-based manhunt—the idea being that if you've got the DNA profile of the assailant, and if you scanned the entire local community, with any luck you'll find this guy. So, they did that, with over 5,000 people volunteering to give blood samples to help track the murderer down. But he damn nearly got away with it because he sent a proxy to give a blood sample to the police. It was quite an elaborate ploy, involving forged passports and swapped photos. But anyway, someone eventually blabbed about this switch and the man was then detected by good police-work. They went up to his front door, arrested him and he confessed, so I believe, on the spot. Subsequent DNA testing confirmed that he was the killer. He's currently serving two life sentences for these crimes.

*What was his name?*

Colin Pitchfork. He was the first criminal ever to be detected through DNA anywhere on the planet. And had he not been caught, he would have killed again. They're fairly sure about that. So, right at the outset, in our first case, DNA testing not only proved one

guy innocent but also caught the true murderer, so preventing the deaths of future victims. This was pretty awesome stuff in a remarkable case. And that was the case that really fired up forensic DNA analysis worldwide. DNA profiling, in about a year or two, had been implemented right round the world. Most major countries were setting up forensic DNA labs and getting DNA profiling going.

*So did all of this eventually lead up to the creation of the national DNA database?*

Yes. The British database was launched in April 1995 and currently stands as, *per capita*, the biggest national DNA database anywhere in the world. Most countries have a criminal DNA database, but our database has about five million DNA profiles on it. And there have been some alarming recent extensions, in particular following changes to the legislation in 2001 and 2003. As it stands, the police are entitled to demand a DNA sample from you—through a mouth swab—if you are arrested with respect to any offence whatsoever. And then your DNA profile will go on the database, even if you're subsequently not even charged with an offence or convicted of anything. So, we're now in a situation where the national DNA database is populated not only by many convicted people, which makes sense, but also by about 850,000 entirely innocent individuals. I've been protesting about this for years, and finally we had a very strong judgment from the European Court of Human Rights last December, saying this was basically out of order— that it was discriminatory, and that it stigmatised people by treating them in the same way as the guilty. The real giveaway was when a Home Office minister was interviewed by John Humphrys, I think, on Radio 4, and was asked *why* these innocent DNA profiles are being retained. And he said, "it's because if these innocent people *re*offend, then we can catch them quickly." And he said it twice! Not "offend" but "reoffend". I think that speaks volumes about how the police and the authorities view the use of DNA for identification purposes.

So, that's basically the story in a nutshell. It's come a heck of a long way. And there are many other aspects to this. You can use DNA identification techniques to establish human origins as well. For example, there is a type of DNA called mitochondrial DNA that's only inherited from the mother—men *never* contribute their mitochondrial DNA to the next generation. So, that gives us a tool to track back your maternal ancestry. So, you got your mitochondrial DNA from your mum, who got it from her mum, who got it from her mum, and we can go right the way back to what we call the "mitochondrial Eve". She was a woman who lived maybe two or three hundred thousand years ago, from whom *all* modern human mitochondrial DNA happens to have been descended. There's nothing special about that woman. It's just the nature of a tree, that if you go back down the tree, eventually you get to the root.

*So is she effectively the mother of everyone on earth?*

No, because mitochondrial DNA is only one tiny part of the totality of your DNA. DNA gets reshuffled between generations. There's a process called "recombination", that shuffles DNA within a chromosome. So, if you look at another bit of your genome, and ask: "who is the common ancestor of all for *that* particular bit of the genome?" then the answer might not be two hundred thousand years ago but rather a million years ago. So, each bit of the genome has its own evolutionary history.

*So, if we trace my mitochondrial DNA back to this mitochondrial Eve, would she be the same person to whom we could trace your mitochondrial DNA or anyone else on the planet?*

Yes, the whole of mankind, tracks back to that one person for that particular bit of DNA—one female, living in Africa. There's another chromosome you can do this for, which is the Y chromosome. That's the one that only men have, it's strictly inherited from father to son. And again, you got your Y chromosome from your father, who got it from his father, who got it from his father, and so on, right the way back to the Y chromosome Adam. One interesting debate at the moment is when and where exactly the Y chromosome Adam lived. Although it was almost certainly a different time and a different place from the mitochondrial Eve.

The Y chromosome is an interesting beast, because there is something else relevant here in our identity, and that's our surname—which is a key part of who we think we are. And of course the surname is also inherited from the father in most societies. There's a colleague of mine, Mark Jobling, who has been looking in great detail at the possible relationship between the type of Y chromosome you have and your surname. Let's suppose you had a surname that was invented once in history. If there was perfect marital fidelity in all the descendants of the man who invented that new name, then all the descendants bearing that name should carry exactly the same Y chromosome. That's the theory. And it does actually work fairly well for some rare surnames. A good example of this is Ketley, which is a fairly unusual Yorkshire-derived surname. It turns out that most Ketleys have the same Y chromosome. So, what that means is: if you find yourself a Ketley, then you can go a long way towards predicting what Y chromosome type he's got, or, if you're at the crime scene and you find that Y chromosome type, that gives you a clue it might be a Ketley. And that, obviously, would be a fantastic lead for the police. Sadly, for most surnames, particularly the common ones, these correlations are weak or non-existent due to names being invented repeatedly, coupled with non-paternity, deliberate name-changing and adoption over the centuries.

*So, it does require a great deal of marital fidelity in the line of descent.*

It does, yes. I have a very good personal example of this. Because this is not just about catching criminals, it is also about genealogy. My family, the Jeffreyses, come from South Wales—Monmouthshire. Now have you heard of Judge Jeffreys—the hanging judge? In 1685 he was responsible for trying individuals involved in Monmouth's Rebellion. He was the Henry Ford of the execution world—he could hang a heck of a lot of people in one day. Now, Judge Jeffreys also comes from Monmouthshire and it's very much our family tradition that we are descendants of Judge Jeffreys. So Mark Jobling and his colleague Turi King put that to the test. They found two men who had very good genealogical evidence that they were descended, by an unbroken male lineage, from Judge Jeffreys. And they shared the same Y chromosome—which will have been the Judge Jeffreys one. We then checked out my Y chromosome and it was completely wrong. So, the family legend has been blown completely out of the water. This changes, albeit modestly, our perception of who we are. It's not a big problem, but it's a little sad to see this possible connection go. What's the explanation? Well, it may have been a naughty Mrs Jeffreys back in history who had brought the wrong Y chromosome into our branch of the family. In theory, DNA could be used to explore this in a lot more detail, though most likely it never will.

Another thing you can do, if you've got about $400, is to send a mouth swab off to a company, which will report back on hundreds of thousands of variations in your genome. This can partly provide a lead for health risks, though this is currently a rather imprecise science. But also, it can give you a report which says: "your genome looks like it's 40 per cent Viking and 22 per cent Mediterranean and five per cent Inuit and two per cent Zulu or whatever." It's great fun and people are quite happy to spend good money on this. However, it does tend to be scientific fluff with little real meaning. For example, people often ask "could you find out through DNA whether I'm descended from a Viking?" And I look at them and say, "right, where were your parents born? Where were your grandparents born?" And they say "Britain, Britain." So I say: "you're descended from the Vikings. I mean, the Danes were Vikings, the Vikings were Vikings, the Normans were Vikings, for heaven's sake! The Battle of Hastings was in part a Viking versus Viking battle, which everybody seems to forget. So of course you've got Viking DNA in you—and probably quite a lot of it." There are a lot of ways in which people get overenthusiastic about DNA when trying to find these very deep connections. I had someone recently asking me if I could test whether he was a descendant of King John, or something like that. For that you don't need a DNA test. King John left a good number of descendants, so yes, you'll have some of King John's DNA in you. Because as you go back up the generations, you have two parents, four grandparents, eight great-grandparents and so on. And so by the time you get to King John, you will have over a billion ancestors. But of course, there weren't a billion people around then, so you're

getting what we call coalescence—a coming-together of different ancestral lineages. So, a person could be your great, great, great, great, great, great, great, great grandfather down one lineage, and your great, great, great, great, great, great, great great grandfather down a completely different lineage. So eventually you will have swept the whole of the UK population into your ancestry—including kings and queens and everyone else. So, DNA is great for immediate identification and sorting out close family relationships. But as you get further and further away, the picture becomes fuzzier and what then starts emerging instead are rather different issues of ethnic group affiliation, geographic origin and the like.

*Kenan Malik, in his book* Strange Fruit, *is very critical of people who describe themselves as "race realists" and who argue that there is a genetic or biological component to race. What is your attitude towards this issue? Do you have any thought on the relationship between race and genetics?*

Oh, we very neatly duck this issue by using the word "population". Now, there is no question whatsoever that mankind isn't a single genetically homogeneous population. There are divisions, from broad continental divisions right all the way down to a much finer scale of divisions. Even just within the British Isles, you can see gradients of gene frequencies over really quite small intervals. So, yeah, the notion that we're all derived from a single, randomly mating population is demonstrably rubbish. Now, whether you want to bring in the "race" word, or not, I don't know. I would rather stick with statements like, "a group of people can be treated as a population because they can be seen to be derived from the same very recent gene pool, and may be geographically isolated from the next population", and so on. These are concepts that I'm comfortable with. "Race" is too loaded a word. But of course, the term "population" is almost a pseudonym for "race". And of *course* there are genetic differences. Nobody seems to get terribly hung up about the fact that the Masai are unusually tall or very athletic, and that these characteristics are likely to be largely genetically determined. However, there are other classes of comparison that can become odious, divisive and indefensible.

*One of the particularly tricky areas has to do with the issue of race, genetics and intelligence.*

Yes. And the problem there is untangling the environmental component of intelligence from the inherited component. Now the idea that all populations on this planet have exactly and precisely the same innate intelligence seems to make as much sense as saying that they all have the same innate hair colour, skin colour, stature, predisposition to heart disease, predisposition to colorectal cancer, and so on. It just seems implausible. But the problem is measuring population differences in intelligence, never mind interpreting such differences in a genetic framework. Even IQ is a very difficult thing to define. Perhaps the only definition of IQ is that it is the result of a test that tests IQ, but that, of course, gets you stuck in a circular argument. So, I'm not terribly sure what they're measuring in IQ tests. And to actually unravel genetic components would be extremely difficult, because the environment is *enormously* important in terms of culture, upbringing, education and the like. So I'm not a fan whatsoever of the idea that science can be meaningfully applied to the issue of race and IQ, and even if it could, what would be the purpose or benefit?

*What are the philosophical implications of your work? What are your ambitions for the future, and what contribution you see some of those ambitions making?*

Well, I'm not a philosopher; I'm a hard-nosed experimental scientist. So, I'm getting onto dangerous ground here! But I've seen people trying to use our discoveries on DNA fingerprinting, for example, to support anti-abortion arguments. Because, of course, your DNA fingerprint is a very simple manifestation of your genetic uniqueness which is created at the point of conception. And that sort of argument just makes me feel thoroughly uncomfortable.

I think one of the things that work in molecular genetics has brought into sharp focus is our extraordinary proximity to the great apes in terms of origin. Before DNA analysis, the general view was that we're descendants of some ape-like creatures but a heck of a long time ago. But if you look at the DNA of a chimp and a human, there's a lot less difference between them than, say, between a rat and a mouse. It's in fact about the same as between two different sub-species of mice. So, if you classify organisms on this planet based purely on DNA sequences—and that could be done—I think you'd almost certainly put humans, chimps and probably gorillas into the same *genus*. And you may be scratching your head asking, "well, the chimp and the human, are these really separate species?"

*Well, there is a philosophical and legal argument, isn't there, about whether chimps should be redefined as human in some legal concepts?*

Yes. That's right. But I'm not going to be led down that road! But I do take the view that there is a respect deserving to higher primates which they do not get. In terms of chimps and humans, the really interesting question, of course, genetically, is not: "what are the similarities?" But rather, "what are the key differences?" So, we may be 98.6 per cent identical in our DNA sequence, but that still leaves millions of differences between a chimp and a human, many of which would have no significance at all. One of the really huge challenges for the future is to try and identify just what variants out there are key to having made humans human. So, everyone knows humans have big brains, the ability to speak, and self-awareness and so on. But chimps probably have self-awareness too. And this is a key issue with identity, because for a long time there has been this almost religious belief that "only humans have self-awareness, a soul or whatever you want to call it." But I think that concept has become more and more discredited. I mean, if you've ever worked with chimps or other higher primates it becomes quite clear that they've got as much self-awareness as we have. I think there's also evidence of this in dolphins and porpoises; elephants too, apparently, have good levels of self-awareness.

*Haven't they just reclassified some cephalods, certain forms of octopus, as being much more self-aware and intelligent than we originally thought?*

Yes, that's right. Yeah. So the problem is: how do you test for self-awareness? I can't test if you're self-aware. I can deduce that you're self-aware by extrapolation from my own personal experience, but I can't prove it.

*The philosopher John Searle talks about the Chinese box. The idea is that you can feed a piece of writing in Chinese into a box and the box might come out with an answer, but that does not prove that the box is self-aware. There may just be somebody in the box who's following a set of instructions on how to respond by rote but who actually has no idea what it is that they are actually writing. So, the machine looks self-aware but actually isn't. And this relates to the whole question of computers and artificial intelligence, doesn't it?*

That's exactly right. I think one of the greatest mysteries of biology is: what is self-awareness? Because one could imagine humans as automata, without self-awareness. And that could work and could probably generate very elaborate societies, and so on. So I don't see that self-awareness as a prerequisite for advanced intelligence, but nonetheless we have it. So, it's some strange, emergent property of an extremely complex nervous system. But it's a property that's been emerging, I suspect, for a very long time during the course of evolution. But now we're getting right out of my comfort zone! It will be an enormous challenge for the future to define the biological basis of self-awareness. Even Francis Crick, who with Watson deduced the structure of the double helix, spent much of his life exploring this issue but with rather little progress. It's too difficult to wrestle with. But it's a key part of what is being human.

Another very exciting area is using DNA as a time machine to go back into the past, by looking at ancient DNA. An institute in Germany will have soon, within the next year, a rough draft of the entire Neanderthal genome, thanks to several Neanderthal remains which, despite being tens of thousands of years old, still have DNA in them. It's there in incredibly small amounts and in incredibly bad condition. But with current technology, it's possible to sequence billions of these DNA snippets and get a rough draft of the Neanderthal genome. Now humans are a very young species. Modern mankind

emerged in Africa about a hundred thousand years ago, something like that. And then we migrated out of Africa and eventually populated the rest of the world. We can go back along the tree of evolution and see at what point chimps and humans separate onto distinct branches. With the Neanderthal sequence, it is becoming possible to place Neanderthals onto this tree and to start answering questions about their fate—did they die out or instead slowly disappear by interbreeding with modern humans? The evidence so far seems to be that there is no evidence for inter-breeding.

So by using DNA, there is huge potential for reconstructing the evolutionary tree of mankind which will of course help answer the question "who are we as a species?", really shining a spotlight on the history of human evolution and on the genetic changes that underpin it. So, there's some *really* exciting stuff ahead.

# ROZ KAVENEY

is a writer of both fiction and non-fiction, and an editor. She was born male but transitioned to being female. She was educated at Pembroke College Oxford. She has been a regular contributor to *The Independent* and the *Times Literary Supplement*. She is a transsexual rights activist and was a founding member of Feminists against Censorship and a former deputy chair of Liberty.

*Who are you?*

Well, I'm a lot of things. I'm the child of Joseph Hugo Kaveney and Joan Mary Kaveney, née Lister. I'm the sibling of Jane McCarthy, the aunt of Michael and Elizabeth McCarthy, and the sister-in-law of Bill McCarthy. I use the gender-specific terms latterly, because that's all I've ever been in those cases, and the gender-neutral ones where there's a more complicated history. My sister sees it much more simply. Once, one of her colleagues said, "so, do you have any family?" and she replied, "oh, I used to have a brother." And they said, "oh, I'm sorry". But she responded, "no, it's great—I've got a sister now!" This is one of those clichéd stories, but it is true. So who am I? Well, I'm someone who realised I was trans. I tend to say "trans" rather than "transgender" or "transsexual" because it's a handy short form and it avoids choosing between two very complicated terms and therefore getting caught up on either side of a debate.

*When did you first feel that you were the wrong gender?*

I sort of knew there was something going on in my childhood, and certainly by my teens I pretty much had it sorted: I knew that I needed a transition, because I wasn't happy with my identity as it had been *provided* to me, and so I was going to have to work on it.

*Was this at a time when it was possible to have a transition?*

Yes, by that point, it was possible. I'm 59 years old now, so when I was younger, the first generation of post-operative trans women and trans men were already around. Though it was still a time when you would read shock horror stories about it in the papers. At that point, there were a number of French women, most of whom had worked as entertainers, who had had surgery in Casablanca—April Ashley was one of them. In fact, a good 15 years had already passed since the first surgeries. The first surgeries that didn't kill the people involved were carried out in the very late 1940s, in this country, in fact. Sir Harold

Gillies, was a plastic surgeon who did an awful lot of war-related plastic surgery, especially on fighter pilots who'd been badly burned. And he carried out certainly the first female-to-male surgery anyone knows about, and one of the very first male-to-female—certainly the first where the person significantly survived. That said, there was Lili Elbe in the 1930s. She had the operation and it wasn't her surgery that killed her, rather it was subsequent surgeries. She tried to have ovaries implanted and they had no idea of the problems with transplants in those days, so that killed her.

So, it meant that when I read the literature about all this in my teens I learnt that there was such a thing as people who were trans, and that it was possible to have something done about it. I also read a lot of the fiction about this. There were various gay novels of the 1960s which had characters in them that fitted the general pattern. And the attitude from these books was, "oh, God, it's all going to be terribly dire and miserable. But you know what? Maybe that's just how it has to be."

*So could you just define what you mean by "trans"? My understanding of the word would have been that a trans person is somebody who has had an operation.*

No, a trans person is somebody who knows that they need to have an operation or some other sort of shift. There are plenty of people who can transition socially and in terms of affect without necessarily having full surgery or by simply restricting themselves to some limited surgery. One of my closest friends has never had genital surgery—she's had a lot of other work done—but because I and another of her closest friends had a lot of post-operative trouble, she got scared and decided to hold off. But because she has the charm of Satan it's never really made any difference, because anyone who's attracted to her, irrespective of their sexuality, just deals with it! But no one would ever say she was male, even after they'd had her dick in their mouth.

But I knew that I didn't want to be the person I was born as. I knew that I wanted to be this other person, who quite rapidly, in my head, was called Roz, or Rosalind. I just thought, "okay, if I'm not this

person on my birth certificate, who am I?" And that was the name that came to me almost instantly, so that's who I decided I was. And everything after that was a matter of thinking: "well I will go on lying to everyone for as long as is convenient, but that's not who I am—the name on my passport is not me. It is this person I have to be in the short term."

*"Short term" being until you were old enough to...*

...find ways of doing something about it, yes. I was very fortunate, because I managed to make contact with a bunch of post-operative trans women in Manchester, who were working-class, most of them were whores. And they were very good to me, and they said to me: "look, our lives are shit. You have the chance to have a life that's better. We're not saying, 'don't do it', we're just saying, 'leave it until later. Get yourself through university first.'" So, whilst I was in the sixth form in Leeds, I would escape off to Manchester whenever I needed to. And when I look back on that period it's quite unbelievable because I was successfully leading a significant double life. I was telling my friends and parents in Wakefield that I was spending weekends in Leeds, and I was telling my friends in Leeds that I couldn't come to things there because I was busy with stuff in Wakefield. I was playing the two places off against each other with everyone I knew, in order that I could go off to Manchester for the weekend and hang out with my trans friends. And the extent to which I managed to avoid quite significant disasters was quite remarkable! And then, all the time I was at Oxford University, I carried on going up to Manchester whenever I needed to in order to get away from London.

Also around that time I discovered the Gay Liberation Front, which had started in London. And because my politics were generally of the left, I thought I'd investigate this, because it sounded like the right sort of thing to be involved with. And one of the consequences of that was that I found this trans group attached to the Gay Liberation Front. It was what we'd now call a trans group, what we then called a TVTS group.

*What does TVTS stand for?*

Transvestites and transsexuals. You know, drag queens and people who were gender queer and people who were ambiguous—all those sorts of people went to that group. And for the first couple of years of the Gay Liberation Front, both here and in the States, trans people were very involved and very active. We only got ousted later. After all, what, for a while, many people tended to avoid mentioning was that the Stonewall riots were populated mostly by drag queens—many of whom would identify as transsexual then—or with young, butch dykes, many of whom would now identify as trans men. There was a very heavy trans presence in the Stonewall riot—it was mostly trans people. People do sort of accept that now, but the more bourgeois and respectable end of the gay movement has always been embarrassed by this fact.

Unfortunately, the consequence of being very involved with the GLF was that some of the earliest theoreticians of gay liberation, like Dennis Altman, and a lot of early feminists, turned vehemently against transsexuals and the whole concept of transsexuality. And because of this, I let myself get guilt-tripped out of being who I was for much of my 20s. It really was a matter of my feminist friends deputing a senior and eminent lesbian feminist to invite me to her college rooms and explain to me why I was wrong. And that was just what it was like in the 1970s, and I knew this was bullshit, but I let myself be guilt-tripped.

*So, if they didn't accept any trans identity, what did they see you as, then? A man?*

They saw me as a man who had been deluded by the patriarchy into thinking it's possible to be something else. By the time I did transition, incidentally, several of those women had become some of my most serious supporters, and many of them said to me: "we were talking the most terrible crap. It didn't make any sense to see you as a man, and the more you tried to be a man, the less we saw you as one!" Now, during that period, I was still sleeping with men and I was mostly going out and sleeping with tranny chasers. I had one heterosexual relationship in those years, which confused me, no end, and didn't lead to me behaving especially well. My only defence, is that it was with my closest friend, and she was trying

to save me from myself, as she saw it. But we came to the agreement that this was a terribly bad thing, it was a big mistake, because after all, she wasn't a lesbian. Whereas, possibly, I was!

*So, did you initially think you were a gay man?*

I was trying to be a gay man, but I was trying to be a gay man who mostly had sex dressed as a woman. Other people couldn't convince me that I didn't want to be a woman. They just convinced me that I couldn't be—briefly. Now I did sort of assume, when I had surgery, that I would go on mostly sleeping with guys, and I accepted reluctantly they might well be guys who have a bit of a thing about trans people. But it was the view of a number of my friends, including some other people who had tried quite hard to persuade me not to transition, and who were themselves all lesbians, that "oh, well, of course Roz is going to be a lesbian eventually." And when I did come out as a dyke, I told them and they said, "well, yeah". I said, "oh really? I didn't assume that would be the case." They said, "well, we did. That was just your affect."

One of the problems I faced was that essentially, my surgery went radically wrong, and I had to have about 20 corrective surgeries, and I nearly died several times. The consequence of that was—and this is relevant to the question of identity—that where I had previously been skinny and cute, I then put on about 12 stone, because I'd been mis-prescribed cortisone. They were using cortisone ointment on skin grafts that weren't taking, and the result was that it was going directly into my bloodstream, and I was allergic to cortisone. But the people who were doing this were surgeons, and they didn't work out that they'd messed things up until a comparatively late stage, and at that point they weren't going to admit it, were they? But they'd messed up and there were post-operative infections and thromboses and God knows what else. I was a malpractice suit waiting to happen. But I never pursued it because, as a matter of principle, my view is that you don't sue the National Health Service. That's a tough call when you've been badly screwed around, but it comes down to socialist principles! And then, of course, I experienced a second piece of serious surgical malpractice, which happened at the end of my 40s, when a simple question of an operation on an exploding gall bladder ended up giving me a surgical hernia the size of several footballs. And this is all relevant, particularly in relation to female identity, because our sense of identity is so bound up with our looks, and with being presentable in our society. So we have to come to terms with "looksism" in our society.

Of course, one of the other things that has been particularly relevant to identity is the internet. Because on the net, you really do get to choose who you are. But I made a decision, when I started to be involved online, that I would be totally and in every respect the same person. I thought it was particularly important not to bullshit in any way, not even in those little ways that most people do. I couldn't afford to play any identity games online, because I wanted to try and write prose that was as close to who I am as I could. I think that is partly because of what Orwell says, about writing prose that is as honest as you can make it, and I do think that the internet hasn't helped that generally.

*How long was it between your decision to have surgery and beginning the operations themselves?*

There was a period of three years when I was living as a woman but hadn't had genital surgery. Though I actually had, at a very early stage after I changed social role, breast augmentation.

*As a boy, or a young man, what were your ambitions for your identity, and, having tried to fulfil some of those, did the reality meet your ambitions?*

Well the crucial point for me was the realisation, when I was 13 or 14, that I was only temporarily a boy. That being male was never a real option. It never even really became an option when people tried to bully me. Even then, I just thought: "oh, let's see how this works out. I really don't think this is a good idea. Oh, screw it. Oh, I'm so miserable. Oh, what am I going to do?" I never really believed it. The thing is, it was caught up with all my other ambitions. My gender identity was only one of my ambitions. I always meant to be a writer, ideally a writer of fiction—although that's an ambition that is only partly fulfilled as yet.

I always intended to write for the *New Statesman*, and I did for a while but then had to stop for that as a matter of principle after a disagreement with the then literary editor. I've managed to construct my life in such a way that I don't compromise. I do walk away from situations I disapprove of, as much as I can. And that's as much to do with the ambitions I had for my identity when I was a teenager.

*Do you see yourself as a woman, full stop, or as a trans woman?*

I see myself as a woman with trans history. I often say "trans woman" simply because that way it gives both halves a voice. And I don't regard my identity as a woman as being exactly equivalent to that of someone who was born and socialised as a woman from the word go. I do argue quite strongly that socialisation is not merely passive. Everyone talks as if we were that *tabula rasa* that Locke writes about, and as if we don't choose a fair measure of our socialisation. I knew I wanted to be female when I was five or six. At infant school, I didn't want to play with boys, I only played with girls. It was a matter of heartbreak to me when, at junior school, they segregated us at breaktimes. I would spend most of break-time at the end of the male part of the playground, talking through the fence to my female friends, to the extent I used to get bullied for it. So in what sense was I not being socialised there? There was a series of attempts being made to socialise me as male, and, in fact, one of the reasons that I was perpetually bullied at every school I ever went to was because bullying is a form of forced socialisation of perceived birth identity. That's one of the reasons I try and take a very hard line on bullying. Schools can sometimes regard bullying as a necessary form of policing. I know this, because I've been a teacher, and I've seen colleagues turn a blind eye to bullying, for all sorts of reasons.

*Do you find that your identity means that you have a lot in common with female-to-male trans people? How do you relate to those kinds of people?*

I have female-to-male friends and trans friends and while I'm aware of their history, they're blokes. They're some of the few blokes I actually get on with. But even in the case where I actually knew them before they were out, (and some of my closest trans male friends are people I knew when they were presenting themselves as lesbians) I still see them as blokes. That's not just me making a political decision that they're blokes. They're just blokes. And I don't have that many close male friends. I do have some, but I'm very selective about it. And the reason I've acquired a few trans male friends, in the last couple of years, is simply that I've started knowing a lot more trans men than I used to, simply because the social environment that I live in, in London, has changed. I'm very much more involved with the trans community than I was three years ago. I used to feel quite alienated from the trans community in the 1980s and 1990s, because it was dominated by people who identified as heterosexual. And they were quite snooty about the minority of us who identified as dykes.

*Why was that? Was that because they felt that you weren't really trans?*

Something like that, or they thought we were rocking the boat. Or maybe they were saying "if people knew how many of us are lesbian, they might stop providing surgery." This was all very noticeable. I was on the parliamentary forum that negotiated trans law reform and the Gender Recognition Certificate and so on. And certainly harsh words did get spoken in the course of that parliamentary debate between those of us who were primarily concerned about the right to get married, and those of us who said, "well, hang on— we need to reserve a position on civil partnerships, at the very least." Because around a third of the trans community identify as queer, post-transition, irrespective of who they slept with beforehand. On the other hand, there's now an environment in London where not only is there a trans scene, a significant part of that trans scene is queer identified. And that's in addition to the people who don't identify as trans so much as gender-queer, or in any other way.

*Do you ever grieve for...*

... the person I might have been otherwise?

*Yes.*

Well, I actually grieve more for the person I would have been if I'd transitioned much earlier, rather than the person I would have been if I'd never transitioned. Because by transitioning later, and betraying myself in that way, I acquired a measure of cynicism about myself that has become a general cynicism about human motivations.

*Betrayal is a very strong word. Were you as clear then, as you sound now about this core self that you felt you were betraying?*

I do feel that, yes. If I look back at things I wrote then, I've got some of my notebooks from my teens, and it does pretty much seem like that. And given that I was actually censoring my notebooks in case my parents found them, it's pretty clear.

*Who do we think you are? How are you perceived by others in society?*

It varies a lot. My neighbours think of me as Roz, and some of them know about my background and some of them don't. Their kids are more likely to know than they do, and some of the kids are cool with it, and some of them are a pain in the arse. But I always operate on the assumption that everyone knows my background. I've always been pretty upfront about my background, partly because I'm so involved in politics, particularly gender politics. So I haven't been able to afford for there to be any bullshit.

*And are there preconceptions that people have that define you in a way that you want to correct?*

The thing is, it varies so much. But here's a story. As I said, I tend to assume people know about me. I am, after all, six foot four, I've got size 12 feet and hands to match, my voice is not little and squeaky. So, I work on the assumption that people know that I'm trans. And yet a lot of the time they don't. For example: some years ago, I was at a wedding—it was rather a posh, literary wedding. And all sorts of the great and the good were there. And there was one woman there called Laura, whom I had known at Oxford. She hadn't known me sufficiently well to understand anything about what had gone on with me, but she was someone I had known socially, from parties. And I thought, "well, there's someone I don't need to speak to, so let's avoid any embarrassment." But then, someone actually dragged us together, and said, "Roz, Laura, you must have been at Oxford at the same time." And so we made nervously polite conversation, and I said, "oh, hello Laura, how are you? I haven't seen you for years, what's going on with you?" And she looked more and more baffled, and then she said, "I'm sorry—it's clear you know me, but I can't remember you at all." And I said, "oh, we knew each other through Louise—I was a flatmate of hers." And she goes, "sorry—I remember Louise, obviously, but I don't remember you as one of her flatmates." And then she said, "what's your name again?" And I replied, "Roz Kaveney", and then she asked, "what was your surname before you married?"! And I said, "ah. I think we are labouring under a misapprehension here. Let me explain!"

*What was her response when you did explain?*

"Oh crumbs!" But before things got too complicated and embarrassing, her sister came over, whom I didn't know and whom I'd always wanted to meet, and so we moved on to talking about other things.

*Do your thoughts on how you feel in terms of your sexual identity, transfer to how you feel about larger questions of identity—for instance your Englishness or your Britishness?*

Well I've been fascinated by that whole vein of philosophy and neurology that one finds in the work of Daniel Dennett and elsewhere. I'm not a Freudian, but various of my friends who are intellectual and trans, have tried to reconcile their identities with a sort of Lacanian psychoanalysis, and I think that is a waste of intellectual effort and time. I don't think it can be reconciled, I mean you just have to look at the trans-phobia of most orthodox French Lacanians to see that. It's also that, much as I admire Freud as a writer and thinker, I don't actually think that, on general questions, as opposed to one or two specific areas like parapraxis, Freud was right. Freud lost touch with his attempt to be a scientist at an early stage. My position is that Freud was a charlatan, but

I don't mean that in a negative sense! So accordingly, what you have to ask is, how is identity constructed? How is a sense of the self constructed? Clearly, it's a narrative. Our mind and our identity are narratives that a portion of the brain tells itself. It's the only explanation that makes any coherent sense. And gender identity is another of those narratives, and the evidence, from brain studies, is that trans identity is innate. Now I'm often sceptical of brain studies, because I've read Stephen Jay Gould's *The Mismeasure of Man* just like everyone else. But the work people have done on the brains of dead trans people does seem to indicate there are particular structures that we have that other people don't have. And I relate that to the particular narratives that the brain tells itself.

I blogged about all of this some time ago when Julie Bindel, *The Guardian* journalist, who's viciously anti-trans, did a rant about it on Radio 4. When that happened, some of us organised for the audience at that recording to be made up of a great deal of trans people and we also politely handed out leaflets to those people who weren't trans! But Bindel was very keen on saying, "gender identity is socially constructed and not biologically innate", to which my response in my blog was, "this is our old friend, the false dichotomy." Because how on earth is anything that is socially constructed, not socially constructed in the context of what is biologically innate? The narratives we tell ourselves about identity in different societies are both biologically innate, inasmuch as the sheer capacities to tell stories about ourselves is biologically innate; and they are socially constructed, because the stories available to people are to some extent a function of their culture. And this relates to the broader question you ask about Britishness. What also has to be added is that the stories we tell ourselves do not only come from the hegemonic or dominant strain in a particular society. There are a number of different vocabularies available to us. And, to some extent, we get to choose what those are. I mean, the ways in which people identify as straight or gay varies a lot. And it's because there are several narratives that people can provide themselves with. People don't choose their gender-object choice, (though they may choose more than they think they do). What they choose is the way they perceive that object choice. There is that wonderful line of Michael Caine's about Richard Gere. Someone once said to Caine in an interview: "so, you live next door to Richard Gere in Hollywood. Is he gay?" And Caine replies, "well, I really wouldn't say he's gay. Mind you, if they were short-handed, he'd help out!" And, like many of the best jokes, that is actually quite perceptive. Not because it has anything specific to reveal about Richard Gere, but it's very interesting in what it reveals about how Michael Caine sees sexual-object choice, not for himself but for other people—that there are grey areas, and a lot of people inhabit those grey areas.

*Do you think that the trans community is closer than other communities?*

Well it's divided. One of the things that divides it is sexuality. Another thing that divides it is that, and this is partly an ethical thing and partly a practical thing, some people make the decision to live "deep stealth". That is to say, they never acknowledge they're trans; they go out of their way to sever themselves from any connection with anybody who knows anything about their past; and they—with varying degrees of denial or non-denial—believe that nobody knows. Though that belief may be accurate in some cases, it may not be accurate in other cases. Whereas I made the decision a long time ago that, if I wanted to do what I wanted to do, in terms of being a writer, I just had to accept that I was always going to live in a world where a lot of people would know. That was always going to be a difficult thing for me, I just made the decision that it was never going to be a secret. And I would live with the consequences of that, whatever the consequences would be.

*In different circumstances, might you have made a different decision about whether to reveal yourself or not if you thought you could?*

I don't think so. The fact is, as I say, there were reasons apart from the practicalities of things like my height, that just meant it wasn't on. I was at Oxford for five years; I was active in political and literary circles for five years in my previous identity. There's absolutely no way that that wasn't going to come

back and bite me. Absolutely no way in the world. The only way I could have done so would be if I had moved to the States, never tried to be a writer, and changed my maiden name. But the things that I am interested in writing about and working in—poetry and science fiction—are small villages within which everyone gossips. So I am sure I would have been discovered eventually!

# KENAN MALIK

is a writer, lecturer and broadcaster. He was born in India, brought up in Manchester and now lives in London. He is presenter of Analysis, BBC Radio 4's flagship current affairs programme and a panelist on the Moral Maze. He used to present Nightwaves on BBC Radio 3. He has also written and presented a number of radio and TV documentaries. His books include *From Fatwa to Jihad*; *Strange Fruit*; *Man, Beast and Zombie* and *The Meaning of Race*.

---

*Who are you?*

I don't think that's a very useful question, because the question "who am I?" depends on context. So, for example, the question "who am I to my daughter?" is very different from "who am I to you?" And identity is about, in a sense, someone's relationship to other people. And that's always changing. It changes in two ways: firstly it changes over time, of course, but it also changes in the sense that how you define yourself and how you want other people to define you depends on who they are. So, the way I want you to see me is very different to how I want my daughter to see me, and my relationship with my daughter is very different to my relationship with you.

So I don't think "who are you?" is a very useful question in abstract, it is only useful in context. But, in broad terms, I am the sum of my relationship to other people. And you shape both the way you want to be seen and the way others see you. And the way others see you clearly shapes how you see yourself too. So, it's a complex question, in that sense.

From another perspective, given that you are developing this project with Billy Bragg, it might be worth talking about this in relationship to the notions of Englishness or Britishness. Personally, I see Englishness as a *faux* identity, in a sense. It's come about, not because there is anything deep and meaningful, it seems to me, about English identity, but rather, because the notion of British identity has broken up: nowadays you just have lots of regional identities. Suddenly, people who might never have thought of themselves as English have begun thinking, "the Scots have their identity, and the Welsh have their identity, so I want my identity." So, in that sense, this sudden rush to find an English identity actually expresses the absurdity of the way we think of identity. Now I live in England, but I don't feel English in any way, I don't have any organic relationship to Englishness. Though I'm sure people like Billy Bragg or Roger Scruton probably do. They have a kind of organic relationship to a sense of Englishness. But I can't understand that, I have no sense of that.

*Why is that?*

Well Englishness is meaningless to me. I have no idea where I'd begin with my relationship to Englishness. I can see myself as a Londoner, but I see myself as a Londoner simply because I've lived for many years in London. So, I have a particular relationship to that place which I call "London". But to me, there is no such distinct place called "England" to which I have a specific relationship. But let's look at this in a broader sense in terms of the debate about Britishness. There's been much discussion recently about creating a sense of Britishness, but I get the feeling a lot of it is a false debate. The idea that people can come in, take part in immigration ceremonies, sign on the dotted line, and suddenly feel more British because they can answer questions about how you pay gas bills seems to me absurd. Because identity is not about a sense of belonging, it's not about signing on a dotted line. It's about, as I said, your relationships. Your identity emerges organically out of the relationships you have with other people. To say that people do not have a core sense of identity in relation to their Britishness means that their relationship to other people who are British is in some way strained or constrained. And that needs to be addressed. But this is not the question of saying, "you are British because you know British history." Of course it helps to know British history, but ultimately that seems to me to be immaterial.

So it is true that I have a British passport and so I am British in that sense. But it would be much more interesting if you were to ask me: "what are the traditions which animate me?" Interestingly, for instance, if I see the Union Jack, I have no emotional response. But if I see the Tricolour, or the American

Stars and Stripes, I have a much greater emotional response to them, even though I don't think of myself in any way French or American. Why is that? Because both flags have a certain symbolic resonance for me, they're rooted in a certain particular history and in particular political traditions. The Tricolour represents something, which is very important to me, because part of what I am is shaped by my relationship to the ideas of the Enlightenment which shaped the French Revolution. So I have no attraction to being French, but I have a certain symbolic attraction to the idea that their flag represents. It is the same with the Stars and Stripes. So, at a contractual level, a legal level, I'm British. But at a philosophical level, what I'm animated by are the ideas that are European, or at least European in a more universal sense. I don't feel European in the sense of the debate about the EU. I feel attached to the ideas of the Enlightenment. And more broadly, from a cultural point of view I feel attached to 'modernism'. Now, nobody thinks about modernism as an identity. But clearly, modernist ideas are part and parcel of who I am—the way I think about the world.

*What do you mean by "modernism"?*

Two things. Firstly there is what we call "cultural modernism" which, as I say, is the product of the late nineteenth, and early twentieth century—with the work of writers like Dos Pasos, James Joyce, early TS Eliot—these are people whose work is, I think, quite remarkable in allowing us to think about the modern world. And there are painters who do this too, such as Picasso, Braque, the Constructivists, and Rodchenko and so on. So, one can define it culturally, in terms of certain cultural figures who I think are important in shaping the way I think about the world. And secondly, and in a broader sense, one thinks of modernism as that package of ideas that came out of the Enlightenment—notions of progress, universalism, and equality. So, that's a slightly different notion from the cultural modernism, and I feel an attachment to both of them. But all I'm trying to say is that how you see yourself, the ideas that shape you, the emotions that shape you, take place at different levels. And so, to say, "I am British" or "English", doesn't do justice to the kind of ideas that shape anybody.

*So you've landed on a kind of an intellectual and to an extent a political tradition as something that defines how you see yourself.*

You're using the words "intellectual" and "political" as if they're simply an abstract thing. But of course, the way one feels about these things is deeply *in* you, it's part of you. There's this idea, for example, that religious ideas are deeply felt and humanist ideas are not, but I just don't see it that way. Your attachment to your ideas are part and parcel of who you are, and therefore political ideas and intellectual ideas, are not just 'out there' they're part of you.

*You have an ongoing debate with Ziauddin Sardar on things like multiculturalism and so on. And one thing you have not yet mentioned at all about who you are, but which some people might pick out above everything else, is that you are an Asian man. So what does 'Asian-ness' mean, or is that question itself enforcing something on your identity that you don't want?*

Well, I quite deliberately didn't mention that, precisely because it's what people expect you to say. People used to ask me "where are you from?" So, I'd say, "I live in London." And then they would say: "no, no, where are you really from?" So I would reply "I was born and brought up in London" but they would persist asking "no, no, where are you really from?" And when I said "I was born in India" it was as if suddenly, they'd found me, they knew who I was, they'd found my essence. And that's what I resist. There are things about India I like but actually, those

things are the very opposite of what most people associate with India. It's not the tradition of it that I like about India, it is that it's resisting those traditions for the moment. There's a sense of it being a global player, a sense of it wanting to make a mark upon the world, a sense of it being modern. But if you ask, "what does my Asian-ness mean?", well I've got a mother and father who were born in India, but I don't have an attachment to the conventional ideas of what India is. I'm very sympathetic to aspects of the Indian tradition, but I do resist the idea that, in some way, you can define me by my Asian-ness.

When I grew up I called myself "black", as many of my peers did, because blackness was not an ethnic term, it was a political term. It was a term to define those who were non-white and fighting against racism. And when I say this at meetings, there are people of a certain generation, who grew up in the 1980s, with certain political beliefs, who understand exactly what that means. But these days, if I call myself "black", people would look at me, as if I was mad or something, because blackness has become purely an ethnic term. So, I'm attached to the political notion of blackness, and to a certain extent, I'm attached to the political notion of being Asian. The notion of being 'Asian' developed in Britain, in response to racism, just like the notion of blackness did. And the notion of blackness, as it developed in Britain in the 1970s and 1980s, is very different from the notion of blackness in America, or in India. In America, it was *both* an *ethnic* and a political term. And in India no one would think of calling themselves black. So "Asian" refers to a very peculiar kind of identity that grew up in Britain under specific circumstances such as immigration and racism. And insofar as that's the case, I'm happy to be Asian, but I have no attachment to what most people would imagine when the terms "India" or "Asia" are used.

*In your book* Strange Fruit *you talk about the so-called "race debate". Can you take us through what that is?*

Well, crudely put, the debate about race is about the question, "does race have a biological reality?" And there's two sets of answers to that. One is that we are biologically divided into distinct races, and that you can genetically show that race is a biological reality. The other side says that there is no such distinction, there is no biological reality to race, and science has proved that race does not exist. And I think both sides are wrong. I think the categories into which humans are parcelled up are social, they are not 'natural' categories. And this is because of things like migration, intermarriage, adoptions, assimilation, and so on. All these things shape the way that human populations are thought about and so there's no such thing as a natural human population. Nevertheless, social beliefs about human populations have biological consequences. And that's because the way we define human categories, whether by race or ethnicity or faith or nationality, geographic or whatever, has biological consequences because people tend to marry within those groups more than they do outside of them. And that inevitably will have certain biological consequences. So, if you take almost any socially-defined group, and look at the genes, you'll find that there's a distinction between that group and any other socially-defined group. So, in that sense, both sides are wrong. Race is not a biological category, and yet social categories can have biological consequences. And that's a very difficult concept to get hold of, to grasp, which is why, I think, there is this great debate about race.

*So biology follows social reality, and if the social reality changes then the biological reality will change. And that is opposed to this race realist idea that biological reality precedes or is the basis for social groupings?*

That's right. Absolutely. And you can, very easily, detect genetic differences between what we call 'races'. But, as I said, you can also detect genetic differences, if you want to, between the people of Pisa and the people of Florence. So the fact that you can detect genetic differences, in and of itself, is not an expression of the fact that those are our natural categories, which is what race realists argue. Now those population differences are important in all sorts of ways. They're important for understanding diseases, they're important for developing new medicines, for understanding human history, and so on. They can be important in all sorts of ways. But the fact that they're important doesn't alter

the fact that these are not natural categories. That's the peculiarity of being human.

*And why were you interested to spend so much time investigating this and devoting so much thought to it?*

Well, because the idea of race has been very important in shaping the modern world and Western thought. Up to 1945, it was the dominant idea of the way we understood relationships between groups. I can't think of many people prior to 1945 who didn't have a racial view of the world.

*Though in* Strange Fruit *you do say that further back, in Ancient Greece for instance, the world wasn't defined in terms of race but rather in terms of those who were civilised and not.*

Yes, this is a modern view. The definition or discrimination between human groups by virtue of their biological inheritance, which is in a sense what we mean by "race", is a very modern view. The Greeks, as you say, distinguished different groups primarily as civilised and barbarian and biological inheritance played no part in that. In medieval Europe, the distinction was in relation to faith—between those who were part of the body of Christ, as it were, and those who were outside of it and again, it was not related to any kind of biological inheritance. It became an argument, eventually, about biological inheritance when there was a discussion about whether Native Americans could become Christians. The idea was raised that they could not, that they did not have the natural capacity to become Christians. But interestingly, the Catholic Church, the Pope, all argued that they did and that they should not be enslaved.

So this idea of race as a biological category is a very modern one—it's post-eighteenth century. But you could say that in order to have a notion of racial differences, you first have to have a notion of equality and common humanity. The notion of racial difference and racial inferiority makes no difference in a world where you don't have the notion of equality and a common humanity. And it was through the Enlightenment that those notions really hit deep. Of course, these ideas of equality were there in

Christian thought prior to that, but there were very circumscribed. So it was through the Enlightenment that these ideas became a major way to think about the world. And, in a sense, the idea of race grew from a contradiction or a conflict, between an abstract belief in equality and the reality of an unequal world that the new capitalist world threw up. In the eighteenth century, most Enlightenment philosophers believed that progress could overcome social divisions. They also believed that if you took somebody from Africa and brought them to Europe, then his or her skin colour would change because it was just a surface thing that had nothing to do with an underlying identity. But two things happened. One was that that the attachment to equality, began eroding, because of a political fear of social disruption, social change, and so on. And secondly, empirically, not only did people's skin colour not change, but those social divisions became deeper than ever.

*Was this, presumably, because different groups of people were suddenly coming into close contact and became very aware of their differences?*

Well it's more than that. In a sense, the idea of race originated not in relation to Europe and its colonies, but rather within European nations themselves. Nowadays, we think about race as being synonymous with a question of skin colour. But for the Victorians it wasn't. Not until the late Victorian era did it become synonymous with skin colour. It was during the early to mid-Victorian era that the idea of race really began to take off. And it was as much a question of social status, and class, as it was about skin colour. The rural poor, the working class, were seen as racially distinct. And I read one interesting story, in relation to this, about the Governor of Fiji and his wife. And their nurse thinks that the Fijians are despicable and below her and so on. And the Governor's wife says, "poor nurse. She doesn't understand that the royalty of Fiji are the same as us, but she will never be the same as them." And so, that shows a kind of interesting clash of class and race and it demonstrates the degree to which class ruled the way people thought about biological divisions. Although we no longer think of class as being about biological inheritance.

But to go back to the question of "why am I interested in this?" Well I think many of those ideas about human differences have given rise not just to biological notions of race, but to cultural notions of identity, too. They're both rooted in the same romantic view of human differences. And the problem with this is that if you define people according to a particular category then you will treat those people according to the category you put them in, rather than according to who they are or what their particular needs are or what their particular aspirations or their particular goals are.

*How would you relate all of this to your critique of multiculturalism?*

Well, for example—Muslims in Britain are treated as if they belong to a single group, called "Muslims", and are all entirely driven by their faith. So, when the Prime Minister wants to say something to 'the Muslim community', what does he do? He goes to the local mosque; or he talks to the Muslim Council of Britain. He doesn't do what he would do with any other citizen of Britain, which is: talk to them as citizens of Britain, who are motivated by as many different fears and aspirations as anybody else. We've come to believe that diversity stops at the edge of minority communities. Britain's a diverse place but we've come to believe that minority communities, somehow, are homogenous wholes, where everybody thinks the same, believes the same, and is driven by the same things. Yet Muslim communities are probably more diverse than any other communities in Britain. And yet, public policy, and the whole political system, is based on the idea that there is a thing called "the Muslim community". And that is the problem with society treating identity in this fashion.

*There are two slightly separate responses to that. Firstly, it is true that Muslims in Britain are a heterogeneous bunch. And we should speak, at the very least, of Muslim communities, rather than a Muslim community. But within Islam, there is also an idea of the Umma—the global identity or group to which all Muslims belong. So how does that relate to your argument? And secondly, Ziauddin Sardar has been quite critical of what you might call the left-wing critique of multiculturalism which says that all it does is to entrench differences. He says that often that is simply a veiled attack on British Muslims and certain British Muslim values. Now, he's obviously somebody who is not an advocate of very extreme forms of Islamism, but he still feels very sensitive about the way the multiculturalism debate is going. So how do you respond to that?*

Well, in terms of the point about the Umma, you've got to realise that again, we take the politicised notion of Islam to be the one that everybody holds about Islam. But most of those in my parents' generation didn't have a notion of an Umma to which they are attached. They hardly went to mosque, and most of the men drank. They didn't make a song and dance about any of this, but they did it and nobody was ostracised because of it. And yet, they saw themselves as pious, devout Muslims. So, it's only very recently that this idea has emerged that Muslims have this intense attachment to the Caliphate, to the Umma, and to a political notion of Islam. But that's a very, very new notion. Obviously it's an old notion in the sense that it comes out of the break-up of the caliphate in 1924, but it's a new notion, in that it's one that's been politicised only very recently. And people like Gilles Kepel, the French sociologist will say that what has driven this is globalisation, and the break-up of any common identity. And so this has created a desire to find a new common identity, and I think there's a lot of truth in that. There's a belief, for instance, that Islam is a total worldview—that all Muslims believe that you cannot separate faith from the state for instance. But go to America. American Muslims have absolutely no problem in separating faith and the state, and in seeing faith as a private matter. So, it depends on the specific circumstances—Islam is not a single monolithic view that all Muslims have.

On the second issue, it is clear that there is a critique of multiculturalism which is rooted in a hostility to Islam and a hostility to immigration. But I think part of the problem is that both sides in this debate confuse the notion of values and the notion of peoples. In other words, on the one hand you'd have

the nativists who'd say, "in order to have common values in this culture, you have to have an ethnically homogenous nation." On the other, you have multiculturalists that would say, "because we have people from different backgrounds, we can't have a set of common values." I think both are wrong, because both confuse people with values. There's no reason why, if you come from a different background, you cannot have common values. So I think that, in that sense, there's a commonality between the arguments of the nativist, if you like, and the arguments of the multiculturalist, where they both confuse the notions of people and values. And part of the problem has also been a conflation of the debate on immigration with the debate on multiculturalism. A part of the problem is that you tend to find, in general terms, that on one side of the debate, you have people who are anti-immigration, and anti-multiculturalism; and on the other side, you have people who are pro-immigration, and pro-multiculturalism. Now, personally, I am a massive fan of open borders, but I am opposed to multiculturalism. So I don't accept the way that the debate's framed. I think that when we talk of multiculturalism, we often confuse two things: one is the diversity of lived experience, the other is multiculturalism as a political process. Now, diversity as a lived experience is a very good thing, and it's an argument for open borders.

*How would you define "diversity" in that context?*

It's what happens when you have a great deal of immigration to your country, and people with different values, different beliefs, and different lifestyles. And I think that's all for the good, because it allows one to broaden one's horizons—to think about the way other people may do things. Multiculturalism as a political process is about asserting, in the public sphere, cultural differences. It says, "these cultural differences should be institutionalised; they should be the basis of public policy" and so on. And the problem, actually, is that multiculturalism as a political process undermines what is good about diversity as lived experience. Because the question that is never asked is "what is good about diversity?" And what it can do is allow one to break out of our own little ethnic box, to think about the way other people do things, to engage with them, to broaden our horizons. By arguing with them, having dialogue with them, and making judgments about them, we can, paradoxically, through that process create a more universal language of citizenship. The problem with multiculturalism as a political process is that it makes such a dialogue and debate much more difficult precisely because you've been put in these little ethnic boxes. And so you're only seen as an authentic member of a group if you act in the way that the label on the box says you are supposed to.

There's a Danish MP called Nasser Khader who was opposed to the protest against those Danish cartoons. He was completely in favour of *Jyllands Posten* printing them. And he tells this story about how he meets an editor of a rival paper in Denmark who said to him: "all Muslims in Denmark are opposed to the Danish cartoons." And Khader said, "well, no—I'm not opposed." And so the editor replied, "but you're not a real Muslim!" There is this kind of concerted argument which says "only if you believe in certain things are you a Muslim. Anyone else, who doesn't believe them, isn't a real Muslim." And therefore, if you define identity only through people authentically believing certain things, then the diversity of those communities gets completely missed out. And I think that's what multiculturalism does, as a political process. It reduces that diversity. It forces you into a box and it defines certain specific ways of being, which I think is a problem. So that is why I'm for diversity as a lived experience but against multiculturalism as a political process.

*Your interest in the diversity of lived experience and your ambitions for that as a way of living seem to demand a certain kind of political society which isn't totalitarian in its views, and which is based on certain principles and values. Could you outline what some of those values are?*

There are a whole host of different values. Take equality, for instance. One of the interesting things about multiculturalism, it seems to me, is that it has transformed what we mean by "equality". When I was growing up, "equality" meant "the right to be treated the same despite one's differences". Now, it means "the right to be treated differently because of

those differences". So it seems that the whole notion of equality has been transformed in a way which is deeply regressive. So, yes, the notion of equality is very important. As is the notion of democracy—the idea that people should be treated as citizens of the country, and should have a say, as citizens of the country, about how it is run. So the democratic process is important, and that means that the state must not just have a relationship with community leaders but with the people themselves so it can understand the diversity of their views.

*Can you say something about what the idea of "home" means to you?*

Well, home's an interesting concept. Because "home" derives, in a sense, from the same thing that identity does, which is your relationship to other people. That's what defines who you are and what you are and what you think of as home. To a certain extent, one's biography is also important. I mean I grew up in Manchester and so I support Lancashire in the cricket. Now, there is no reason why I should do that, it's a purely tribal attraction in that sense. Although I support Liverpool in football actually, which is strange for somebody who grew up in Manchester! But again, this comes down to tribal attachment. I came here before knowing anything about Liverpool/Manchester rivalry, yet Liverpool happened to be the first team I saw play, and because these things are irrational, I ended up living my life as a Liverpool supporter. But these are irrational tribal attachments and we all have them. And part of the problem, I think, is that we confuse important aspects of one's relationship with the outside world and with other people, with what are fairly minor or trivial attachments. So I will get devastated next week when Liverpool fails to win the Premiership, but that is minor compared to the broader things that are important. And part of the way, I think, that identity has changed, is that those broader, political or philosophical attachments have become less important, and those minor attachments have become more important. But going back to the question of home, I can think about home in the same way that I can think about identity. Our sense of home can be as variegated as our identity. We will call different things home, depending on who we talk to, what the context is, and so on. So Britain is home to me. When I go abroad on holiday or whatever, I feel like a stranger because these are places where I don't know the customs, I don't have a history of living there, I don't know their people, and I can't speak their language very well. I'm part of their culture—if I watched their TV, I wouldn't understand the jokes, I wouldn't understand the sitcoms. All of that plays in to how you think of home. So what I'm saying is: you have certain relationships which are important, which surround you and which give you a certain sense of purchase on that society in which you live. There is your history, the way you understand the culture, and so on. But I could quite easily have grown up in France or Italy, in which case, I would have come to Britain, seen Fawlty Towers and not understood the jokes there at all. So, in some ways, when you talk about home it is all contingent. So, even though I see Britain as home, and I relate to British culture, it's only an accident that I don't see France as home or Italy as home, in which case they would be equally important to me, but also equally contingent to me.

*And is it that awareness of contingency that allows for us to avoid any sense of chauvinism when it comes to an idea of home? If we accept that something is ultimately contingent and, in that respect, arbitrary, it can, presumably, prevent arguments about one place being intrinsically more valuable or better than another?*

Well, there are places which I do think are better, because I have a greater attachment to them. And there are places which I think are better, even though I don't have an attachment to them. I mean, I happen to like New York—I think it's a great city, a better city than most cities in the world—but that's not because I have an attachment to it. It's because there's a feel about it that I like. So does that sense of contingency mean that I'm not so chauvinistic? I don't know. I don't think it's a question of contingency. It's more to do with my political-philosophical beliefs, in terms of what I think is important. But those beliefs, also, lead me to recognise that what I call home is important, but it's also contingent, in that sense—"arbitrary" is a good word.

*So, for you, "identity", in the most important definition is something that can be forged and actively chosen?*

Not necessarily. I haven't chosen to be British. I haven't chosen to live here. My parents came here, and I've grown up here, and as I've said, my parents could have settled in France or Italy or America or elsewhere, in which case, you'd be talking, in one sense, to a very different Kenan Malik.

*But for you, the things that you considered important at the very start of this conversation were relationships, not just to people but to ideas.*

Well you can choose a relationship to ideas. But not all your relationships are chosen. I mean I know people who are atheists, but who were brought up as Catholic, and they still have this residual attachment to Catholicism, which is something that they find very difficult to shake off. So, for instance, I've had debates with people about euthanasia, for instance, where people's residual attachment to religious beliefs, even though they might be atheist now, shape the way they look at the issue. So, I don't think it is entirely chosen, but certainly a bit of it is chosen, and I think that is because we are not entirely rational—we are rational, but we are not *entirely* rational. We have emotional as well as rational attachments to ideas. But the important thing is that we are *able* to choose in some contexts. And so I think there's a distinction to be drawn between saying "everything's chosen" and saying "one is able to choose some things". And because I don't accept that everything is chosen, I think that the choices we do make are important in shaping who we are and what we are.

# THE HINCH TWINS

Hugh Aldersey-Williams

Twins challenge our notion of individual identity. We find identical twins interesting because they are clones, not only in the strict biological sense, but also in the popular use of the word: the one often appears and behaves so like the other that we think of the two of them as interchangeable. In our excitement at seeing twins, we implicitly regard each sibling as something less than a full individual in their own right. Is this fair? What does this perception of ours do to each twin's sense of self?

Scientists too have a strong interest in twins. By comparing pairs of identical and non-identical twins, they can begin to tease out the influences of our genes and our environment, both of which interactively determine our character, health and behaviour. Large-scale twin studies around the world are devoted to the goal of identifying the genetic factors in diseases, but their remit often runs well beyond this, and twins' responses are sought on everything from preferences in art and music to religious predilections—matters that might seem to have no biological component.

All of this special attention reinforces the idea of twins as freaks and eats away at their individuality. The Hinch twins, Charlotte and Emily, in their turn, challenge this preconception of what it means to be a twin. At the time of writing, the two girls are respectively aged one and four. They are biological non-identical twins because their eggs were released and fertilised at the same time; one was frozen and later implanted in the mother's womb. Unlike most twins, then, Charlotte and Emily won't grow up wearing matching outfits, which is something that many pairs of twins continue to do into adulthood, playing up to the performative aspects of identity, "acting the twins".

The girls provoke us to wonder whether our feeling that twins are special is a matter of semantics rather than something based in observed reality. To an embryologist, they are twins regardless of the different dates of their birth, and yet they are of no interest to scientists involved in twin studies because they break the standard condition of growing up at the same time as well as in the same family.

Charlotte and Emily's father, Julian, is an identical twin. He and his brother Jeremy did grow up in this typical way. They were dressed alike, given identical toys, and shared a private language. But in adolescence they began to assert their individual identities, consciously expressing different preferences in clothes, hairstyles and music. Yet in some respects, their lives too have been markedly different from the moment of birth: Jeremy came out of hospital soon after he was born, but Julian had to stay in for several weeks, and attributes his phobia of cotton-covered buttons to his frequent exposure to nurses' uniforms during this spell.

It is clear that both genes and environment are very powerful forces influencing our development. Which is the more powerful? More to the point, perhaps: why are we asking? Are scientists bent on proving that it's nature over nurture in order to vindicate theories of genetics, a field over which they have only recently gained some degree of mastery? Are the rest of us hoping that nurture wins out because it leaves us the hope that we ourselves can exert control over our own lives?

And where does this leave twins? Are they only interesting because of the coincidence of their births? In a scientific sense, the answer is sometimes yes. But in general, perhaps, we should be more mindful that twins are individuals too.

192/193
194/195
196/197
198/199
200/201
202/203

Charlotte (left) and Emily Hinch are the twin daughters of Julian Hinch and his wife Lisa. They were born in 2005 and 2008 respectively following in vitro fertilisation. One fertilised egg was implanted immediately, while others were stored, and a further egg was implanted later. The difference in age immediately subverts our received notions about what it means to be a twin. We tend to regard twins born at the same time as curiosities because they are clones, and to undervalue their individual identities correspondingly. Charlotte and Emily should be spared this indignity.

All images courtesy of the Hinch Family.

Julian and Jeremy Hinch as infants, 1966. Though 'identical', Julian and Jeremy's lives were markedly different from the very moment of birth. Jeremy came out of hospital soon after he was born, but Julian had to stay in hospital for the first month of his life. His sojourn left him with an aversion to the cotton-covered button of nurses' uniforms, and suggests that, contrary to much anecdotal evidence, twins do not always share their passions and phobias.

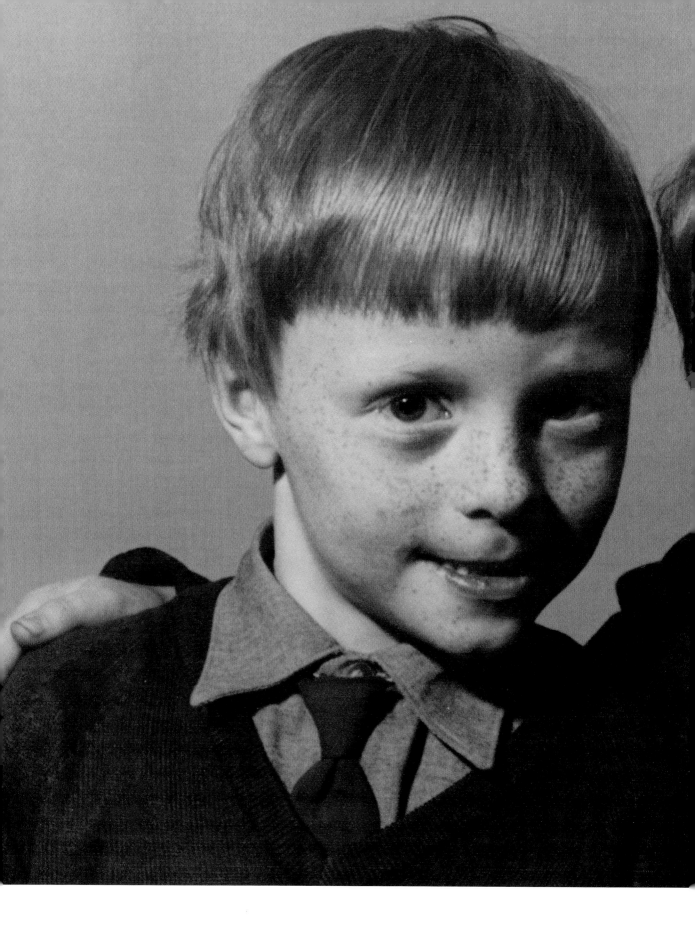

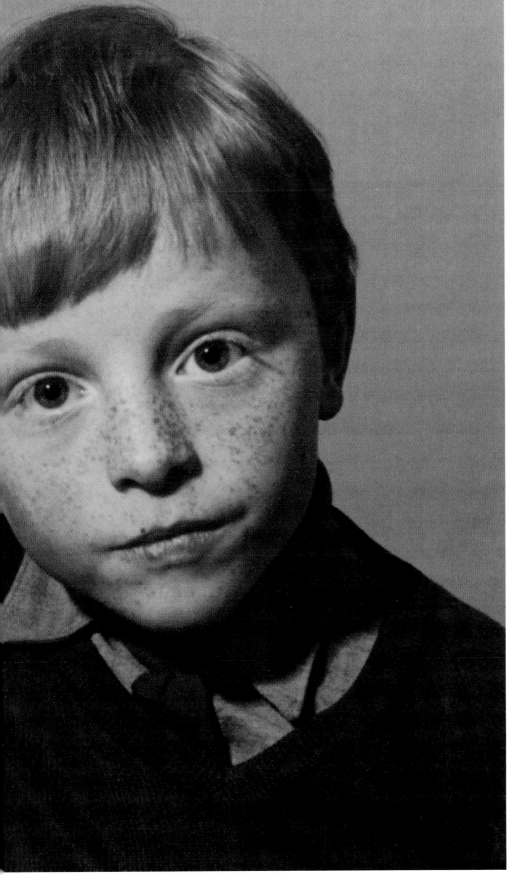

Julian (left) and Jeremy as schoolboys.

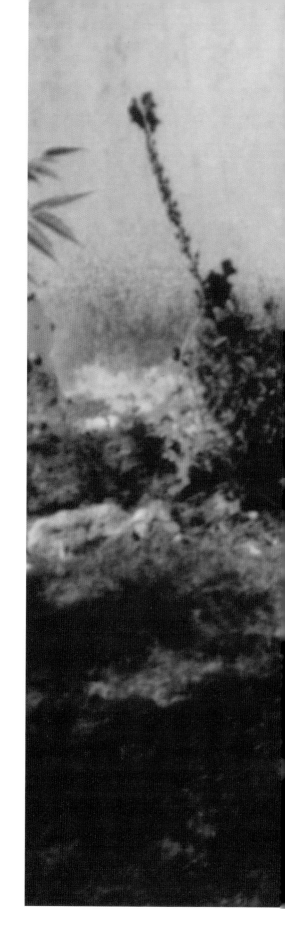

Jeremy (left) and Julian playing. Like most twins, the boys were often dressed alike.

Julian (left) and Jeremy as teenagers. At this age, Julian expressed a preference for jeans,
Jeremy for pale trousers.

Jeremy (left) and Julian beneath a poster for *Quadrophenia*.

Lisa and Julian Hinch have taken frequent photographs documenting their daughters, Emily (left) and Charlotte (right), as they grow up.

# ZIAUDDIN SARDAR

is a scholar, writer and cultural critic who specialises in the future of Islam, science and cultural relations. *Prospect* magazine has named him as one of Britain's top 100 public intellectuals and *The Independent* newspaper calls him: "Britain's own Muslim polymath". He has written or edited 45 books over a period of 30 years. Recent titles include *Balti Britain: a Journey Through the British Asian Experience*; and *How Do You Know: Reading Ziauddin Sardar on Islam, Science and Cultural Relations*.

---

*Who are you?*

Well that is a very loaded question. I don't think it is ever simple to say who you are. It has always been a complex question, but I think it's even more so today, because of all the changes that have taken place through globalisation and so on. And this is not just true of me—I think it's true of most people. Nobody these days would say, "I'm this—full stop." You are by definition a number of different things, and some of the things that you are may be contested. So, you might say, "I'm a white guy—full stop." But the moment you say, "actually I'm a white gay guy and a gay guy" then that becomes contested, you see. Because as a white guy, you have certain rights which most people will recognise. But they might not recognise that you have those rights if you are gay as well. So, that second category that you might apply to yourself means that your identity immediately becomes contested and problematic. So, the point I'm trying to make is: there is no simple identity. So, I cannot simply say, "I'm British and Muslim" because both of these identities are contested.

That said I probably would not say that I'm English. On the whole, Indians and Pakistanis don't say "we are English Pakistanis or English Indians". We always say, "we are British Pakistanis or Indian Pakistanis". Whereas in Scotland they will always say that they are a Pakistani Scot, or an Indian Scot, and it is the same with the Welsh. This is because the Welsh and the Scottish identities are less contested and much more open, inclusive and flexible. Whereas English identity is far more fixed and exclusivist—it's connected with Middle England, it's connected with foxhunting and the House of Lords and all that kind of stuff. And most Asians do not identify with that. But if your identity is connected with things like Hogmanay and haggis, well it is very easy to enjoy Hogmanay, and very easy to eat haggis and so on. But we don't find it as easy to incorporate Englishness. Because Englishness has that aloofness about it, does it not?

If I say I'm British, then I can define myself in one way. But if I say I am a Muslim, then that becomes a very problematic category. Because immediately I have to say: "and actually, I'm one of those liberal Muslims", because I don't want to be associated with the fundamentalists and the Taliban. And then I have to say, "well, basically, even though they've got the Taliban in Pakistan—the Taliban are trying to take over Pakistan—I am a non-Talibani person of Pakistani heritage." So, I think that our identities are much more problematic nowadays than they ever have been and they are much more contested and interconnected than they have ever been. So it is never easy to say who you are. The answer is not going to be a universal answer, it is contextual. And it can depend on where you're asking me the question. So, if you ask me the question, say, at an Indian wedding I will say, "actually, I'm a Pakistani from Lahore", or if you ask me who I am at an expats' dinner in Kuala Lumpur where I lived a long time I'd say, "I'm a Londoner." Because everybody there are expats, they know that we're all from the UK and so there is no point telling them you're British. They really want to know whether you're a Yorkshire lad or a London lad or, if you come from the valleys.

So, the answer depends on the context that you ask the question. And that context can be both environmental or geographical. The answer is always multiple, because we are never one thing. We are always multiple things. Sometimes we can be contradictory things, and sometimes we can be complementary things. But we are always several things at the same time. I think the problem that most people find is that they like to put everybody in a box. We still have this very strange notion that everybody is one thing. And that's very scientistic— that notion that we can put people in boxes.

*Could you talk about this in relation to the question: who do we think you are?*

Yes. But first of all, we have to ask why do we need these boxes? This comes from a very long tradition of Western thought—going back to the Enlightenment—that believes that in order to understand a problem, you have to isolate it. You have to put it in a nice little neat box and then you can handle and solve it. That's how most scientific problems up 'til now have been solved. So the belief is that in order to understand somebody, you must understand them scientifically, which means isolating them, and putting them in a box. So if someone puts me in a box saying: "this guy is a Muslim", then you automatically assume that you know or understand me.

You see this kind of thing all the time in the study of anthropology. The white man invented two social sciences: sociology and anthropology. The function of sociology was to study white society and keep the working classes and labour classes apart from the aristocratic and land-owning classes—the ruling elite. Sociology studies working classes. It never studies society as a collective thing. It is a discipline that was designed to gain knowledge of the working class to keep them in one place. Equally, the function of anthropology is to study *non*-white societies and its aim was to learn how to manage and control them. The attitude of those who founded anthropology in the eighteenth century was: "we need to learn to manage these people." The question for the administrators in India, the Raj, was: "how do we turn these people into the kind people we can understand?" So they said, "we need to develop an education system that turns them into little Englishmen who are brown. That way we will be able to understand them." You see? They didn't know what to do with the complexity of the Indian culture. It was too mind-boggling and complex for them.

So, this idea of putting peoples into boxes comes from sociology and anthropology—from a scientistic way of thinking. And the assumption is that if you put the people in a box, then you can basically understand, manage and control them. So, if people look at me they might say: "this guy looks Asian. So, he must be either Indian or Pakistani." Then, if they ask me who I am and I say, "I'm Pakistani", then I

am immediately put in a "Pakistani" box. And this means that, if they have some understanding of Pakistan, they will think that they can understand me and relate to me in a way that makes them feel at ease and so on. But even if this analysis worked in the past—30, 40 or 50 years ago—it certainly doesn't work nowadays. Because if we put five people in a box and labelled them "Pakistanis", they could still be totally different. One of them might be a Talibani who hates you; another could be an Anglophile, who comes from a family of Raj-supporting people, and who loves you and so on; the third could be an American Pakistani who grew up and lived all his life in America; the fourth could be a British Pakistani, like me; and the fifth one could be the product of some mixed marriage. Yet you've labelled them all exactly the same. You see?

So, putting people in boxes doesn't work as a way of identifying them. What it does do is to give power to other people. So, if you put me in a box labelled "Pakistani", then it makes you feel as if you can represent me, or, it allows you to think that you understand how I'm going to represent myself. So many of the ways that we have of identifying people inevitably involves some element of control and management.

*Is it a better question to ask: who, or what, are you not?*

Yes, in some respects. But if you ask what you are not, you are not asking a universal question. By definition, the question is a contextual one. After all, you're not asking me, "are you a glass" or "are you a train?" You're asking me a very contextual question. But because of this, it may be easier to answer, generally, than "who are you?" Because that question is a universal rather than a contextual one.

*What do you mean when you say you are British?*

Well I mean that I am loyal to the state. But I do not believe that there is a monolithic notion of identity called "Britishness", or that all British people are exactly the same. I am British in the sense that I am loyal to Britain. I grew up in Hackney and Britain made me who I am. Britain gave me primary schooling which was free, it gave me university schooling which was free—I got a grant without which I would not have survived or lived, and then I got a grant to do a Master's degree and to do a PhD. So Britain made me and I owe a great deal of allegiance to the state here. Without that state, I would not be here. But if you were to tell me that Britishness means I should uncritically accept everything the state says, then my answer would be no! Because I have a mind of my own, and amongst other things, Britain also taught me to think! So that's why I cannot accept certain oppressive things that the state does. So I can be critical of the state, but my criticism of the state does not necessarily mean I am disloyal to the state.

*You frequently debate the issue of multiculturalism with your critics. Could you explain what that word means and how you respond to their position on this?*

Well first of all, I think that my critics have a very simplistic and rather monolithic notion of multiculturalism. They think multiculturalism is one simple thing, and that it is a policy of the British Government to promote ethnicity and to promote equality and opportunity within ethnic communities. And I don't think multiculturalism is anything of the sort. I think multiculturalism is about how we empower all the different segments of our society. These segments may be multi-ethnic, multi-religious, multi-sexual orientation, and multi-age. Nowadays age differences are vast. I mean, sometimes differences in age are much more prominent than, say, differences in sexual orientation. So how do you get these different segments to participate in society—not just in the public space but in society as a whole—in terms that are equal and inclusive? That's what I think multiculturalism is all about. It means any viable mechanism that brings all the diversity of the society together but does it in such a way so that there's equality of opportunity.

I think you need two things to enable that. One is power. Now, in all the discussions about multiculturalism, power is never mentioned. My critics, for example, never ever talk about power. For me, multiculturalism begins with power and ends with power. It means that you as a totally different kind of individual, and me as a totally different kind of individual, should have equal power to participate. If I am marginalised and live in a ghetto, and you live in Hampstead but are a lesbian or gay individual, then it might be that neither of us have equal opportunity to participate, but that does not mean that we are equally excluded. And all of this does not necessarily have anything to do with ethnicity. I went down to Oldham recently, and there are three communities there fighting each other: white, Pakistanis and Bangladeshis. They all live in three different enclaves, but all three have the same problem. So you can't say that multiculturalism is simply about the Pakistanis or the Bangladeshis, because the whites, they are just as marginalised. That's why the BNP is making so much progress. The whites are just as marginalised and they need jobs and social housing and so on as much as anyone else.

So, multiculturalism is not just about focusing on ethnicity. It is about power. Multiculturalism is about the equality of power. And in any particular context, you can show that certain marginalised elements of a community will have more power, and certain other marginalised elements of a community will have less power. So there are two different levels of disadvantage or marginalisation. But whereas one group may be disadvantaged in psychological but not economic terms, the other group may live in abject poverty and might find it difficult to find enough sustenance to ensure their physical survival.

Now, I'm not saying that the psychological isolation is not important, but everything needs to be seen in context. I recently wrote the introduction to a book which a friend of mine has edited about gated communities. There are more and more of these communities—where people effectively lock themselves up—emerging. And there was the case of one of these communities in Birmingham being told by the council that they had to pay more for their rubbish to be collected because the nature of the way they were living meant that it was harder for the bin men to reach them. And these guys in the gated community used the argument that other minority communities were gated as well because they were ghettoised. And so they tried to claim that they should pay no more than those in the ghettos. But this is obviously problematic. A ghetto may be gated in a different way. But the survival level of a person in a ghetto is not the same as that of someone who has chosen to live in a gated community. They are different kinds of ghetto. They're both ghettos because they're both isolated. But one exists by choice, and the other comes out of necessity. Those people who are poor will do anything to get out of the ghetto, whereas those people in the gated community will do anything to get into their ghetto! You can't look at both of these ghettos in the same way. So, I think the power equation has just totally been missing and is not understood. Different minority communities have different degrees of power, and we really do need to tackle that.

My first point is that there's no multiculturalism without addressing questions of power. Then the second point is: there's no multiculturalism without addressing the question of self-representation. Power and self-representation in my way of thinking go hand in hand. And again, my critics overlook the no notion of self-representation.

*What do you mean by that?*

Well take the various groups that might be disadvantaged or excluded. If you go to a group in a ghetto and say: "these are your problems, and we are going to solve them", the people in that ghetto might say, "no—hang on. These are not our problems. These are your perceptions of what our problems are. Our problems are actually this, this, this, and this." Only the minority that suffers can know what those problems are. You can't impose on them your notion of what their problems are. In the same way you can't impose your notion of who I am on me. To understand who I am, or to appreciate who I am, you need to listen to who I think I am. Even if what I think about myself is wrong.

So unless you have that notion of self-representation, you are not going to balance the power equation. The power equation requires self-representation. If you come to me and say: "oh you poor lot, we know you don't have any power so we are going to help you out" then that would be patronising. Rather, first of all, you need to allow me to represent myself. You need to let me say who I think I am. After all, you may think that my problem is that I am an unemployed person living in a ghetto and that I need to get off benefits. But I might think that my problem is that I should stay on benefits, because, given the fact that I do not have many qualifications, the job I would end up getting would pay less than the benefits. My solution would be not to get me employed, but to get me educated. You should not insist that I should be off the dole—because if you do that, I'm going to resist it. But I could be totally open to the idea of getting some qualifications. So, unless you listen to what I have to say, you will not discover what the solution to my problem really is. So, self-representation is a vital part of multiculturalism. My notion of multiculturalism is not fixed. Multiculturalism, just like identity, is fluid.

*Your suggestion that multiculturalism needs those two things, equality of power and self-representation, seems to demand a certain type of society that will encompass and encourage that.*

Yes. You see, multiculturalism is not an empty notion. It demands certain political concessions. For example, how can we have multiculturalism without redistribution of wealth for example?

*Can you unpack those things that it requires and also why you think those are good things?*

Yes. Well, I think the redistribution of wealth is good because I believe in equality—equality's good. But that doesn't mean that I believe that every person is equal to every other person. It's not a question of "*a* equals *b*", because clearly, some people are more educated than others for example. Or some people can do certain jobs better than others. Some are cut out to make good television presenters, but others hate publicity—they are very private. So, I'm not talking about a kind of "*a* equals *b*" equality. But I do believe that a society which enables an equality of opportunity will be a much healthier, more sustainable more prosperous society that one that does not. And there is research to prove this. I'm not saying anything specifically original. There's a recent book called *The Spirit Level* by Richard Wilkinson and Kate Pickett which shows that a society with a more equal distribution of wealth is an economically better society. And so, my notion of multiculturalism cannot be divorced from our culture, more generally. And there are several different notions of multiculturalism, but the one that is operating today in Britain, we got from America. And it began with the 1960s student movement when they began to chant: "hey, ho— Western culture has to go!" That was the slogan of multiculturalism. It was all about teaching different cultures in the universities and changing the way courses were taught. Their point was basically that you cannot look at everything in the world from the perspective of a single Western culture. But even this notion was absurd, because Western culture is not a single thing either. American Western culture is probably very different from British Western culture, which is probably very different from French Western culture. But even if you just look in America, there are different 'Western cultures'. In political terms, if you look at the Democratic culture and the Republican culture—they're like two bulls in a ring, they couldn't be more different from each other. And there is a huge contrast between East Coast and West Coast; California's totally different from Texas, and so on and so forth. So, the idea of a monolithic Western culture is meaningless, it doesn't exist. But the way various academic disciplines are structured, can lead us to think that there is a single Western culture which comes out of Enlightenment. And this is what my critics, like Kenan Malik, argue—that there are universal values of the Enlightenment. But I find this to be absolutely rubbish. First of all, there's nothing really Western about the Enlightenment, and second, there is nothing particularly enlightening about the Enlightenment. Because from an Islamic perspective, the Enlightenment took the best of what we had, and inverted it. Muslims have always believed in reason, but we always believed that reason has to be tempered with some sort of ethical norms and values. And that was the great debate in Islam between philosophers and theologians. Islam discovered Greek philosophy when it was first translated in the early eighth century. And this led to a mushrooming of Islamic philosophers. But then they began to find problems with what they were reading. They would say: "hang on—we don't like this idea of pure blood in Plato's *Republic*, because that does not allow for equality as we understand it in Islam." They were actually identifying notions of eugenics in

Platonic thought and were very concerned by it. And they would ask "what is this natural law in Aristotle?" Because many of them were aggressively anti-slavery, because the Koran said, "free the slave". And so they found the Aristotelian idea of slavery quite repellent from an Islamic point of view. So, they were great believers in reason. Indeed, Ibn Rushd wrote the greatest defence of reason—better than any Enlightenment thinker like Kant or anybody else. But right at the end of his book, he concludes by saying: "I know not; God knows best." And what that means is that reason should make you humble, at the end of the day—you need certain amounts of ethics to guide you.

*And those should be enshrined in society?*

Yes they should be enshrined in society. But what the Enlightenment did, was that it took the Muslim ideas of reason and all that from us and then, totally disconnected it from the idea of any ethics and value. For us, metaphysics and physics went together. You couldn't do physics without doing metaphysics. But they said, "no. Physics is a different discipline from Metaphysics. They are different phenomena, the two are not related." If someone was to go to a rational philosopher and scientist like Ibn Sina and say "I need you to make some poison." He would say: "my science teaches me how to make poison, but my religion and ethics teaches me not to make it. So, I am not going to make it for you." There is a sense of 'ethics in action' throughout his science. But what we have now is an idea of reason which is totally and absolutely instrumental, and so, you can justify anything in terms of reason.

*Could you say something about extreme forms of identification—maybe with reference to the Taliban and other fundamentalisms. What is their appeal?*

For me, any identity that is seen as monolithic immediately becomes oppressive and problematic. And you don't even have to go to the Taliban—it could be anybody or anything. Unless you allow for some flexibility, or a certain amount of uncertainty, you risk extremism. The problem is this idea of a world where things are certain, and everyone knows their place, and everything was in its place, is wrong. That does not exist and has not existed for a long time. We just do not think like that anymore. So, uncertainty is built into our world. And so uncertainty must be coupled to identity, as well. You can't say that your identity is certain. I mean perhaps it is if you live in the middle of England, and you don't go to the next village, and you've spent all your life there and you were born there and you know you'll die there. But for most people that world doesn't exist anymore. But even if you did live like that, the world will infringe on you, because the moment you go inside your house, and switch the television on and watch some American TV show then that will change your identity—because you will begin thinking of yourself in a different way. You will change your notion of who you are, simply by looking at the television. And then, the moment you leave your little village and go to Oxford or London or Edinburgh or Glasgow, you will come across people from all over the world. And that might make you want to change the way you live or your job or whatever. You will discover things which you would never have discovered had you remained in that little village, and so, you become something different in that sense. There can be no notion of a certain, fixed identity, that it's fixed and certain forever. And any identity that is seen as fixed and certain forever becomes nasty and brutish and oppressive. It's not just about the Taliban.

*Does a fixed identity have to do that in order to sustain itself?*

Yes. I mean, why are the Taliban so nasty and evil? Basically, they're absolutely cruel and brutal because they think you must believe what they do. But if you are a great scientistic individual who thinks that science equals truth, and you go around saying that, then you are doing exactly the same thing as the Taliban. True, you're not engaging in violence, but that is the next step. Don't forget that the Nazis were very heavily into eugenics and science and all the rest, so, it's not that far removed. Basically, the Taliban are no more different from the settlers in Israel. Those settlers have a very fixed identity—it is non-negotiable, and fixed in time and place forever. And the settlers are some of the cruellest people you'll

come across. Or, if you go to Middle America, you'll find these Christian cults who have a very single, fixed notion of who they are.

*Can you say something about the idea of "home"?*

The idea of home is very, very interesting now. We have multiple identities, which are all fluid. And sometimes we want to play games—we want to use the identity that suits us at a particular time. Sometimes, we might want to hide some of our identities. So, from that point of view, the idea of having a fixed home can become problematic. Now, the idea of "home" should not be seen as the idea of "roots". Home is not necessarily where you have roots—we are not like trees fixed in that sense. So, we are capable of making different homes. But my idea is that the home now is always the displaced home. All homes are displaced homes. And you can put down roots wherever you want to. For example, I lived in Kuala Lumpur for seven years, and that's my home. I set my roots there and I always take a bit of Kuala Lumpur with me wherever I go. I wrote a book on Kuala Lumpur, I love the place. And I miss it when I'm not there, because I laid the roots there. It's part of me. But then I lived in Chicago for three years and I just did not take to the place in that sense. So, I don't go around with Chicago on my shoulder, but I do go around with Kuala Lumpur on my shoulder. So, homes are always displaced homes, they are not fixed homes, in that sense. And the moment you make your home fixed, then problems arise. The most brutish sense of this can be seen with the settler who says, "God gave me this piece of land, and it's mine, and this is my home." And that will mean that you will have to forever defend that little patch of sacred land from everybody else and so there will be perpetual warfare, as it were. Or its like the Taliban saying, "God has made this an Islamic State." If "home" relates to a fixed idea of a nation, then you could end up defending the idea of a nation, and that is very, very problematic.

*But there are certain principles that you would think are good to defend?*

Principles and home are not necessarily related. You could have the same principles wherever you may want to put your roots down or have your home. But home is also about being part of a community. And community nowadays need not be a physically or geographically located community. We need to belong to communities of real people with whom we feel in touch. And that could mean being part of a network of 40 or 50 people who meet regularly and have a connection with each other—even if you only meet once a year, or whatever. And that community then becomes your home. So, home is not necessarily a physical location.

*Why do you write about these ideas and these issues? What are your ambitions in contributing to these debates?*

Well, if I have an ambition, it's to open people's minds in order to enable them to perceive themselves as more than one thing and to see others as more than one thing. I was speaking at the Asia House recently to a mostly Asian crowd. And I kept on saying, "now, look. I don't identify myself with Pakistan, really. I don't identify myself with India, really." What I really identified with, at the end of the day, is the idea of India as a civilisation—which included India, Pakistan, Bangladesh, Sri Lanka, Nepal, Bhutan and even Burma. It was something that was multi-civilisation, multi-ethnic, multi-linguistic, multi-religious. It was a civilisation where you could be different things in different places, and nobody would question that you were that. Rather, they would all acknowledge that difference and thrive on it. But I think this is true for most civilisations.

People in Britain don't realise how diverse indigenous British cultures are. For people like me, the Scouse accent, for example, is incomprehensible! It's like moving from Delhi to Tamil Nadu and coming across a totally different language. But this kind of diversity is what makes our identity and the civilisations within which we live so interesting. So the question I want to ask people is "why do you want to define yourself as one thing?" I guess, at the end of the day, I want my readers or audience to think "I'm far better than I thought myself to be". And hopefully that realisation will lead them to think, "actually, Britain is so much richer than I always thought it to be".

# JOHN SEARLE

is the Slusser Professor of Philosophy and Mills Professor of Philosophy of Mind and Language at the University of California, Berkeley. He is widely noted for his contributions to the philosophy of language, philosophy of mind and social philosophy. He received the Jean Nicod Prize in 2000, and the National Humanities Medal in 2004. His books include *Consciousness and Language; Freedom and Neurobiology*, and *Mind: A Brief Introduction*.

---

*Who are you?*

Who am I? Well, I guess the way you normally answer that question is just by giving your proper name. But if you're asking me as a philosopher, "what is a philosophical conception of my own identity?" then I'd have to say something about my background and my ideals and the various activities that I'm engaged in. So, there's different ways of interpreting the question, "who are you?" and they're not all equivalent.

From a philosophical point of view, I'd distinguish between certain general features that I have. Such as: I'm a Professor of Philosophy, and I was educated at Oxford, and I have written a number of books, and I'm interested in certain kinds of things. And then I might also insist on certain idiosyncratic features of my identity, such as the fact that I care a lot about some things and less about others. So, that's how I would go about answering that. I mean, to answer it in any detail, I'd have to write you an autobiography. So, I'm afraid I have to give you rather a short answer at this time!

*Some people would answer that question by saying, "well, I'm a white American and..."*

Yeah, those categories are less interesting to me than the ones that I was mentioning to you. The colour of my skin and my national origin are, to me, less interesting than the values I have and the kind of activities that I engage in. But I think, as you say, it would depend on who's asking the question and what's the purpose of asking it. If I'm applying for a passport, and they say, "who are you?", then I might give my old passport number.

*So, in general terms, then, how do you understand the word or the term "identity"?*

Well, identity is formally defined very simply. There are certain laws of identity. One is: "everything is identical with itself. If two things are identical, they have all their properties in common. And, if *a* is identical with *b*, and *b* is identical with *c*, then *a* is identical with *c*." So, you get that transitivity, reflexivity and what's called "extensionality"—that is to say, if two objects are identical, and one has a certain property, then you know the other one must have that same property.

*How does that relate to our individual sense of identity? Perhaps you could start by telling us what you see the term "consciousness" as meaning?*

Well, okay. I think "consciousness" is actually very easy to define. Conscious states consist of those states of feeling or awareness that we experience. They typically begin in the morning when you wake up from a dreamless sleep, and they go on all day until you fall asleep again, or die, or otherwise become *un*conscious. In this definition, dreams are also a form of consciousness, even though the characteristic of dreams is different from waking consciousness. So, consciousness, in a common-sense sense, is not hard to identify. But, of course, what we want from a scientific account is a scientific definition in terms of the sorts of brain processes that are identified with consciousness.

In terms of our sense of our individual identity, the features of consciousness that are interesting to us are: first of all, that it has this qualitative character. Every conscious state has some characteristic feel to it. So, drinking beer is different from listening to Beethoven. And then, furthermore, this qualitative character gives consciousness a kind of subjectivity. I mean, I have my consciousness—I can't have your consciousness. And all conscious states come to us as—except in extreme forms of pathology and brain damage—part of a single, unified conscious field. So, I don't just hear your voice, but I hear your voice at the same time as I feel the pressure of a shirt against my back, I hear certain sounds coming from outside, and I see things going on in this room. So, all of our conscious states come as part of a single, unified conscious field. And then, finally, there's this other feature of consciousness—namely, conscious states are typically *about* something. That's what philosophers call "intentionality". Conscious states have intentionality.

Then there is a separate question of: what is it that constitutes our identity over time? What is it

that makes me the same person as the person I was a few years ago or ten years ago or 20 years ago? And there are a number of features that we must consider here. The most important in practical terms is: I have to have the same body. There has to be a continuous body for me to feel that I have the same identity. The second feature we need to consider, if I'm going to preserve my *sense* of myself, is memory. I have to be able to remember that things have happened to me in the past. If I become terribly amnesiac, if I've forgotten absolutely everything, then there's a sense in which I would have lost my identity—I would have lost my sense of myself. And then, I think, there are certain characteristics of a personality that we regard as essential to one's continued identity through time. I do have changes in my personality, but they tend to be gradual, and systematic, and not instantaneous. So, those are the kinds of things that we would actually count if we were trying to decide whether or not somebody is the same person as he was in the past.

*In your writing recently, you make a distinction between consciousness in general and self-consciousness in particular.*

Yes. Some philosophers—like Kant—say that all consciousness is self-consciousness. And I think that's not really true. Often, for human beings, we become self-conscious, and we start thinking about ourselves, and our relationships with other people, and our relationship with our present conscious states to other conscious states. But that's clearly sophisticated and high-level. I don't think my dog, Gilbert, has many experiences of consciousness of himself as a dog. He has conscious experiences. But I don't identify consciousness and self-consciousness. Self consciousness, as I'm using the term, is a very special form of consciousness.

*And do you think that it's impossible to have a sense of identity without a sense of self-consciousness?*

Well, you see, my dog, has a continuous sense of himself engaging in activities, but if you're talking about a higher level sense, does he think, "the experiences that I'm having now are the experiences of the same person, of the same dog, as the experiences that occurred yesterday?" Well that's a difficult question to answer. Humans have consciousness of consciousness, and that's what I'm calling "higher-level", and that consciousness of consciousness is undoubtedly important to our own sense of identity.

*Could you explain to us the difference between ego theory and bundle theory?*

When people talk about the bundle theory, they're talking about David Hume. And David Hume said, "well, really, there isn't anything that makes me the same person as the person I was in the past. It's a kind of illusion that I'm the same person. I'm just a bundle of continuing perceptions, and strictly speaking there is no such thing as personal identity." Now some people say, "no, no, each of us is a separate self, each of us is a separate ego. I am, of course, the one who is experiencing my experiences." Descartes thought that what makes me 'me' is that I am a continuing mental substance.

Now, I'm not sympathetic with either of those views, because I think that they rely on a mistaken conception of experience.

*Could you explain that mistaken conception?*

David Hume had a crazy conception of experience— his idea was that each of our experiences is a separate, independent unity. And I don't think you can make sense of human experiences unless you see that my continuous experience is an experience of the *same person*. I mean, it's like saying that there isn't any difference between one guy having six experiences and six different guys having each one of those experiences. And, of course, there is a difference. If I'm the one guy, I've had those experiences *as part of a single, unified conscious field*.

Now then, in addition to that, I want to say, you can't make sense of human behaviour and human life unless you postulate a self. Because, if you think of what it is to make a decision on the basis of reason, and then to assume responsibility for the decision you've made, then it only makes sense if you suppose there's a single entity, which is conscious, which is capable of reason, which makes decisions, which acts on the basis of decisions, and which takes responsibility. Now, that notion of the self, which I just explained to you, is a purely formal notion. It's not like Descartes' "mental substance".

To postulate a self, we need to postulate a point of view when we have a perception. Whenever I have a visual perception, I see something from a point of view. I don't see the point of view, but I can't make sense of the perception without postulating a point of view. And in the same way, I want to say, we don't experience the self, but we can't make sense out of our experiences unless we suppose there is a self.

And that basically is where I part company with both Hume and Descartes. Descartes mistakenly posited a mental substance, and that's wrong. And Hume says, "there's nothing there, except the sequence of unitary experiences", and that's wrong.

*Could you explain your idea of "biological naturalism"?*

What I mean by this is that consciousness is a biological feature, that it's part of nature. It's not supernatural, as Descartes would have it. It isn't something that God gave us, by tacking consciousness on to our body. It is a straightforward feature of nature. But the right level for describing it is the biological level because consciousness exists as a phenomenon of nature at the biological level—specifically, the level of brain processes.

*How do you know that consciousness is an emergent property of physical matter, rather than it being—as the dualists would say—something separate from it?*

Well, we've got, now, over a century of pretty good work in neural biology, and we have overwhelming evidence that all of our conscious states are caused by neural processes in the brain. Now, it is an empirical claim on my part, and it could be refuted if it turns out that, 100 years from now, you and I are having this conversation in heaven, and we don't have bodies, and I would have to say, "well, I sure made a dumb mistake". I just don't think that's going to happen. There's *overwhelming evidence* that consciousness is caused by brain processes. Now, that doesn't mean you couldn't build an artificial machine that produced consciousness. We just don't know how the brain does it, so we don't know how to build an artificial machine.

*And is that the root of your problem with the computer scientists?*

Well, no, my problem with what I call "strong-artificial-intelligence people" is that they hold a false theory, and it's very easy to refute. Their theory is that all consciousness, or any cognitive capacity, comes from just carrying out the right computer programming—the right sequence of zeros and ones. And I point to the "Chinese-room argument". I imagine that I'm locked in a room, and people give me questions in Chinese. I don't understand any Chinese, but I look up in the rule-book of computer programming what kind of answers I'm supposed to give back, and I give back the right answers, but I don't understand any of it. I don't understand the questions; I don't understand the answers. But now, I'm doing exactly what a computer does. A computer's got no more or less consciousness than that which I have in the Chinese room. But this raises a whole lot of other interesting questions such as "well, what exactly is the right approach to the science of consciousness?"

*What is, in your opinion, the best approach to the study of consciousness?*

The best approach is the one that's being pursued in fact right now by a whole lot of very good neurobiologists. Ideally, the work proceeds in three stages. First of all, you find the Neural Correlates of Consciousness. There must be some biological difference in the brain that correlates with my being in a conscious state from my not being in a conscious state. That's step one. Step two is to see if it's causal. That is, for any putative NCC, you want to know if you can produce a conscious state by producing its NCC, and if you can turn off a conscious state by turning off its NCC. And then step three, you try to get a theory. Now, at the moment, we're still very much in step one. We're finding interesting correlates of consciousness, but we're not yet at the stage where we know which are causal and which aren't. One of the many problems we're having, is that, if you use the current technology, using FMRI, for instance, then there are a lot of differences between the conscious brain and the unconscious brain, but we don't know which of those are responsible for consciousness.

*Could you say something about our social understanding of the word identity?*

Well let's assume we are talking about identity in ordinary speech and we're not talking technical logic here. In ordinary speech, identity has a lot to do with one's social identity. Who am I as a member of society? And there, I think things like ethnicity and skin colour and so on figure largely in people's self-conceptions. One of the features of the conception of social identity you're talking about is what I call "collective intentionality"—that is, the fact that people have a certain sense of themselves as a collectivity.

*In the past you have talked about there being three notions for social reality.*

To give an account of a highly creative society, with money and property and government and marriage, you have to use at least three notions. You have to have collective intentionality—humans need to cooperate. Now, lots of animals have that, lots of animals can cooperate. So, that's not sufficient, but it's necessary. But then, you have to have what I call "the assignment of function". So, we use money, even though there's nothing intrinsically that makes something money. We treat George Bush as President of the United States, even though he's not President of anything. It's just, he's President because we treat him as President. Okay, so we have this assignment of function. But then, there's a very special assignment of function, and that's what I call a "status function". This is where something performs its function—the President of the United States, or money, or private property—only by virtue of the fact that there is a collective recognition of it having a certain status. And then I try to analyse how we do that. How we work our private property and government and universities—all these are created by certain logical, linguistic operations. What I call the "fundamental operation" is where we count something as having a status. We count something as having the status of money, or, in my case, I have the status of a Professor at a university. The car outside has the status of being my car. And those are all the result of human collective intentionality assigning what I call "status functions" to objects and people.

I think this is an exciting field: how human beings create their social and institutional reality, and of course the fundamental institution is language. And the fascinating question is "how exactly do we use language to create the non-linguistic, institutional reality of such things as armies and private property and nation-states and universities?"

*Does this mean that your view of our social reality is dependent on a shared notion of hierarchy?*

I think human beings naturally need to assign certain sorts of statuses to each other. If only so they get a division of labour. I think there is something hierarchical about institutional reality. In a university there's a series of assigned functions. There's a Chancellor and a Vice Chancellor; there are the Professors and the graduate students; there are the undergraduates and the custodial staff. So, all these people have different assigned status functions.

But I'd like to say a little more about the specific role of language. Why is it that language is the fundamental social institution? And how does language inevitably create these other institutions, like private property and government and money? You see, my dog or the chimpanzees can have relatively complex social interactions, but they don't pay income tax and they don't have cocktail parties and they don't go to universities. Now, all those have to be created by language. And I now think I know how it works; how exactly we use language to create all of these things.

Humans have different ways of relating to reality. The philosophers' favourite example is with truth and falsity, what I call—when we use language to represent a state of affairs—"the world-to-word" direction of language. So when we say, "snow is white", or "two plus two equals four", we are using language to represent things. But not all language is like that, for example, orders and promises. There, the aim is to get the word to match the world. We give someone an order, and we hope his behaviour will

change to match the content of the order. And that's what I call the "word-to-world" direction. World-to word can be true or false. Word-to world cannot be true or false.

Okay, but now here's the fascinating thing. In human languages, we have a capacity to do both at once. We can make something the case by representing it as being the case. Now, the most famous cases of that were discovered by my old teacher, and they're what he called "performative utterances". This is where you make something in the world the case by making a promise, or that you adjourn the meeting, by saying, "the meeting is adjourned". He called these "performatives", and those are cases where you create a reality by representing that reality as existing.

Society therefore is a process of speech acts, which I call "declarations". And declarations are the basic linguistic moves by which human institutional reality is created. Human institutional reality, without exception, is created by what I call "status function declarations". When we make something the President of the United States, or private property, or a Professor at a University, we make them what they are by representing them as being that. So, we change reality by representing reality as having been so changed, that is to say, we do it with the word-to-world direction. And we do this over and over, every day, to create institutional sets of power relations. And it goes all the way from swearing in a President of the United States, to such things as giving somebody a glass of beer. I go to the bar, and I come back with two glasses of beer, and I push one over to Betty, and I say, "this one's yours, Betty", and I push one to Mary-Ann, and I say, "this one's yours, Mary-Ann". Now, those are status function declarations: I have *made* it their property by declaring it to be their property.

And basically, I think this particular linguistic move, by which we create institutional reality, by representing it as existing, is the basis of all human civilisations that I know anything about.

*So how does this then relate to statements like, "we are Muslims", or "we are black", or "we are Nigerian"?*

Well this is a crucial point. What all social movements try to do is to create a sense of collective intentionality.

The women's movement did something they called "consciousness-raising". And the idea was to get women conscious of being women together, and of being discriminated against. And similarly with the black movement in the United States—there was a lot of effort to get people to linguistically define themselves collectively, as "the black community". Now, I can tell you, there's no such thing as a white community. The whites are a majority in the United States, and white people don't think of themselves as a collective white people. They might think, "well, I'm a Republican", and "I'm an Episcopalian", but not every general description identifies a form of collective intentionality. In order to make social institutional structure grow, you have to have collective intentionality. And what social movements try to do is induce a sense of collective intentionality. And the way you do that is to get this sense of "we are doing this together".

Again it comes back to status function declarations—and the performatives are the most visible cases. You adjourn the meeting by saying, "the meeting is adjourned". But, I want to say, the phenomenon is pervasive, and it occurs without performative verbs as well. It occurs in all kinds of forms. It says on a dollar bill I have in my pocket, "this note is legal tender for all debts, public and private". Now, that isn't something they *discovered*, by doing an investigation. They *make* that the case, by representing it as being the case.

*How does this relate to the question of human rights?*

Human rights are status functions. And I think the sooner we understand this, the sooner we have a better conception of human rights and how they work. The problem is, a lot of people think, "well, it's only a human right if God gave it to us as a human right." But that won't do. If God gave us the original list of human rights, then he keeps changing his mind, because when the American conception of human rights came about, women did not have total equality, black people did not have total equality. So, human rights are status functions, and they're created by these status function declarations. And now, the question is: how do we justify them? I

think we can, but you have to have a theory of how humans flourish, and what benefits humans, what sort of biological beasts are we? And that's where my biological naturalism comes back in.

The different parts of my philosophy hang together in this way—that human rights will be justified by a consideration of the kind of people we are and the kind of things we value.

We need to understand that the conception we have of human rights is not neutral. You have to realise that some things are more valuable than others, so I regard, human speech and reflection and thought and discussion as especially precious. And it's because I attach a certain value to freedom of speech—that it has to be listed as a basic human right. I think I can justify the claim to that value, but I think we shouldn't suppose that there'd be a list of human rights that everybody would *automatically* accept.

*So is it possible, then, for different societies, to have different and equally legitimate understandings of human rights?*

Well, it's not impossible for people to have different conceptions of human rights. I don't think that all of the ones I know are equally legitimate—that is, for example, there are lots of societies where women simply do not have equal rights. And I think that's unjustifiable. I don't think that I can say, "well, that's just their way of doing things, and they have their way, and we have our way." That's true—they have their way. But I think their way is unjustifiable. So, I have a certain basic conception that if you're going to have the notion of human rights at all, then these rights have to be universal—everybody has to have them—and they have to be equal—everybody has to have equal rights.

So we have to be willing to say that some cultures are just wrong, and I think we ought to be able to justify that claim. I'm not a cultural relativist. I think I can justify a certain conception of human rights, but I can't discover that human rights exist the way I discover DNA, or the way Columbus discovered America. They are social creations.

# MARK WALPORT

was appointed Director of the Wellcome Trust in June 2003. Before joining the Trust, he was Professor of Medicine and Head of the Division of Medicine at Imperial College London, where he led a research team that focused on the immunology and genetics of rheumatic diseases. He was appointed a member of the Council for Science and Technology in 2004.

*Who are you?*

It depends on circumstances. That's what's very interesting about identity. So, talking to you now, I'm the Director of the Wellcome Trust, but at home I'm a husband and father. On Flickr, I'm someone else, and so on. In all sorts of different circumstances, we're slightly different people. On eBay, I have a pseudonymous identity. When I put my PIN card into a bank machine, I have a number. So, I'm a mass of different identities and different personas, depending on what context I find myself in. But I don't get worried about this. I think we can all incorporate our different identities very easily into one persona. So, I'm a single person with many identities.

*Who do we think you are?*

I think that you think that I'm, in the context of this, the Director of the Wellcome Trust. You think that I'm someone who's interesting to talk to, hopefully, in the context of the exhibition that we're putting on on identity. And you probably have some kind of impression of me from your view of the Wellcome Trust and from anything that you might have read about me on the internet or in the media.

*Can you define "identity"?*

Yes. Identity, for me, is all about the question: "who am I?" And that is different from identification, which is the second question that you've just asked, which is "who do you think I am?" And of course, if you were the taxman, you'd know me by my National Insurance number and tax returns. If you were my doctor, you'd

think of me as an overweight middle-aged man with a slightly high cholesterol level. We each identify people in the context in which we meet them. If you were one of my friends, I might be the person that you were an 18-year-old at university with.

*Why do you think identity is important to us?*

Because our identity is our inner being—it's how we view ourselves—how we interact with the world. It's an absolutely critical matter. And it's why issues of identity and identification are so socially sensitive. We each have aspects of our identity that we're perfectly happy to put out on the street or on the internet and post on blogs and so on, but then each of us have aspects of our identity that are private in different contexts. Most of our identity is something that's freely known and exchanged with members of our family. But there can be aspects of identity that people feel extremely sensitive about. And what's interesting about identity is that it is an abiding topic of interest. You can't look at a newspaper or listen to the radio without issues of identity and identification arising. And of course, it's the stuff of literature, it's the stuff of art, it's all-pervasive—because in some sense, it's at the core of being human.

*You're talking about identity in terms of context and in terms of making particular decisions about how people see you or how you present yourself.*

Absolutely, yes.

*So is there a better question to be asked about: "who are you not?" Or, is there anything that you specifically say that you aren't in any context? And does that help us get a better sense of who you are?*

That's an interesting question, and I think it all depends. There may be social circumstances in which you are conscious to identify yourself as not being somebody. And I think in some ways, politicians probably do that all the time. And people may almost do it unconsciously. But yes, identity, of course, is about who you're not as much as it is about who you are. I'm just trying to think if, on a day-to-day basis, I use identification in that excluded sense very much. I don't think I do, probably. But you're absolutely right. Often, you see people protesting, "well, I'm not this", or "I'm not that."

*One of the things that a lot of the people we've spoken to feel is a core issue in the question of who they are is related to notions of, for instance, race and ethnicity, or political identification, or gender. In your personal capacity, but also more generally, how important do you think those elements are to that question of who you are?*

Well, I think that's very interesting. Because in the context of the Wellcome Trust, where we support an enormous amount of research into genetics, we often very quickly get into questions of identity, and particularly questions about origins. It is striking that people make very important distinctions between each other based on social, religious and national identifications, but when you actually look at the underlying biology, you see that we're all essentially the same. I find it quite frustrating that you see an enormous amount of human conflict on the basis of perceived important social differences, where you know that actually the biological differences and differences in genetic origins are non-existent. So, in the Middle East, you look at people of different religions who have very close and intermingled genetic origins and you think, "what on earth is going on here?" But one is brought back to reality when you see the battles that occur between supporters of different football teams in different parts of London, where they know perfectly well that they are socially essentially the same. But they choose to identify themselves in ways that then generate conflict.

*Would you dismiss the idea that there is any genetic basis for race?*

No. There clearly is a genetic basis for differences in populations. And you can see that in very sophisticated ways. So, it's now possible to look at genetic variation in over a million genes, and compare each of us, one to another. And you can then cluster people quite remarkably according to their origins. And you can, in some populations, even distinguish people genetically by what language they speak. And of course another outcome of genetics is that it defines our place with respect to other species as part of the natural world. Genetics shows how closely related we are to other humans—only about one in a thousand of DNA base pairs differs between one human and another. But then, it's only about two per cent of our DNA that differ from that of chimpanzees.

*We spoke to Kenan Malik, and in his book,* Strange Fruit, *he's very critical of notions of race realism—the idea that there is a genetic basis for race. And he tackles this idea of population differences and really engages with it, but he also says that actually, the difficulty with that is that you can define populations in so many different ways. So the population of East London's different from the population of North London, and there'll be genetic variations there, and in the same way the population of Kenya is very different from the population of Britain, genetically. But actually, in terms of social policy or social awareness, it's still not a very helpful way of understanding the question of identity from that point of view.*

Well I agree it can be very harmful in a social context. But sociology is not biology. In a biological context, there are clear differences between populations that have developed in different parts of the world. And these are underpinned by important genetic differences. So, for example, if you look in those parts of the world where malaria is very common, then you see the genetic fingerprint of resistance to malaria has been selected in populations living in those regions. You can see mutations in haemoglobin such as the sickle mutation, which provides very significant protection against severe malaria, you see genetic variation that causes differences in red cell shape and in blood cell metabolism that provides some degree of protection against malaria. Equally, if you look in more Northern populations that have adopted a pastoral way of life, then you see the genetic persistence to adulthood of the ability to digest lactose, which is an important carbohydrate in milk. So, evolution and natural selection has actually adapted populations to living in different parts of the world. And so, yes, there are biological differences that underlie different populations. But, translating that into racial stereotypes, which cause social dislocation, is entirely unhelpful and has no validity. But I don't think one can get away from what are the fundamental observations about genetic differences between people. They do exist.

*Another thing that Malik talks about in* Strange Fruit, *from a biomedical point of view, is the use of things like racial profiling when testing certain drugs. And it appears that certain drugs work better for, say, African-Americans than others.*

Yes. Again, to understand the basis of that you can think of the old adage in the pharmaceutical industry that if you take almost any medicine, about a third of people will benefit significantly; in another third of people, it will have very little effect; and in the final third you might get side effects. Now that's a

gross simplification. But part of the explanation for differences in effects of medicines in different people is that there are genetic differences in the way we metabolise drugs. And as we understand those, then it will be possible to prescribe drugs more accurately. And it's why these genetic studies are so important. Cancer is an extremely good example of that. Cancer is caused by what are called "somatic changes"—mutations in the cells in the body. And if you get a mutation in a skin cell, for example, which gives it a growth advantage, then, that can go on to form a cancer. And if you can identify those genetic changes, then that can give you the basis for genetically targeted medicines. One very good example of this is a drug called Glivec, which is used to treat chronic myeloid-leukaemia. It was discovered a number of years ago that the mutation behind chronic myeloid leukaemia is a reassortment of two genes, BCR and ABL, to give you a gene which is called BCR-ABL and that's then the precise target for Glivec.

*With the advances in our ability to profile or map individuals genetically, there are implications for an individual's relationship with its society or the state. I'm thinking specifically about genetic databases, identity cards, and how that information is used. What are the ethical issues which will become more prescient for us to consider?*

Okay, well, let's take the example of the use of DNA for forensic purposes. I think there are two sets of different questions here. The first set of questions is scientific, "what is it possible to learn about the identity of a person from their DNA?" It was initially discovered, by Alec Jeffreys, that you could use DNA as a 'fingerprint'. But at that stage, genetic fingerprinting gave you virtually no information about the person other than that you could match them to the fingerprint or not. But what's now changing is that, as we learn more about what genetic variation actually tells us about the appearances—the phenotype—of the individual, then the question is: how much more information can you get out of the forensic analysis of DNA? So, to give you simple and straightforward examples: you can clearly detect the sex of the person from whom the blood sample comes, just by looking to see if there are Y chromosomes present. But you can go further. You can actually detect whether they have red hair, because the mutation that's associated with red hair in the general population is identified and can be identified forensically. Amazingly, it turns out that you stand a reasonable probability of being able to work out the surname of a man from a DNA sample, particularly in the case of uncommon surnames. This is because in men Y chromosomes are the inherited counterpart of surnames. So, in the rarer half of surnames in Britain, there's about a 20 per cent chance that you can predict the surname of the subject. So, we're moving very rapidly from a completely anonymous DNA barcode which tells you nothing about the person at all—like the whorl of a fingerprint that you might see on the tips of their fingers—to DNA sequence information that can tell you more and more about what that person might look like.

But then the second completely separate set of questions is about what the extent of the forensic DNA database should be. And we've seen a big public discussion about that. And that is very much a social question, it's not a scientific question. And sometimes, the science and the sociology get confused. Science can discover so much, but it's then up to society to decide how it wants to use that information. And here, the issue of proportionality comes into it. And there's an interesting example to illustrate this: the brick murderer on the M3. In that case, someone threw a brick off a motorway bridge, and a lorry driver, who had the misfortune to be driving underneath was killed when it hit his windscreen. Now, that brick had a tiny trace of blood on it. And when they went to look in the forensic database, they didn't find an exact match, but they found a sample that almost certainly came from a relative. On the basis of that, they approached the relative, and the actual perpetrator of the crime confessed and was convicted. So, the question then is, "well, to what extent does society want to use this information, and what are the limits?" And because this was such a serious crime, there wasn't much of an outcry even though it was actually the relative that was approached first, because the criminal confessed. So the debate at the moment is what the extent of the database should be. My personal view is that I think there are two defensible positions. There's one position where you say that the only people

who should be in the database are people who have actually committed the crimes, and the other position is to say that we should all be in the database. I think it is harder to defend any intermediate positions. But as I say, I think that this is a social debate.

*Why are those two positions defensible?*

Well, I think that in the case of everyone being on the database, then there's no question of discrimination. We're all in there together and it's a societal decision. Though personally, I don't think that's a realistic one. It is easier to justify the other position. If you've been convicted of committing a crime, then most people would consider it reasonable to retain a DNA sample. The trouble with the intermediate position is that there is some social inequality in the way that the samples are being collected.

*Could you just define what you mean by an "intermediate position"? When we interviewed Alec Jeffreys he pointed out there are about five or six million people on the database now, of whom about 850,000 have never been convicted of a crime and are probably innocent. Is that what you mean?*

Yes it is. Though we are reaching a compromise in which samples taken from people not convicted of crimes will be retained for a length of time dependent on the nature of the crime being investigated. You can debate this topic endlessly. But a position has been reached which, to me, seems reasonable.

*It's interesting that you mentioned earlier the idea of collecting everyone's DNA on one database. That is a position that the journalist Johann Hari would defend quite strongly. But isn't the problem with that position, arguably, that it fundamentally changes the relationship between the individual and the state?*

I think that is exactly right. And it wouldn't be my position to have everyone on the database. But this is the other interesting issue about identity and identification. It touches a philosophical divide which is, I think, a very important tension in Britain. And that is the split between the libertarian and utilitarian positions. The utilitarian view would be, "well, for the general good of society, we should have everyone on a database." And the libertarian view of society says, "well, that's my DNA and no one can have it under any circumstances." And again, I think that we see this debate played out all of the time, and the question is "where do you end up on the spectrum between the utilitarian and the libertarian position?"

Last year, I did a review with Richard Thomas, the Information Commissioner, on the whole subject of data sharing, and the issue of whether information should be shared in case law enforcement comes down, again and again, to proportionality. No one objects when surveillance cameras are used to try and detect people committing serious crimes or terrorist crimes. But when a council on the South Coast uses legislation, which is intended for serious crimes, to undertake surveillance to work out whether a young girl is living in a catchment area of a particular school or not, well most people think that's completely unacceptable. And I would agree with that. So, we must use the modern means we have of identifying people in a proportionate fashion.

And this is directly relevant to the work of the Wellcome Trust and to the questions surrounding the use of medical data for research. I think the key issue for medical research and for medical practice is confidentiality. So, to give you an example: the Human Tissue Act was a legislation that made it more complicated (though I think a reasonable compromise has been achieved) to use tissue for research. Now, personally, I would actually be outraged if someone had taken out my appendix, and, didn't then use it in research in the future if it could have been useful for that research. But I would be equally outraged if it appeared in the paper, saying, "Mark Walport's appendix showed this or that." So, the issue for medical research is very much about confidentiality. Confidentiality is absolutely everything. But, if information about my health can be used when aggregated with others to provide information that is valuable for the future treatment of patients or for the health of the population, then I, personally, would be extremely disappointed if my information wasn't used in that way. And it would be very difficult for me to be asked for my consent to do this if it was for research

on a topic that cannot be predicted at present. A good example of this is when new variant CJD, "mad cow disease", came on the scene. And people didn't know how long it had been around, or where it came from. A very valuable study was to actually look at tonsil and appendix tissue that had been taken out in the early 1990s, to see if there was any evidence of mad cow disease in the tissues. Now, no one could ever have asked permission in the early 1990s, when those tissues were taken out, for it to be used for that purpose, because that purpose wasn't known—it didn't exist.

So, I think there's confusion about the issue of consent versus confidentiality. The thing that is absolutely paramount is confidentiality. Consent should always be asked if you are asking someone to participate in a clinical trial, or if you are asking them to do something additional, but when it's the use of anonymised, or key-coded, information about their health, then I think most people in the population, when it's explained how the information is used, think, "well, this is a splendid thing to do." So why wouldn't you do it?

*So in order to have a sense of our identity and a sense of control over our identity, the capacity for privacy is important. How does this relate to the discussion about identity cards? After all, ID cards are slightly different from a database, because in theory it has to be produced on demand.*

Well, I think identity cards are a completely different issue. You have to step back and say, "what is the purpose of an identity card?" And again, I don't think this is in any sense a scientific topic any more. This is a discussion within society about whether, in this democratic society, people want identity cards or not. And it's interesting, because if you look at Britain, the issue has caused an enormous controversy. But then you look at many other countries in Europe and it is a very different story. These countries are equally concerned in different ways about issues of civil liberty, and indeed many of them had been under Nazi occupation, and had seen the very worst of what happens when you have profiling for religious reasons, or reasons of sexuality and so on. And yet, there's no controversy in those countries about identity cards. They just have them. So, I think it's an interesting social issue. But I think it's a quite separate discussion from anything that we've been talking about around genetics and medical research.

*Earlier, when we asked: "who are you?" you said, "well, I would have a different identity on eBay or if I was on a blog" and so on. What kind of impact do you think that wider developments in technology, and not just in the biomedical context, but with things like the internet, will have on our sense of identity as individuals and as a society both now and in the future?*

Well there's a lot we don't know. And there is some evidence of people living quite sophisticated pseudonymous existences in places like Second Life. But there can be dangers in how the net lets you create a new identity—one can see this in terms of the sexual grooming that can go on. So the web creates a great deal of potential for people creating new and fictional identities, which may be completely harmless, but may also be quite harmful, so I think that there are some quite interesting challenges. I think there's another interesting aspect of the web where people seem remarkably willing to post very detailed images of themselves and information about themselves, and make it available to the whole world, without really thinking about the consequences. And it's not that easy to delete information from the web, so I think there are important questions about how people use Facebook, and other social networking sites. All of this is going to raise some quite interesting issues about identity, some of which, I think, may be quite troublesome.

*Are there any areas where science should not allow itself to investigate, because the implications of that investigation could be too dangerous?*

I think that's a very old question, and I think the answer to that is "No". I mean you could easily say, "well, we've discovered this thing called 'fire', and we mustn't use it, because it's dangerous stuff." I don't think that there are limits to scientific enquiry, because I think we should understand the natural world as much as we can. But the flip side of that is

that knowledge has to be used responsibly. So, for example, medical research has to be subject to very, very careful ethical scrutiny so that people *don't* go off and do research without very careful governance and permissions. I think that's very important, and actually, this is something that Britain is extremely good at.

*What if we invert this question about the limitations of science: are there limits to what genetics can tell us about our identity?*

Yes, absolutely.

*So what are the general limits about what genetics can tell us about our identity? And where is science generally not helpful in terms of us understanding our identity? You have identical twins, how do their identities differ?*

Okay, that is an interesting and important question. We are a very complicated mix between our genes and our environment, and, as you said, if you have identical twins then you understand that very well. Because whilst you see the extraordinary degree of physical similarity, you also notice that their personalities are very different—their friends are different, the way they cut their hair is different, and they have very different and unique identities. There was a distinguished paediatrician called Elizabeth Bryan who worked at Queen Charlotte's Hospital, who used to lecture to parents expecting twins or multiple births. And she would show one slide, which had identical twins dressed absolutely identically and she said, "don't do this." And then she'd show a second slide with one twin dressed all in red, holding a Penguin biscuit in a red wrapper, and another one dressed all in blue and holding a Penguin biscuit in a blue wrapper. And she said, "don't do that either." For identical twins, it has to be about bringing them up as individuals, with their own identities. And within a very short time, as parents of twins, you soon learn—they have their own identities, they are completely individual. And yes, of course they have a very close relationship with their sibling, but then most siblings do. So, there are absolute limits as to what genes specify, and our interaction with our environment is absolutely crucial. This is not only in terms of our health, but our personality and everything else. So there is both the biology of identity, and the sociology of identity.

*It could be argued that the word "identity" means two things: it either refers to the way that I identify myself as opposed to other people, but it can also refer to the way I identify with other people. From a biological point of view, what is the current concensus or understanding of us as tribal creatures and as social organisms? I'm thinking specifically in terms of evolution. As I understand it, the idea of group selection is something that's widely thought to not be true these days. That selection happens on an individual basis, rather than a group basis. Is that right?*

Yes.

*But the biologist Edward Sloane Wilson argues that group selection should not be dismissed. And he is, for example, quite critical of Richard Dawkins' interpretation of natural selection which focuses solely on the individual. What are your thoughts on that? Does this argument relate to our tribal identities?*

Well, in a sense, natural selection has to operate at the level of the individual, because you either survive to reproduce, or you don't. Or you either reproduce successfully and have lots of offspring or you don't. So, that is actually the level at which natural selection operates. But one then sees certain behaviours in terms of how groups act to protect one another. So family bonds are extremely strong, and people will put themselves in danger to protect other members of their family. And one clearly sees in society that people will also put themselves in danger to protect their group—be it a nation or a bunch of football supporters. So, we are social organisms, and our behaviour is under selective pressure as well.

But just to come back to identity in a more general sense, I think we all have our inner identity, which if we were introspective, we might be able to explore and write down. But then, we make choices about how we express that identity in different social contexts. So we have a sort of inner identity and that can be different from the identity we express outwardly. And I think we probably make most of those decisions pretty subconsciously.

# FIONA SHAW

Hugh Aldersey-Williams

Fiona Shaw's acting is, she says, a gradual process of "becoming herself". The major dramatic leads she has taken—Richard II, Hedda Gabler, Electra, Medea, Mother Courage—may be milestones on that journey; her occasional comic character roles more in the way of brief digressions from the route. It is also a process of pushing towards physical and emotional limits, in which the sense of exertion is felt as part of the achievement, as it is by athletes.

Actors differ greatly in how they 'find' their character: in some cases they themselves come to believe they are that person, both on the stage, and sometimes beyond. They become the character by extended immersion in that person's physical, social and emotional world. Other actors 'just act', with their true selves retaining a detached view of the impersonation. Fiona Shaw is in this second group. "I too, sometimes, am an audience member", she says. Truly 'transformative' actors of this type are few, but they are, she suggests, "the ones who can reveal something about the world that they could not as people. Charles Laughton was such a one. One was drawn to him, say, in *The Hunchback of Notre-Dame* even as one was repelled, and in there one saw all of 'us'. What strikes me about these actors is the question: what did they have to contact in order to repress so much of themselves to allow the game of a new set of characteristics to emerge?"

Playing Richard II, who must surrender his crown to Henry Bolingbroke, Shaw felt strongly how the "self-abnegation of handing over the symbol of one's primary role and identity releases the self to be another self. Playing Richard, there was a relief and a revolt in that act. And we all have crowns—loves, positions, roles, identities. That was my feeling, and I think the temperature in the theatre changes too, because the audience who have been in resistance to the terror of a spoiled child invested with such power is released from that grip and at last permitted the human feeling of sympathy." Shaw draws a parallel with recent debate surrounding the release from prison of Ronald Biggs and Abdelbaset al-Megrahi on compassionate grounds. "We have all these feelings once we disempower the abuser. I think it is the best of us."

Fiona Shaw in Shakespeare's Richard II at the National Theatre in 1995, directed by Deborah Warner.
All images courtesy of Neil Libbert.

### HUGH ALDERSEY-WILLIAMS

is a writer and curator with interests in science, architecture and design. He curated the Zoomorphic (2003) and Touch Me (2005) exhibitions at the Victoria and Albert Museum. He is the author of many books, including *The Most Beautiful Molecule* (1994), about the Nobel Prize-winning discovery of buckminsterfullerene, and *Panicology* (2007), a timely examination of media scare stories. *Periodic Tales, a cultural companion to the chemical elements* will be published by Penguin in 2010.

### KEN ARNOLD

is a museum professional, who has worked on both sides of the Atlantic. He joined the Wellcome Trust in 1992, and now heads a department that programmes events and exhibitions in Wellcome Collection (a young venue for the incurably curious that explores the links between medicine, art and the rest of life). He regularly writes, lectures and advises on museums and the contemporary relations between the arts and sciences. His most recent book is *Cabinets for the Curious* (Ashgate, 2006).

### RUTH GARDE

is an independent curator, writer and researcher based in London. Her relationship with the Wellcome Collection began in 2003 when she worked on the Medicine Man exhibition held at the British Museum. Over the last two years she has worked on a number of curating projects with the Wellcome Collection and Wellcome Library, as well as contributing research and writing for the Henry Moore Institute in Leeds on Sculpture in Painting, an exhibition opening in Autumn 2009.

# CONTRIBUTOR BIOGRAPHIES

### MICK GORDON

is a theatre director and dramatist. He is the founding Artistic Director of On Theatre and was Associate Director of the National Theatre and Artistic Director of London's Gate Theatre. His plays include On Love, On Death, On Ego, On Religion, On Emotion, Grace, and The Ride of Your Life. His books include *Conversations on Religion* and *Conversations on Truth*.

### JAMES PETO

is Senior Curator of Public Programmes at the Wellcome Trust and one of the curators of the exhibition Identity: Eight Rooms, Nine Lives at Wellcome Collection (November 2009–April 2010). He has co-curated a number of Wellcome Collection exhibitions, including The Heart and War and Medicine, for which he co-edited the accompanying publications. Previously he was Exhibitions Curator at the Whitechapel Art Gallery and Head of Exhibitions at the Design Museum, London.

### EMILY JO SARGENT

is an artist and curator based in London. She is currently Curator of Temporary Exhibitions at Wellcome Collection, London and has curated a number of temporary exhibitions including The Heart (2007) and Skeletons: London's Buried Bones (2008). She contributed to the BMA award-winning book *The Heart* (published with Yale University Press, 2007) and edited an accompanying catalogue to the Skeletons exhibition.

### CHRISTOPHER WILKINSON

is an award winning theatre director and journalist. he has written for the *Financial Times*, *The Scotsman*, *Prospect* and *The Guardian* (online). His books include *Conversations on Religion* and *Conversations on Truth*. He is the Associate Director of On Theatre.

# ACKNOWLEDGEMENTS

Our gratitude to the following people without whom this book would not be possible: Rikki Arundel, Natalie Zemon Davis, Timothy Longman, Geoffrey Marsh, Keith Roberts, Nikolas Rose, Sophie Erskine and Iona Firouzabadi and especially: April Ashley, members of the Hinch family, and Fiona Shaw.

© 2009 Black Dog Publishing Limited, London, UK, Wellcome Collection and The Authors.
All rights reserved.

Black Dog Publishing Limited
10A Acton Street
London WC1X 9NG
info@blackdogonline.com

Edited by Hugh Aldersey-Williams, Ken Arnold, Mick Gordon, Nikolaos Kotsopoulos, James Peto and Chris Wilkinson.
Designed by Emily Chicken.
Design assistant Ben Jeffreys.

All opinions expressed within this publication are those of the authors and not necessarily of the publisher.

British Library Cataloguing-in-Publication Data. A CIP record for this book is available from the British Library.

ISBN 978 1 906155 86 5

Black Dog Publishing Limited, London, UK, is an environmentally responsible company. *Identity & Identification* is set in Scala and is printed on an FSC certified paper.

architecture art design
fashion history photography
theory and things

www.blackdogonline.com